Brazil in the International System

Also of Interest

† Available in hardcover and paperback.

Westview Special Studies on Latin America and the Caribbean

Brazil in the International System:
The Rise of a Middle Power
edited by Wayne A. Selcher

In recent years, Brazil has grown greatly in international status, and all indications are that it will continue to do so. The authors of this book evaluate Brazil from a "Brazil in the world" viewpoint, placing the country in the current international system in relation to its capabilities, effects, and interest positions. On the basis of their conclusions, the authors go on to assess the extent and direction of Brazil's potential to exert international influence in the future.

Wayne A. Selcher is associate professor of political science and department chairman at Elizabethtown College. He is also a prominent writer on Brazil and, in addition to many articles and studies, has written *The Afro-Asian Dimension of Brazilian Foreign Policy, 1956–1972* and *Brazil's Multilateral Relations: Between First and Third Worlds* (Westview Press, 1978).

Brazil in the International System: The Rise of a Middle Power

edited by Wayne A. Selcher

Westview Press / Boulder, Colorado

Westview Special Studies on Latin America and the Caribbean

Copyright © 1981 by Westview Press, Inc.

Published in 1981 in the United States of America by
  Westview Press, Inc.
  5500 Central Avenue
  Boulder, Colorado 80301
  Frederick A. Praeger, Publisher

Library of Congress Cataloging in Publication Data
Main entry under title:
Brazil in the international system.
  (Westview special studies on Latin America and the Caribbean)
  Includes index.
  1. Brazil—Foreign economic relations—Addresses, essays, lectures. 2. Brazil—
Foreign relations—Addresses, essays, lectures. I. Selcher, Wayne A., 1942- . II. Series.
HF1513.B7   337.81   81-1686
ISBN 0-89158-907-4   AACR2

Printed and bound in the United States of America

Contents

Tables and Charts

ix

Foreword

Ronald M. Schneider

Is Brazil now or is it soon to become a major power? What is the degree of correspondence between this continent-sized country's aspirations and its capabilities in the international sphere? No clear consensus has yet developed on these and related questions, but their relevance has become increasingly evident as Brazil's upward mobility within the international system has been dramatic over the past decade and little less than breathtaking over the past twenty years. In this first edited collection of essays on Brazil's foreign relations, Wayne Selcher and his associates comparatively examine the position of Brazil in the global international system and the significance of its particular location, determining whether or not it is unique and examining changes that may be taking place, the effects of these changes on other countries, and methods for determining the answers to such questions. Drawing upon the literature of international politics, they systematically place Brazil within the structure of international affairs with respect to capabilities, effects, interests, and status. Particular care is given to distinctions between middle powers and major powers and to Brazil's place among the so-called new influentials.

Serious attention to Brazil's current foreign relations in the general literature of international relations is a very recent development, dating at best to the late 1970s. Prior to that time scant attention was paid even by Latinamericanists to this subject, with very little research done and that chiefly by doctoral candidates. H. Jon Rosenbaum began to publish a series of articles at the end of the 1960s, and Roger Fontaine completed a Ph.D. dissertation on "The Foreign Policymaking Process in Brazil" at Johns Hopkins University in 1970. This was followed by Keith Larry Storrs's "Brazil's Independent Foreign Policy, 1961-1964" (Ph.D. dissertation, Cornell University, 1973). By this time Wayne Selcher had also completed a dissertation, subsequently published as *The Afro-Asian Dimension of Brazilian Foreign Policy, 1956-1972* (Gainesville: University of Florida Press, 1974). In 1972 the Foreign Policy Research Institute (FPRI) in Philadelphia developed an interest in this subject and started several young scholars working along with such relatively old hands as myself and Wayne Selcher. Perhaps more important than the FPRI's two-volume mimeographed report—*Brazil's Future Role in International Politics* (June 1973)—was the fact that two of these young scholars, Michael Morris and William Perry, would continue their research along this line into their subsequent academic careers.

The thesis that Brazil was a potential major power or even a candidate for eventual great power status was launched at the August 1973 World Congress of Political Science by Norman A. Bailey and me in a paper on "Brazil's Foreign Policy: A Case Study in Upward Mobility," subsequently published in the spring 1974 issue of *Inter-American Economic Affairs* (Vol. 27, pp. 3–25). This was followed shortly by David M. Landry's "Brazil's New Regional and Global Roles" (*World Affairs*, Vol. 137, Summer 1974, pp. 23–37) and Riordan Roett's article on "Brazil Ascendant: International Relations and Geopolitics in the Late 20th Century" (*Journal of International Affairs*, Vol. 29, 1975, pp. 139–154). Other aspects of Brazil's international relations were explored in Fontaine's *Brazil and the United States: Toward a Maturing Relationship* (Washington, D.C.: American Enterprise Institute for Public Policy Research, 1974); Brady Tyson's essay in Harold E. Davis and Larman Wilson (eds.), *Latin American Foreign Policies* (Baltimore, Md.: Johns Hopkins University Press, 1975); and Perry's "Contemporary Brazilian Foreign Policy: The International Strategy of an Emerging Power," Foreign Policy Papers, Vol. 2, no. 6 (Beverly Hills, Calif.: Sage Publications, 1976).

Since the end of 1976, literature in this field has begun to proliferate and to be reflected in some of the general international politics works. My own *Brazil: Foreign Policy of a Future World Power* (Boulder, Colo.: Westview Press, 1977) was soon joined by Selcher's *Brazil's Multilateral Relations: Between First and Third Worlds* (Boulder, Colo.: Westview Press, 1978) as well as Norman Gall's influential article, "The Rise of Brazil," in *Commentary* (January 1977). The third edition of K. J. Holsti's *International Politics: A Framework for Analysis* (Englewood Cliffs, N.J.: Prentice-Hall, 1977) included the "growth of Brazil as a major power" as an item in a list of eight causes of change in the global system, while Ray Cline ranked Brazil as number 6 in "perceived power" in his comprehensive *World Power Assessment* (1975 ed., Washington, D.C.: Georgetown University Center for Strategic and International Studies; subsequent eds., Boulder, Colo.: Westview Press). Most notable among the specialized studies following this upsurge of interest was Morris's *International Politics and the Sea: The Case of Brazil* (Boulder, Colo.: Westview Press, 1979).

The present volume grew out of a panel organized by Wayne A.

Selcher for the April 1979 national meeting of the Latin American Studies Association. Substantial interchange of ideas among the contributors has provided an intellectual cohesion lacking in many multi-author works. Taking advantage of the freedom stemming from being something of an intellectual "godfather" to several of the scholars collaborating in the volume rather than an active participant in its organization, I will add a few of my own thoughts for broadened comparative perspective in commenting upon each chapter and its relation to the basic themes of the work.

Frank D. McCann has provided in Chapter 1 the essential background of historical trends in Brazil's foreign relations, including the evolution of its goals and the changing views of its foreign policy elites. As he comes down to the present, he reviews foreign perspectives on Brazil's significance and status in the world at different junctures during the present century. Although his chapter is not specifically addressed to U.S.-Brazilian relations, it does portray the problematical special bilateral relationship that has been a keystone of Brazilian foreign policy until very recently.

I would like to add the perspective that the vaunted "special relationship" was essentially one of Brazil's subordination to the United States and that it was an obstacle to Brazil's playing a larger role in international affairs. Indeed, the appropriate question is not why it came to an end with the short-lived, acrimonious confrontation of 1977–1978, but rather how it lasted so long in the face of repeated abuses on the part of the United States. Taking office in 1953, the Eisenhower administration chose to forget Brazil's role as an ally in World War II and repudiated any responsibility for helping Brazil implement the recommendations of a joint commission that had been working during the Truman years to draw up integrated plans for Brazil's economic development. Adding insult to injury, U.S. policy sought to court Argentina, Brazil's historic rival, passing over the fact that under Juan Domingo Perón Argentina had been more than friendly to the Axis cause. Washington's primary objective came to be destruction of Brazil's newly created government oil corporation, Petrobrás. This would prove to be an unattainable goal, and its continued pursuit would foster the development of an anti-U.S. strain of nationalism.

On a personal note, I remember vividly the prevailing attitude in Washington during the late 1950s, when key individuals responsible for U.S. policy toward Brazil spoke of it as the world's largest banana republic and ridiculed then-president Juscelino Kubitschek for his "absurd" pretensions, which were nothing more than to set Brazil on the path to becoming a modern industrial nation. "Keep Brazil on a short leash" and "Give aid with an eye dropper" were favorite Foggy Bottom sayings in 1959, as concerted efforts were made to force Brazil into an austerity program of the type favored by the technicians of the U.S. Treasury and the International Monetary Fund. When Kubitschek chose to push ahead with the program that provided the basis for Brazil's post-1967 "economic miracle," this was interpreted as a sign of perversity, if not megalomania, by the dominant faction of the Brazilian specialists in the State Department.

Ironically, the pronounced inclination of the Kennedy White House to view Brazil as a potentially significant country was thwarted by the suspicions engendered by João "Jango" Goulart during his accidental presidency and also by the premature death of President Kennedy. Brazilian dependency was underscored during the mid-1960s because of the economic crisis inherited by the military regime. A decade later, U.S. policy under the direction of Henry Kissinger recognized Brazil's increasing importance and sought to reaffirm the "special" nature of the relationship between the two countries—at least symbolically. The effect, however, was to heighten Brazilian feelings of disillusionment and betrayal when the Carter government immediately resorted to a diplomacy of self-righteous high-handedness that linked the issues of human rights and nuclear proliferation. This was ameliorated only in part by the conciliatory attitude displayed by Carter during his 1978 state visit to Brazil. Since that time, the salient feature of U.S.-Brazilian relations has been an increasingly widespread view in Brazil that the United States cannot be counted upon to provide adequate leadership for the Western alliance—yet another reason for Brazil to act independently of Washington on many international issues. The extent to which this perception is shared by other countries will be a factor in the equation of challenges and opportunities facing Brazil in a changing international environment, conditioned, of course, by the policies of the Reagan administration.

Selcher's systematic and quantitative approach to a global ranking of Brazil's foreign policy capabilities and international status in Chapter 2 is a model of coldly objective analysis. His stress on tangible factors alone leads to a positioning of Brazil just below the top ten countries in the international system as of the mid-1970s. This is certainly reasonable, as is his recognition that Brazil is continuing to move upward in this regard. He does not see it entering the ranks of the great powers during the coming two decades—yet this is a most exclusive family composed of only the United States, the Soviet Union, the United Kingdom, the German Federal Republic, France, Japan, and China. Thus, the picture that emerges from his analysis still grants that Brazil—perhaps the most important and certainly the fastest-rising of the middle powers—may occupy a position as high as eighth in the world today. This, I submit, is by no means a poor showing for a country until recently all but ignored as a factor in international affairs.

As Selcher concentrates upon the 1970s, by way of perspective it might be well to recall that only a little more than a century ago Germany joined Great Britain and France as a great power (while Spain, Austria-Hungary, and the Ottoman Empire dropped out of this exclusive company). Shortly thereafter the United States emerged as the first great power outside Western Europe, followed almost immediately by the arrival of the Soviet Union and Japan. Since the triple breakthrough of the United States, the USSR, and Japan was consolidated in the 1920s, only China has joined the ranks of the great powers—largely on the basis of location, sheer size, and population. History has shown that although the emergence of new great powers may sometimes appear to take place rather suddenly, it can occur only upon the foundations of impressive power capabilities that have been built up gradually over a long period. Moreover, a coherent national strategy, skillfully executed, has been a major factor in each case of a rise to great power standing, particularly in light of the existence of rival upwardly mobile middle powers and opposition on the part of the established great powers. Thus, although Ray Cline, for example, may ascribe too much weight to national will and strategy in presently ranking Brazil behind only the two superpowers in perceived power, these qualitative factors need to be borne in mind in assessing the heights to which Brazil may rise in the 1980s and 1990s.

Even within the framework chosen by Selcher, whose views are reflected in the other chapters through his having chosen the authors and subsequently functioned as editor, Brazil is seen to be moving ahead somewhat faster than is indicated by official comparative international statistics, with their inevitable timelag. Thus, Brazil's current agricultural production is far beyond the 1976 figures used in this study, and the same is true for many of the indicators of industrial development. Hydro-electric projects well under way, for example, will more than double installed generating capacity, while the mineral riches of the Carajás region alone may by the end of the decade add as much as $10 billion yearly to Brazil's exports. In many other facets of development, current rates of movement are greater than simple extrapolation of the statistics in this book would indicate. For example, Brazil's exports in 1980 are nearly double those of 1977—the cutoff year for most of Selcher's quantitative indicators. Similarly, the gross national product (GNP) continues to grow at more than 6 percent a year, while the United States and Great Britain experience declining GNPs. Thus, significant dents have been made already in the gaps between the great powers and Brazil, as shown in Table 2.10.

Brazil's military power is certainly a topic upon which too little has been written, with almost nothing framed in a meaningful comparative context. Max G. Manwaring, in Chapter 3, makes a significant contribution in this respect. Lest the rich comparative data displayed in a time series mask the dynamics of the current situation, recent developments are again worth mentioning. Thus, for example, Brazil's merchant marine is no longer number 12 in the world; having nearly doubled over the author's figure to better than 7.2 million tons, it is fast closing in on Spain for 8th position. More importantly, production of well over one million tons per year (plus exports) from Brazilian shipyards puts that country in a position to move up at least even with France and West Germany during the present decade, passing Italy in the process. As this would place Brazil immediately behind the United States, it would culminate a very significant development in light of the fact that Brazil's construction of a world-class merchant marine really got under way only in the mid-1970s and is just now really hitting full stride. Moreover, Brazil's aircraft industry is likely to duplicate this achievement during the present decade. Already it has begun to export both civilian and military aircraft, including passenger models to U.S. airlines. Similarly, developments in the arms industry, noted by Manwaring, are only now really beginning to build up significant momentum, with dramatic growth still ahead. Annual export sales now exceed $1 billion and even the United States and the Soviet Union, as well as China, are seriously considering weapons acquisitions from Brazil. Then, too, Brazil's diversified industrial base and fairly sophisticated capital goods industry have great potential military relevance.

In Chapter 4, grappling with the question of how Brazil can translate its vast economic potential into influence in the international system, Martin T. Katzman takes a much more speculative and future-oriented approach than do the other contributors. His scenario of Brazil, frustrated in seeking satisfaction in the international arena and becoming aggressively expansionist along its western frontier is, to say the least, provocative. Providing unity to some of his considerations is the recurring theme of the dilemma between economic development and dependency, related by the author to the contradictions between the theoretical approaches of classical national capability analysis and the new political economy of interdependence. In this respect he takes the hopeful view that interdependency will reduce interest conflict and bring about less hostile use of national political potential. I see little reason to believe that nations will cease striving for advantage, using whatever means they can to prevail within a "semianarchical" international system. Moreover, contrary to what Katzman implies, capability analysis can provide insights into political-economic as well as military competition.

The facts seem clearly to support Katzman's conclusion that Brazil will end the century as the dominant power in South America, but in my view his contention that it is not likely to play a major role in world affairs is based upon a set of rather static assumptions about continuity in the established international system. The full impact of the Chinese decision to participate actively in an international system they scorned for over a quarter century has not yet been felt, and China's eventual emergence as a third superpower would profoundly affect the situation of an aspirant great power such as Brazil.

On the foundation of the historical and systematic global analyses by McCann, Selcher, Manwaring, and Katzman, the next group of authors moves away from primary concern with establishing Brazil's international position and determining its actual and potential influence on the rest of the world. Adopting a "Brazil-as-seen-from-abroad" focus as a unifying theme, they investigate specific bilateral relationships with countries above, roughly on a par with, and below Brazil's level of development, stressing the impact of Brazil's mobility on each type of relationship.

Robert Bond, in Chapter 5, analyzes Brazil's relations with the northern tier Latin American countries, emphasizing problems in the management of conflicts stemming from Brazil's consolidation of regional supremacy. The Venezuelan (Venezuela is the richest and most democratic of South American nations) and Mexican (Mexico is the largest and most populous of the Spanish-speaking countries) dimensions of the question receive particular attention. In raising some valid criticisms of efforts to portray Brazil as an emerging major power, I feel he goes much too far in the other direction. Reflecting perhaps his considerably closer contacts with Venezuelan and other Hispanic American circles—at least in comparison to a quite limited direct familiarity with Brazil—he perpetuates the myth of Brazilian isolation from its neighbors. In fact one of the most significant developments in recent years in the international relations of Latin America has been the vast improvement in Brazil's relations with its Hispanic neighbors. Indeed, this has been so extensive as to open up the possibility that the generally frustrated efforts at economic integration undertaken in the 1960s may experience a new era of success during the 1980s. The fruits of visits to Venezuela and Argentina by the Brazilian president in late 1979 and mid-1980, followed almost immediately by the arrival of Mexico's chief executive in Brazil—on the heels of Pope John Paul's prolonged tour of that subcontinental country—add further substance to these trends. The return visit of the president of Argentina in August underscored the abandonment of that nation's traditional policy of hostility toward Brazil in favor of cooperation on a broad range of matters. Certainly the success of Brazil's Amazonian diplomacy as reflected in the October 1980 meeting of foreign ministers in Belém commemorating the second anniversary of the Amazon Basin Pact gives the lie to the view that Brazil remains isolated from its Spanish-speaking neighbors.

Bond does a good job of summing up the challenges facing Brazil and outlining its economic problems as they impinge upon its international position. One problem that neither he nor the other authors explore is Brazil's foreign debt and its far-reaching ramifications. Brazil's foreign debt, approaching $55 billion, is relatively low in relation to gross national product but quite large in proportion to export earnings (roughly $20 billion for 1980). Major U.S. banks may be uncomfortably overextended in loans to Brazil, and their Western European counterparts hesitate to increase their involvement. Brazil's borrowing needs will again rise sharply in 1981, and pressure is growing from the international banking community—or at least its Anglo-American leading component—for Brazil to turn to the International Monetary Fund (IMF). This Brazil is reluctant to do, perhaps more for political than economic reasons. Should Brazil be able to withstand these pressures or even to obtain special treatment from the IMF, it would be further evidence of Brazil's increased international standing.

Carlos J. Moneta and Rolf Wichmann concentrate in Chapter 6 upon the range of countries from Argentina through Peru, with particular attention to their perceptions of Brazil's growing significance. They clearly define the challenge to Brazil's diplomacy of establishing a predominant status in the region as an essential step toward becoming a great power or a leader of the developing countries' campaign for a new international economic order. Here a good appreciation of the internal political factors in several South American countries is demonstrated as the authors identify areas of actual and prospective cooperation and conflict. Moneta and Wichmann conclude that inept diplomacy could catalyze a reaction against Brazilian hegemony on the part of Hispanic American countries. Yet Brazil has played its cards very well in this respect and is likely to continue to do so. This can best be seen in the skillful utilization of subregional multilateral arrangements to reinforce bilateral ties. Thus, in reading these chapters, with their almost exclusive concentration on bilateral relationships, it should be borne in mind that in addition to being the linchpin of both the Amazon and La Plata Basin pacts, Brazil has also recently managed to become a valued partner of the Andean Pact—which was originally directed in large part against it. In dealings with fellow members of these organizations Brazil takes advantage of Venezuela's remoteness from Southern Cone concerns and the exclusion of Argentina from the Amazon and Andean pacts. At the present stage of partial redemocratization Brazil can be viewed with some degree of affinity by both the more democratic regimes and the more authoritarian ones in this politically very mixed continent.

It is undeniable that the Federal Republic of Germany and Brazil enjoy a close and important economic partnership, and its various dimensions are explored in depth in Chapter 7 by Wolf Grabendorff. This policy-attuned German scholar underscores the Federal Republic's assessment of expanded bilateral relations as "an investment in the future" against the possibility that Brazil will not only be the leading regional power but also become an important industrialized nation. Still, he objectively analyzes the future divergences that may result from Brazil's concern with North-South issues and the priority given by Germany to the East-West conflict. Certainly Grabendorff's emphasis upon the transitory nature of the near-identity of interests that drew these two countries close together during the 1970s is a valuable corrective to assumptions that this relationship will naturally broaden and deepen in the future. Yet the progress being made by Brazil in improving relations with Hispanic American countries and the increasing tendency of these countries to accept the fact of Brazil's greater importance in world affairs—along with the continuation of the transition toward democracy begun in Brasília in the late 1970s—may remove some of the obstacles to an even closer Brazilian-German partnership. A relevant factor neglected by the author is the common concern of the foreign policy elites in both these countries with the decline of U.S. leadership and the possible need to adjust to this as a permanent factor (rather than just a temporary aftermath of Vietnam, Watergate, and the ensuing Carter administration).

Ideally, this analysis of the effects of the special relationship between Brazil and West Germany on the former's striving for upward mobility in the international system would be complemented by a similar study of Brazilian-Japanese relations. The absence of such a chapter is the result of the lack of serious scholarship on this subject. Not only is Japan third behind the United States and West Germany as a source of foreign investment for Brazil, but trade between the two countries is growing steadily. The visit of Brazilian President Ernesto Geisel to Japan in late 1976 was the occasion for announcement of a three-year program of nearly $3 billion in new investments, and in mid-1980 a very large Japanese trade mission visited Brazil to identify new areas for expansion of trade and investment. The basic long-run complementarity of economic interests between these two countries will be a major factor in the future role of Brazil in world affairs. Present exports of iron ore and foodstuffs to Japan will be augmented by exports of other minerals and growing quantities of steel as Japan opts to invest in the expansion of Brazil's steelmaking capacity rather than build in the overcrowded and pollution-plagued home islands.

Brazil's foreign minister recently completed a tour of the "front line" African nations, and President Figueiredo is expected to visit Africa during 1981. Although quite a bit has been written from the Brazilian perspective on the affinities between Brazil and the countries of sub-Saharan Africa, less attention has been paid to the degree of African acceptance of Brazilian initiatives. Anani Dzidzienyo and J. Michael Turner probe this question in Chapter 8, with attention to African perceptions of the Brazilian racial situation and Brazil's concern with establishing the foundations for cooperation in the field of South Atlantic security. In this regard, relations between Brazil and Nigeria receive special attention, and the authors stress that several contradictions will have to be worked out in the early 1980s, particularly with respect to South Africa.

In the final chapter, the comparative roles of Brazil and India as "Third World middle powers" are thoroughly analyzed by Michael A. Morris. This innovative type of paired comparison yields significant results in the hands of this knowledgeable scholar who, like most of the contributors to this volume, resided in Brazil at some point in the 1970s. Morris's generalizations concerning the role of middle powers among the developing countries are something of a bonus in a study focusing upon Brazil. I would argue that, in fact, Brazil only partially fits in the same category as does India. In the first place, India's role as the premier power in South Asia is much more limited by the geographic proximity and political-military presence of the Soviet Union and China than is Brazil's role in South America, more distant from the United States than is Western Europe. Moreover, Brazil has managed to engineer an accommodation—bordering on an alliance—with its chief traditional rival, Argentina, while Pakistani hostility remains a major restraint upon Indian foreign policy. Then, too, Brazil's international trade (approximately $33 billion in 1979 and over $42 billion in 1980) is far more significant and diversified than that of India.

Looking to the future, India seems destined to remain a Third World middle power, but Brazil retains the option of possibly entering the club of industrialized nations. Brazil's emergence by the mid-1980s as the developed world's leading single source of both foodstuffs and minerals will project it well ahead of India, a trend not brought out by Morris's admittedly "factual and present-oriented" comparison. Yet one of the virtues of this study and all the other contributions to the book is careful restraint, with sober consideration of constraints and problems a major unifying theme. Readers can have confidence that Brazil is at least as important an actor in the present international system as these scholars indicate, for none errs on the side of overoptimism or emotionalism about the rise of Brazil.

The Contributors

Robert D. Bond, a fellow at the Council on Foreign Relations and an international political consultant, is the author of numerous publications, including *Contemporary Venezuela and Its Role in International Affairs* and articles on Latin America in *Orbis, International Organization, Foro Internacional,* and *Worldview.* He lectures frequently throughout the United States and Latin America.

Anani Dzidzienyo is on the faculty of the Afro-American Studies Program and the Center for Portuguese and Brazilian Studies at Brown University. He has researched and written about blacks in Brazilian society and in other Latin American societies.

Wolf Grabendorff, senior research associate for Latin American affairs at the Stiftung Wissenschaft und Politik (Research Institute for International Affairs), Ebenhausen, West Germany, is coauthor of *Brasilien: Entwicklungsmodell und Aussenpolitik* [Brazil: development model and foreign policy] (1977) and has published widely about the foreign policies of Brazil, Mexico, and Cuba, as well as on Latin American international affairs in general. He has been appointed a visiting research fellow for 1980-1981 at the Center of Brazilian Studies, School of Advanced International Studies, Johns Hopkins University.

Martin T. Katzman is professor of political economy and environmental sciences at the University of Texas at Dallas and is the recipient of a Guggenheim Fellowship for 1980-1981. He taught at the Instituto de Pesquisas Econômicas of the University of São Paulo from 1970–1972 and has published extensively on urban and regional development in Brazil. His *Cities and Frontiers in Brazil: Regional Dimensions of Economic Development* was selected as one of the best academic books of 1977 by *Choice.*

Frank D. McCann is associate professor of history at the University of New Hampshire. His *The Brazilian-American Alliance, 1937–1945* (1973) won the Society for Historians of American Foreign Relations 1975 Stuart Bernath Prize. His articles have appeared in such journals as *Hispanic-American Historical Review, Inter-American Economic Affairs, Journal of Inter-American and World Affairs, Foro Internacional* (Mexico), *Diplomatic History,* and *Journal of Latin American Studies* (London). In 1976-1977 he was visiting professor at the University of Brasília. He is the 1979-1980 chairperson of the Committee on Brazilian Studies, Conference on Latin American History.

Max G. Manwaring, Lt. Col., U.S. Army, is a graduate of the Army War College. He was formerly associate professor of political science at Memphis State University and president of the Midwest Association of Latin American Studies. He has written "Career Patterns and Attitudes of Military-Political Elites in Brazil: Similarity and Continuity, 1964–1975," *International Journal of Comparative Sociology,* Vol. 19, pp. 233-248, and *RAMP, A Relative Advantage Military-Political Simulation Dealing with the Major Types of Limited War* (Ft. Leavenworth, Kans.: U.S. Army Command and General Staff College, 1975).

Carlos J. Moneta, presently a Special Fellow at the United Nations Institute for Training and Research (UNITAR), has been professor and researcher at universities in Argentina, Mexico, and the United States. He has held various public posts, including the presidency of the National Argentine Commission of the La Plata Basin Treaty. He has published numerous articles on Latin American foreign relations and world order studies in specialized Latin American and European journals.

Michael A. Morris is currently on leave from his position as associate professor of political science at Clemson University as a research fellow at the Stockholm International Peace Research Institute. He is the author of *International Politics and the Sea: The Case of Brazil* (Westview, 1979), as well as numerous articles in professional journals.

Ronald M. Schneider is chairman of the Latin American Area Studies Program and professor of political science at Queens College of the City University of New York. His writings on Brazil include *Brazil: Foreign Policy of a Future World Power* (Westview, 1977) and *The Political System of Brazil* (1971). He is now working on a major study of transitions to democracy, focusing particularly upon the present Brazilian experience.

Wayne A. Selcher, associate professor of political science at Elizabethtown College, has published articles on Brazil's foreign relations and national security doctrine and policies. He is the author of *The Afro-Asian*

Dimension of Brazilian Foreign Policy, 1956–1972 (1974) and *Brazil's Multilateral Relations: Between First and Third Worlds* (Westview, 1978) and has participated in several U.S. government–sponsored studies on Brazil's international role.

J. Michael Turner, program officer, Office for Latin America and the Caribbean, the Ford Foundation, was formerly assistant professor of history, College of the Holy Cross (1973–1978) and professor-colaborador, Departamento de Geografia e Historia, Universidade de Brasília (1976–1978). He has conducted research on Brazilian historical influence in West Africa, in Benin, Nigeria, Togo, Ghana, Senegal, and Brazil.

Rolf Wichmann, assistant professor of political science at Boston College, was previously a researcher with UNITAR and a research assistant at the Institute of International Studies of the University of California at Berkeley. He has had extensive research and journalistic experience in South America, especially Chile.

1
Brazilian Foreign Relations in the Twentieth Century

Frank D. McCann

Underlying the history of Brazilian foreign relations has been an effort to use foreign policy to achieve recognition of national greatness. The methods, indeed the intermediate goals, have changed with time and circumstance, but the ultimate objective of *grandeza nacional*, or national grandeur, has endured. Throughout the imperial period (1822–1889), the European monarchies looked upon the Brazilian empire as a tropical oddity, while the American republics regarded it with either suspicion or indifference. In the twentieth century suspicion became paramount among its neighbors, while the powers tended to treat Brazil as an economic or political pawn that could be dealt with according to their needs. Brazilians sought to mitigate the suspicion and worked to have the powers take Brazil seriously and admit it to their ranks. The concern with national prestige is a keystone of Brazilian policy, its other characteristics clustering about it.

Continuities in the Colonial Administration and the First Republic

Brazil's colonial heritage included, in rough outline, the present national territory. There was little need to demarcate the nearly 10,000 miles of frontier until this century when population began to spread into the continent's interior. Still, the successful conclusion of negotiations, arbitrations, and military maneuverings employed to draw exact boundaries without major conflict was a remarkable achievement that stands as testament to the brilliance of Foreign Minister José Maria da Silva Paranhos, the Baron of Rio Branco, who set the tone and direction of twentieth century Brazilian policy.

Linked to the policy of secure frontiers was that of seeking to prevent

1

Brazil's neighbors, especially in the Rio de la Plata, from forming a coalition against it. This required maintaining the status quo in the equations of power among its neighbors. For the most part this has meant keeping Argentina in check and preventing it from achieving its dream of reconstructing the Viceroyalty of the Rio de la Plata. It has also led to intimate involvement in the internal politics and economies of Paraguay, Bolivia, and Uruguay and to an informal but consistent alliance with Chile. This policy of division, of keeping its neighbors disunified, reaches back into the last century. Involvements in the civil war in Argentina (1852) and in the war against Paraguay (1865–1870) were in support of it. Ambassador Heitor Lyra's 1951 observation that Argentina is "the nerve point of our foreign policy" holds true to the present.[1] Recent efforts toward neighborly cooperation in the Amazon and with the Andean countries and in energy development in the Rio de la Plata are only a seeming departure from the rule, developed in the course of negotiations over the frontiers, that Brazil should never sit down with more than one neighbor at a time, in the belief that the Spanish-speakers would join forces against the Brazilians. This rule encouraged Brazilians to seek an alliance with the United States to offset potential isolation among the Spanish-speakers. In the Amazonian and Andean situations Brazil has carefully developed bilateral understandings before moving to the stage of multilateral agreement. Its approach to Pan-Americanism was conditioned by the belief that hemispheric unity, with its accompanying legal mechanisms for preventing and containing armed conflict, would lessen the possibility of anti-Brazilian coalitions.

Diplomatic efforts in support of economic development are another element of continuity in Brazilian foreign policy. The nature and perception of development have changed since Brazilian diplomats worked to fend off British suppression of the slave trade in the first half of the last century, or, later on, to assist Paulista planters to obtain European immigrant workers. In the twentieth century they sought to defend coffee and cacao markets, developed complicated subterfuges in the 1930s to maintain trade with antagonistic powers, and supported industrialization from the 1940s onward. Of course, in socioeconomic terms the segments of society influencing and benefiting from this diplomacy changed composition over the decades as the economy slowly shifted from a total colonial-style export orientation to an increasing internal-market orientation, but in broad terms that seems less significant than the tendency to provide diplomatic support for the economy.

Still, examination of the socioeconomic and regional backgrounds of Brazilian diplomats over the decades shows that they were consistently drawn from the dominant elites of each era and that they represented the interests and attitudes of those elites. Under the empire, fifteen out of forty-two foreign ministers came from Bahia, while with the republic and the shift in the focus of power from the Northeast to the Center-South, Minas Gerais and Rio de Janeiro became common sources of foreign ministers and diplomats. There may have been psychosocial as well as economic and political reasons for the regional elites' interest in diplomacy. Bahia, Minas Gerais, and Rio de Janeiro were heavily Africanized, and yet their elites tended to reject the reality around them and to function instead in an imaginary white, Latin society. As José Honório Rodrigues has suggested, the foreign ministry and diplomatic service was an ideal environment in which to create a false reality, where French could replace Portuguese, where judicial procedures and international topics could shut out the illiterate, dark-skinned world about the elites. Even the office furniture of the Itamaraty was deliberately imported from England.[2] The expression *para inglês ver* (for the English to see), the creation of a European facade to cover the reality of Brazil, flowed from a mind-set in which the whitening of Brazil was a basic desire.[3]

Their shame at the darkness around them made the elites feel inferior to Europeans, so the diplomats tried to convince their European colleagues that Brazil was a new country with a society in formation. Yet, strangely enough, until the 1930s European travelers would comment that they felt more comfortable there than in Argentina or the United States exactly because the society appeared older, more rooted, more hierarchical. The idea of newness has been joined since the 1950s with notions of internal expansion and economic development to project an image of dynamism that seems to put aside any sense of inferiority.

Because foreign policy has been the creature of a restricted segment of society, it has tended to preserve its underlying characteristics. There is a consistent tradition of legalism, of juridical solutions, in part due to the law school training of many diplomats and in part due to Brazil's military weakness that prevented recourse to arms. Also there is the tradition of nonpartisanship; foreign policy was not normally a political football. This latter was less the result of a conscious policy than of the historical circumstance of rule by restricted elites, whose interests were more complementary than competitive, and the consequent lack of competitive, representative government.

The Rio Branco era (1902–1912) was more than a period in which the frontier lines were fixed. The breadth of the baron's vision set the tone for the following decades. Clearly the boundaries were essential for determining exactly where Brazil began and ended, but even more important than the series of successful negotiations and arbitrations

themselves was that they served to alert the powers that Brazil was drawing lines over which they were not to intrude—this during the heyday of
imperialism when Africa, Asia, and the Caribbean had been forced
under European or U.S. flags. The baron urged reform of the Brazilian
army and navy because he understood that without military
preparedness territorial claims could not be sustained. To this end, he
and General Hermes da Fonseca (president, 1910–1914) sent young,
reform-minded officers to train with the Imperial German Army. And to
enhance Brazil's prestige, the baron convinced Rome of the wisdom of
conferring the first Latin American cardinalate (1905) on the archbishop
of Rio de Janeiro.

In the economic sphere Brazil was in an awkward position. The principal customer for its coffee was the United States, but Great Britain held
its 1898 "Funding Loan" note (between 1883 and 1914 Brazil had bor-
rowed over $120 million, of which it still owed over $100 million in
1925). British banks financed international commercial exchange, and
down to 1930 British investors accounted for 53 percent of total foreign
investment in Brazil. Rio Branco and his successors sought to set tem-
poral and physical limits to dependency by diffusing it among the
powers. Encouraging closer economic and political ties with the United
States provided a hedge against the British, and eventually, in the first
Vargas period (1930–1945), would allow a shift from the London to the
New York financial orbit. The military ties with Germany involved purchases of expensive field equipment that encouraged trade relations. In
that era of infrastructure building, the purchase of foreign-made
machines and equipment was seen as a necessary stage of internal
economic development. Rio Branco saw this diffused dependency as temporary; once developed, Brazil would achieve full independence.

Participation in the Pan-American movement and the Hague conferences had the objective of increasing Brazilian prestige to lessen the
possibility of imperialist attacks and of creating an image of independent
action that would inspire national confidence. By standing with the
United States in its Caribbean adventures and by arguing for acceptance
of arbitration in the settlement of disputes, Brazil at once sought to protect itself from similar U.S. abuse, to convince its neighbors that the
United States was allied with Brazil, and that Brazil would not threaten
them militarily.

Rio Branco's lengthy chancellorship provided the basis for what
would be henceforth nodded to as the Itamaraty tradition, but not
all administrations understood it; some confused its tactical elements—dependence on foreign loans and investment, Pan-Americanism, and alliance with the United States—with its strategic sub-

stance—the pursuit of independence and national greatness.

World War I found Brazil in a quandary. Its officer corps had been partially reinvigorated and Germanized; its troops used German drills to train with their Mauser rifles, while at Vila Militar outside Rio the very kitchens were German in style and equipment. Yet economics, the U.S. decision for war, and German submarine attacks on Brazilian merchantships pushed Brazil into the conflict on the side of the Allies in 1917. Though Brazil mobilized, it lacked the ability to place units on line in Europe quickly, so its war was limited to naval demonstrations, the supply of some medical personnel, and the exploits of a few officers who served with the French forces.

The peace, however, provided opportunities. At Versailles, Woodrow Wilson embraced the newly elected Brazilian president, Epitácio Pessoa (1919–1922), exchanged correspondence with him, and sent him home on a U.S. warship. For a short while it seemed as if Brazil and the United States would form a New World team in the League of Nations. Unhappily, Wilson failed to convince the Senate and so Pessoa led Brazil into the League alone. There Brazil was consistently elected to one of the Council's nonpermanent seats and its diplomats played active roles in League business, enhancing Itamaraty's image. In Geneva the Brazilians' legalistic mentality served them well, but ability alone was not sufficient to overcome European resistance to Brazilian pretensions to permanent Council membership. In 1926, when Germany joined the League and received a permanent seat, Brazil withdrew, partly in protest, partly from wounded national pride.

In the Western Hemisphere, the Pan-American conferences provided their own form of frustration. At the end of 1922 the Arthur Bernardes (1922–1926) administration, wishing to cut its military expenditures in order to balance the budget, had invited Argentina and Chile to discuss mutual arms reduction prior to the upcoming inter-American conference in Santiago. Argentina had declined, claiming a lack of time to prepare, while Chile had accepted. The Argentines felt squeezed and their press launched a propaganda campaign painting Brazil as a militaristic country with hegemonic designs on the continent. Argentina had remained neutral during the recent war, betting on a German victory. Its military officers had looked on with irritation and suspicion while Brazil had established obligatory military service, reorganized its army, constructed new training areas and barracks, purchased modern weapons, and contracted to obtain a French military mission. The Bernardes administration saw its good intentions placing Brazil in the uncomfortable position of having to defend its military program, not only to Argentina and Chile, but before all the American republics. The Brazilian army's report on the conference observed that "the Brazilian delegation encountered a deliberately prepared hostile milieu in Santiago" thanks to "Argentine propaganda." The report accused the Argentine government of using "Brazilian armaments" as a device to squeeze arms funding out of its congress and to weaken the position Brazil had developed in the League of Nations.[4]

Though Brazil wished to be regarded as "the most powerful state in South America," the U.S. military attaché reported that "a war of aggression would not meet with popular favor, nor is the Brazilian army prepared to take the field against an organized force."[5] Even so, seeing the French and Americans advising the Brazilians in the reorganization and modernization of their army and navy had to have an unsettling effect on the Argentines. Tension between Argentina and Brazil and continuous maneuvering for superior positions of influence in the buffer states of Paraguay and Uruguay were, and are, characteristic of their relations. For this reason a third of the Brazilian army has been traditionally stationed in Rio Grande do Sul.

These experiences did not encourage Brazilian faith in a rigid Pan-Americanism. In the League of Nations Brazil opposed creation of regional arbitration and security pacts, arguing somewhat deceptively that an unshakable peace reigned in the Americas. Rather, it favored worldwide pacts because expanded Western Hemisphere ties to other continents only increased the possibility of future intercontinental conflicts that regional agreements would be powerless to stem.[6]

The World War I era and the 1920s also saw an expansion of Brazil's ties abroad. The United States had raised its Rio de Janeiro legation to embassy status in 1905, while Great Britain and Italy were the first European states to do likewise, in 1918. By 1926 Brazil had relations with thirty-four countries and was receiving a stream of distinguished visitors, such as Prince Humberto of Italy and General John Pershing of the United States. Brazilian coastal cities were standard ports of call for the British, German, U.S., and Argentine fleets, while European and U.S. universities, museums, and zoos sent expeditions to study its geology, flora, and fauna.

Also by the mid-1920s, Brazil was caught in a struggle to develop a reasonable balance between its customs receipts and government expenditures; more attention was being focused on the national debt, most of which was owed to British banks. Not surprisingly, since the United States was taking half of Brazil's exports by 1926, there was a gradual shift to financial ties with U.S. banks as part of the process of moving out from under debt obligations to British and French institutions. Between 1921 and 1927 U.S. banks came to hold nearly 35 percent of the foreign debt. The process speeded up in the next decade and was completed during World War II. Interestingly, the Bernardes administration, while not supporting complete import substitution based on customs barriers, did favor protecting existing industries. And it urged cutting down on imports to halt the outflow of convertible currency, to maintain debt service, and, especially, to reduce the frequency of foreign loans. Moreover, Bernardes saw the importance of developing the internal market, pointing in his 1925 report to the increasing volume of interstate coastal trade. With pride, he declared that "in equal conditions of climate, natural resources, and population density, no other people could have created, in a century of independent life, a more prosperous nation than ours."[7]

However, the so-called *tenente* rebellions of the 1920s marred Brazil's image. In Bernardes' words it was "difficult . . . to maintain the country's good name . . . [while] the insurrections against legally constituted authority" diminished "the nation's international image" and caused "the most incredible and malevolent rumors to the detriment of national credit."[8]

The Vargas Period

The first half of the 1930s would do little to alter the image of instability, but by decade's end the powers were wooing Brazil as the republic played a pivotal role in the pre–World War II jockeying for position. From 1930 to 1954, Getúlio Dornelles Vargas dominated the political stage and shaped or influenced Brazilian foreign relations. His task was even greater than that of his predecessors because he had to deal not only with internal problems, such as the 1932 São Paulo rebellion, but also with a destabilized world economy in which all nations were seeking ways to protect themselves. The deepening depression emphasized Brazil's vulnerability due to its dependence on coffee exports.

Vargas was confronted with conflicting pressures from Britain, the United States, and Germany. The English Rothchilds sent a representative, Sir Otto Niemeyer, to protect their interests, advising the government on how to obtain sufficient funds to maintain debt service. From his office in the Treasury Ministry, Niemeyer urged the purchase and destruction of surplus coffee to support its price on the world market. Washington, always opposed to foreign governments maintaining price supports, protested against this and measures aimed at encouraging Brazilian-flag shipping. As Brazil's gold supply dwindled, Vargas found himself facing a United States seeking a reciprocal trade agreement that would, in classic Open Door fashion, reduce Brazilian tariffs on a wide

range of U.S. products in exchange for *continuation* of free entry into the
United States of the principal Brazilian products, coffee and rubber. It
was a form of blackmail disguised as liberal free trade. Brazil was to
make concessions to keep what it already had, but at a double cost: First,
via most-favored-nation agreements other coffee-producing nations
would move into the U.S. market, cutting Brazil's share; and second,
Brazilian industry would have to compete with U.S. products. Further,
such an agreement would give the Americans an edge over the Europeans.

The Europeans (Germany, Italy, Sweden) came forward with trade
deals of their own. The German mechanisms revealed considerable imag-
ination. Germany proposed an exchange agreement based upon a nonconvertible (compensation) mark system that allowed the two to sell to
each other without recourse to gold or internationally accepted currency.
Vargas signed both the U.S. and German agreements and, until the war
ended the game, skillfully played the two powers against each other.

To conduct the increasingly complex diplomacy of the era and to bring
some revolutionary breezes into the Itamaraty, the Vargas government
reformed the foreign ministry. It fused the diplomatic and consular corps
and made requisite a regular rotation from posts abroad to ones in the
ministry. It also established entrance examininations and a rigorous
training program for those seeking a diplomatic career. The reforms
ended what Foreign Minister Oswaldo Aranha regarded as the ministry's
isolation on an "island of fantasies and traditions" and drew new talent
to the diplomatic service.[9]

Though Brazilian diplomats dreamed of a continent untainted by
hegemony and joined in an "economic confederation,"[10] the reality of the
1930s was war in the Chaco and unease in the Amazon. The former involved Bolivia and Paraguay in a struggle for supposedly oil-rich lands,
while the latter resulted from Peruvian cession of Leticia to Colombia
and tension between Peru and Ecuador. During the Chaco war Brazil
feared possible Argentine-Paraguayan collusion because of their close
military ties. Since then it has been an objective of Brazilian policy to
minimize Argentine military influence in the neighboring countries.

General staff officers believed that Amazonia would have "a role of
great importance in the future" and would be an area where varied international interests would converge. Because of its vastness and thick
jungle cover, aviation would be the key to military control. And so the
"military interests of Brazil counsel the maintenance of *de facto* monopoly of the aerial life of Amazonia, especially since the internationalization of river routes noticeably restricts our sovereignty."[11]

Regarding relations beyond South America, a 1934 general staff situation study suggested that Brazil might be pulled into another world war as an ally, or that the "various expansionist currents" could make it a cause for, or a theater of, such a war. The study specified the Japanese, Germans, Americans, and Italians as "serious threats." The Japanese threat was the "most dangerous, because it is the most systematic and methodical, most clearly absorbing and best directed." Germany was an old threat that intensified with the current racist spirit and scientific-military philosophy. The U.S. threat was above all economic, and although it did not directly threaten political independence, it "tended to make us vassals." U.S. expansion, the report argued, was largely by means of commerce and the export of capital and clashed in Brazil with the Japanese, who exported labor to expand. "The clash of these two currents could result in an action against our independence or, at least, against our integrity." The Italian was the least dangerous, though the accumulation of Italians in certain regions could "indirectly threaten to break the national unity of the people" and influence public opinion in case of a European war. The preventative measures that Brazil adopted when war broke out in Europe in 1939 closely followed those suggested six years earlier: control of immigration to lessen regional accumulation of any one nationality; neutralizing foreign assistance to immigrants; obligatory use of Portuguese; and "intense nationalization" of immigrant children.

Army thinking probably reflected accurately Brazilians' underlying distrust of the United States. As the only people of Portuguese origin in the hemisphere, the Brazilians should, the staff analysis argued, count solely on themselves in the event of a world war. Though there were, they admitted, certain similarities between Brazil's situation and that of the United States that had served as the basis for a "more or less intimate approximation" that gave Brazil U.S. support in international questions, it had not been "without grave inconveniences." "Economically we are their dependents." Indeed, the economic arrangements were precarious because coffee was not a necessity and could be dropped in case of war. Moreover, recalling U.S. interventions in the Caribbean and Central America, the general staff cautioned that "we must consider that the United States itself could constitute a threat for us . . . in view of the evolution of its post-war international policies." The conclusion was that Brazil had to prepare itself militarily.[12]

From this type of analysis developed the foreign policy of drawing support from Germany and the United States simultaneously. The matter has been studied elsewhere[13] so only a summary is necessary here. Military officers and civilian capitalists joined efforts to shield the German agreement because it allowed the former to buy arms without draining away gold and currency reserves and the latter to increase and diversify export markets for foodstuffs and raw materials. Of course, it did not contribute to the accumulation of reserves, which U.S. bondholders and businessmen wishing to remit profits were quick to note. But because the U.S. Congress was then severely limiting arms sales, military support for the compensation trade could not be weakened. Vargas's close friend, Oswaldo Aranha, had the task, as ambassador to Washington, of keeping the Americans mollified.

With the outbreak of war the German trade faded but Vargas continued to play his Berlin card to secure concessions from the United States. Throughout, his style was one that would become a feature of postwar neutralist diplomacy—playing the powers against each other to obtain maximum advantage. The result was a U.S. drive to secure an alliance with Brazil, which provided U.S. financing for the Volta Redonda steel-mill complex, market guarantees for Brazilian products, an improved transportation infrastructure, and U.S. arms, planes, and ships. As a result Brazil became the only Latin American republic to commit troops in Europe. It would come out of the war the strongest military power of South America, with an economic infrastructure on which would be built the rapid development of the postwar era.

By early 1943 Foreign Minister Oswaldo Aranha had drawn up Brazil's wartime objectives. The list can be read as the underlying policy objectives of the following thirty years. He had advised Vargas that Brazil should seek

1. A better position in world politics;
2. A better position in the politics of the neighboring countries via consolidation of its preeminence in South America;
3. A more confident and intimate solidarity with the United States;
4. An increasing ascendancy over Portugal and its possessions;
5. The establishment of maritime power;
6. The establishment of air power;
7. The foundation of a war industry;
8. The establishment of light industries—agricultural, extractive, and mineral—complementary to those of North America and necessary for world reconstruction;
9. The extension of railways and highways for economic and strategic reasons;
10. The exploitation of essential fuels.[14]

Brazil's active participation in the war heightened Brazilian nationalism. When the expeditionaries took Monte Castello, a key point in the German line, the press was in ecstasy, predicting that Brazil would be invited to join the big five in the Supreme Allied Council, thus advancing to great power status.[15] Although that notion soon proved an illusion, Brazil was able to use the war to advance its position in South America. Brazil gave Paraguay free-port privileges in Santos, a move that began the gradual rerouting of Paraguayan commerce through Brazil away from the Rio de la Plata, and declared "nonexistent" the debt that Paraguay owed Brazil from the War of the Triple Alliance (1865–1870). The Brazilians opened a branch of the Bank of Brazil in Asunción and sought to improve ties via scholarships, training programs for Paraguayan officers, the donation of a radio station, the signing of a trade and navigation treaty, and discussion of extending the São Paulo railway to Paraguay. In similar fashion the Vargas government worked to strengthen links with Bolivia, where Brazilians were building the rail line from Corumbá, on the border, to Santa Cruz de la Sierra, which would give Bolivia access to the Atlantic via Santos.

Relations with Argentina had deteriorated steadily as internal crises brought Juan D. Perón to power in Buenos Aires. During 1944, as Argentina increased the size of its army amidst parades and newspaper references to territorial expansion, Brazilian agents reported that several thousand Axis officers and technicians were helping to mobilize war industries and train the armed forces. An Itamaraty analyst noted the rehabilitation of Juan Manuel de Rosas (1829–1852) and warned that revival of his dream of resurrecting the colonial Viceroyalty of the Rio de la Plata would be a nightmare for Brazil.[16] Though it never came to a fight, the Vargas government used the Argentine threat to secure additional U.S. military aid to build up its forces and base facilities along the southern frontier.

The Second Republic

In the immediate postwar period Brazilian diplomats focused on making their mark in the United Nations. Though Brazil did not secure the permanent seat on the Security Council for which the Vargas administration had worked and for which the press had cheered, in 1946 Brazil was elected by an impressive margin to a two-year term as a nonpermanent member. In 1947 the General Assembly elected Oswaldo Aranha president of its second session; thus his name and that of Brazil were associated with the UN's recognition of the state of Israel.

That same year the American republics' foreign ministers met in Rio de Janeiro and Petrópolis to draw up the Treaty of Reciprocal Assistance, or Rio Pact, condemning aggression and calling for immediate intervention on the part of the UN Security Council in cases of invasion. The pact validated Brazil's opposition to war as an instrument of foreign policy and provided arbitration mechanisms, while insuring security via commitments of international response to aggression. It altered Brazil's military relationship with the United States by giving it a more multilateral aspect.

Brazilian relations with the United States during the Eurico Dutra administration (1946–1950) were intimate, but with an edge of caution. Harry Truman and Dutra exchanged visits, giving the latter the opportunity to be the first Brazilian president to address the U.S. Congress. And building on the work of wartime studies of economic potential, the two governments set up a mixed commission to study and make recommendations for economic development projects. U.S. economic specialists saw "Brazil as a pilot area to test modern methods of industrial development."[17]

Ties with the United States were tightened in the military area as well. Army, air force, and naval officers entered U.S. training programs in large numbers and the armed forces were reequipped with surplus U.S. equipment. However, some activities pointed toward a more independent future. The army sought, where possible, to acquire locally produced weapons and equipment "to liberate itself from foreign dependency."[18] Graduates of the Escola Técnica do Exército were beginning to make their presence felt in arms production, in the steel industry, in hydroelectric projects, and in petroleum research. The establishment of the Centro Técnico de Aeronáutica in São José dos Campos laid the basis for Brazil's current aeronautics industry. Perhaps most important was the 1949 creation of the Escola Superior de Guerra, a "national institute of higher studies" where military officers and civilian leaders would study "the development of national economic potential, the coordination of our foreign policy with the necessities of security and . . . the combined employment of the armed forces."[19] The era also saw the establishment of the Instituto Rio Branco for the training of diplomats, underscoring the continued improvement and professionalization of the diplomatic service.

Economic relations became increasingly complex in the postwar world. The Dutra administration paid off half Brazil's foreign debt but found itself compelled to print more money to keep the internal economy functioning. As a result, inflation continued unabated. Between 1945 and 1950 currency in circulation increased by 84 percent. Moreover, the war had left Brazil with accounts of nonconvertible funds in a variety of countries, which it expended via a series of bilateral agreements in 1947. It also developed barter arrangements that had India swapping jute for

Brazilian rice and Norway exchanging codfish for coffee. Brazil began to experience the dilemma of depreciation on a large scale. It had to depreciate its currency relative to the dollar to make its exports cheaper in the world market, thereby increasing sales and production. But to maintain expansion implied costly outlays for transportation facilities, improved technology in agriculture and industry, and education and training of the labor force. Continuous internal expansion would require continuous export increases to pay for it.[20]

The 1950 elections swept Getúlio Vargas back into the Catete Palace. In his first year in office there were the continuities of close ties with the United States and active participation in the United Nations, where Brazil was reelected to the Security Council with fifty-seven out of fifty-nine votes, and in the Organization of American States. By March 1951, when it opened missions in Haiti, Honduras, El Salvador, and Nicaragua, Brazil had resident diplomats in every Latin American country.

Observers have underrated the impact of Vargas's second presidency on foreign policy, assuming that Jânio Quadros and João Goulart effected the major departures of the postwar era with their "independent foreign policy." Vargas certainly maintained, and even strengthened, military and economic ties with the United States, attempting to capitalize on a relationship that had paid dividends in the war years, but he knew well the dangers of tacking too closely to Washington's course. In 1951 he emphasized the necessity of "the new policy of international economic cooperation, whose objective is to give to the underdeveloped countries means of intensive expansion, with which to correct their deficiencies and to compensate the natural disadvantages responsible for their retardation." If something were not done to correct the imbalance between the rich and poor countries of the Western world, "sooner or later," he warned, the unity of the West would break and "social revolution would come." The era when the highly industrialized countries could exploit the backward ones was over. The democratic world would not survive, he declared, if it did not overcome the exaggerated inequality among the areas that comprised it.

Brazil, he said, viewed its own "intensive economic development" as an "undelayable imperative."[21] To this end, in 1952, he proposed that Congress create a national economic development bank as part of "a general plan of investments for the economic and social progress of the country."[22] And he was clear in asserting that although Brazil was ready to cooperate economically with others in the hemisphere, its conduct would be conditioned by the reciprocity of "our allies" in helping Brazil's economy.[23] He was signaling that the developmentalism that marked the Estado Novo (1937–1945) would be continued and would be an element of Brazilian foreign policy. Moreover, he expected the United States to help.

But even more strikingly, he announced that, given the changes in the world, "Brazilian interests are not only close to [Brazil's] frontiers, but in every corner of the world." Especially, he called attention to Africa as "a new force surging forward on the international scene. . . . All colonialism," he said, "should be considered an undesirable leftover on today's international scene." In 1950, to emphasize its position on colonialism, Brazil recognized the independence of Indonesia, Laos, Cambodia, and the government of the emperor of Vietnam. And to support the stepping up of Brazil's international efforts Vargas asked the Congress to increase the Itamaraty's budget allocation.[24] A 1951 law tightened regular rotation from assignments abroad to ones in the foreign ministry to insure that it would be staffed with people who had fresh field experience.[25]

The themes stressed in his first annual message to Congress were sharpened in succeeding years as Vargas urged Brazilians to realize that Brazil had become a world power and that national greatness demanded a foreign policy compatible with "our destiny as a great power." Further he pointedly linked foreign relations to "the economic development of Brazil."[26]

Policy positions that would be highlighted during succeeding administrations were already being assumed by early 1952. Note the topics that Brazilian diplomats at the Sixth General Assembly emphasized: "the colonial question, the financing of economic development by international entities, the agrarian question, social progress, the preservation of peace and disarmament." Vargas pointed to the vulnerability of the Brazilian economy in confronting the international crisis which the Cold War and the Korean conflict had produced and called on the United States to strengthen the economy via investments in transportation, energy, and foods.[27] The government followed closely the situation in the Mediterranean, the Near East, and Africa and looked with sympathy on nationalist movements in Morocco, Tunisia, Egypt, Ghana, and Nigeria. In the UN it took the initiative in seeking a solution regarding Morocco and Tunisia.[28] And arguing that the UN should establish a special fund to subsidize economic development with low-interest loans, Brazil also advocated the idea that nonautonomous territories should be developed and prepared for independence. In 1952 Brazil voted in the UN against racial discrimination in South Africa, and in 1953 it supported Puerto Rican autonomy.[29]

The period also saw an improvement in relations with Argentina, although Vargas's aides maintained that contacts with Perón did not go beyond those that protocol demanded.[30] In 1954 Brazil sponsored the first world congress on coffee and participated in conferences of sugar and cotton producers seeking to stabilize market conditions and fix prices. It also completed the São Paulo–Santa Cruz de la Sierra rail line, begun during World War II, which would gradually bring eastern Bolivia into Brazil's economic orbit.

Meanwhile, U.S. policy had begun to run counter to Brazil's. The Eisenhower administration's position on development aid was that it must come from the private sector, ending the Mixed Brazil–United States Commision for Economic Development set up under Truman. This repudiation of aid, coupled with demands for easier access for U.S. investment money, was an irritation into the 1960s. Even so, U.S. investments more than doubled between 1950 and 1958,[31] as President Juscelino Kubitschek (1956–1961) continued Vargas's developmental tradition.

But the Americans wanted more access than the Brazilian government could give. Eisenhower urged Kubitschek to ignore Petrobrás, which he seemed to regard as communist-inspired; John Foster Dulles and Allen Dulles urged closer ties between the Central Intelligence Agency (CIA) and Brazilian secret services. Ironically, from the perspective of 1980, Ford and General Motors refused to set up plants in Brazil, arguing that there was not a sufficient market for automobiles. U.S. business had little enthusiasm for Kubitschek's notion of fifty years' progress in five; so he turned to Europe, where the Germans especially were ready to increase their presence in Brazil. Between 1951 and 1961 West Germany invested 17.6 percent of its total foreign investments in the country.[32]

It should be noted that Kubitschek all but ignored the African struggle for independence and embraced the cause of Portuguese colonialism. José Honório Rodrigues charged that his government limited itself to simple de jure recognition of independent status. It is curious that an administration so committed to development failed to grasp "the unity of the struggle against underdevelopment."[33]

The change in U.S. policy coincided with, and contributed to, the rising tide of nationalism in Brazil. The Brazilians could not understand how the United States could rebuild its former enemies while ignoring its ally's desire for development assistance. Earlier, in 1951, their resentment had bubbled up when Washington requested troops for the Korean conflict. Vargas had told an aide: "We fought in the past war and were entirely forgotten and cut out in the division of the spoils."[34] The Brazilians never tired of reciting their contributions to the Allies in World War II and noting bitterly how fast Americans had forgotten. The various binational developmental study groups that Washington mounted to satisfy

U.S. economic needs had raised Brazilian expectations for continued economic cooperation and assistance. The Republican administration's refusal to make good on what appeared to be U.S. commitments seemed to Brazilians to be aimed at retarding their nation's emergence as a world power.

Brazilian and U.S. perspectives were rather different. A State Department intelligence report worried that Brazilian nationalism tended to be directed against the United States and "in its extreme form poses a threat to Brazilian-U.S. relations."[35] In Kubitschek's view the United States not only did not aid Brazil but upset its negotiations with the International Monetary Fund.[36] Relations with the IMF were difficult enough. Kubitschek accused it of trying to force a national capitulation that would deliver industry into foreign hands. Kubitschek's 1958 Operation Pan America created new friction as Dulles and Eisenhower did their best to ignore this Brazilian call for U.S. aid to Latin American development. Still, after Vice-President Richard Nixon's disastrous tour of South America in 1958 and Fidel Castro's victory in Cuba, Washington had to do something. So Ike flew down to Rio and the IMF loosened up.

But Brazil stood on the edge of a disaster of its own in 1960. Jânio Quadros (1961), who had so captured the popular mood in the elections, could not match Kubitschek's imaginative leadership. While taking millions in aid and loans from the nervous Kennedy administration, Quadros opposed efforts to isolate Cuba, sought friendly relations with the communist countries, attempted a leadership role in Latin America, and expressed solidarity with the struggle to end colonialism, especially in Africa. Each of these moves was based on traditional Brazilian diplomatic principles, such as self-determination, nonintervention, and commerce with all, but in the heated international atmosphere Quadros's flamboyant style made them appear more radical than they were. His sudden August 1961 resignation pushed Brazil down the slope toward military rule.

João Goulart (1961–1963) continued the policies of his predecessor. Though he completed arrangements for an exchange of ambassadors with the Soviet Union, he took pains to explain to the U.S. Congress in 1962 that Brazil identified "with the democratic principles which unite the peoples of the West." Brazil's foreign policy sought to find solutions to the country's development problems. Brazil was open to foreign capital and technical assistance, he declared, but "the eradication of the difficulties which we are now undergoing depends upon *our work, our energy, and our sacrifice*" (italics added). He saw the Alliance for Progress as the fulfillment of expectations Latin America had nurtured since World War II and was hopeful that it would have the impact on the region that the Marshall Plan had had on Europe. "It is my deep conviction," he asserted, "that good and well-defined relations between Brazil and the United States are both desirable and necessary."[37]

The policies of the Goulart administration, like those of the Quadros government, were based upon the following: (1) preservation of peace through coexistence and progressive, general disarmament; (2) strengthening the principle of nonintervention and self-determination; (3) broadening of Brazil's markets via tariff reductions in Latin America and intensification of commercial relations with all countries, including socialist ones; (4) emancipation of nonautonomous territories, regardless of the legal forms used to subject them.[38]

The Military Republic

The political mobilization of the population so alarmed the Brazilian elite, and Goulart's apparent tolerance of indiscipline in the armed forces so unsettled the military leadership, that the latter intervened, deposed the president, and checked the society's drift toward radicalization. The revolution of 1964 ushered in what Riordan Roett has termed the "military republic." The sixteen years since have seen five generals-president sitting in the Planalto Palace.

Humberto de A. Castello Branco (1964–1967) reversed many of his predecessors' policies. He broke relations with Cuba, obtained Brazil's first standby agreement with the IMF in three years and its first World Bank loan in six, sent troops to participate in the U.S.-sponsored Dominican intervention, and made such broad concessions to foreign firms that the Brazilian left accused him of being an *entreguista* (one who sells out his nation). The record of those years is only beginning to be made available to historians, making observations tentative, but some can be attempted. The interpretation of Brazilian policy in the 1960s is clouded by partisan rhetoric. Quadros and Goulart used foreign policy to improve their credentials with the left. However, their baiting of the United States must be balanced with the image of Goulart traveling to Washington to secure loans and to convince officials that "anti-Americanism has never caught on here and never will."[39] Considering that the United States had blatantly intervened in internal affairs via the "islands of administrative sanity" policy providing aid monies to friendly state governments, Goulart was either extremely patient or helpless to stop the affront to Brazilian sovereignty.[40]

Castello Branco was sure of military and political support after the coup and could pull aside the veil that Goulart kept over American relations. What was not clear at the time was the degree to which he was pursuing an independent course. In July 1964, he told the graduating class at the Instituto Rio Branco that sovereign states had to have an independent foreign policy, which for Brazil meant that it "had to have its own thought and its own action . . . [which] will not be subordinated to any interest beyond that of Brazil's own."[41]

In several areas Castello set Brazil on courses that at the time appeared retrogressive but, as they came to be played out, allowed Brazil considerable room to maneuver. The decision to send troops to the Dominican Republic is pointed to as the ultimate proof of Castello's embrace of U.S. policy. Yet the experience was a negative one, at least for senior army officers who resented the Americans' attempt to make a puppet of General Hugo Panasco Alvim, while placing him in command of the Inter-American Peace Force. In his first encounter with Lt. Gen. Bruce Palmer, he made it quite clear to the American, who had addressed him in English, that he had better get an interpreter or learn Portuguese because that was to be the language at headquarters. Negative military feelings and popular distaste contributed to Castello's refusal to send troops to Vietnam when Lyndon Johnson requested them in December 1965. In the Organization of American States (OAS) Castello pushed for the "renunciation of any unilateral action" and the creation of a formula that in each instance would allow the call-up of an inter-American force with specific objectives and oversight powers limited to the period of intervention. This may have been a ploy to extend Brazilian influence, but it would also serve to prevent the United States from again acting alone and would warn Cuba that its sponsored guerrilla movements would be opposed by all.[42]

Castello reversed the Quadros-Goulart anticolonial stance in the UN in deference to Portugal, urging instead the formation of an Afro-Luso-Brazilian community. To that end Brazil signed a commercial treaty with Portugal that opened the ports of Portuguese Africa, allowing Brazil, as Portuguese rule collapsed in the next decade, to expand its commercial and investment activities there. Nearer home he favored an Argentine-Brazilian common market, a topic discussed at the ministerial level, and the formation of multinational enterprises such as a steel mill at Corumbá, Mato Grosso do Sul, that would involve Brazilian, Argentine, Bolivian, Paraguayan, and Uruguayan participation. The controversy with Paraguay over the boundary at the Sete Quedas on the Paraná River was resolved with the June 1966 Act of the Cataracts that formed the basis of agreement for the vast Itaipu hydroelectric project. And Castello placed Brazil on the path to the Tlatelolco nuclear nonproliferation treaty, while urging the development of atomic energy for peaceful purposes.

In short, Castello Branco's brief administration cannot be dismissed as simply regressive; rather, it was an active period whose policy initiatives are still coming to fruition. Further, it must be remembered that two aides on whom he had great intellectual impact, Ernesto Geisel and João Baptista Figueiredo, would govern Brazil between 1974 and 1984, and that all three would have as adviser Golbery do Couto e Silva, Brazil's leading geopolitician.

Castello's immediate successors, Arthur da Costa e Silva (1967–1969) and Emilio Garrastazu Médici (1969–1974), were mildly antagonistic to Castello and more enthusiastic than he was about maintaining military control of the system. Costa e Silva responded to increased civilian opposition with repression. Army intellectuals at the Escola Comando e Estado Maior do Exército and the Escola Superior de Guerra began to think that the roots of agitation were not only in foreign-inspired "subversion" but also in the society's socioeconomic inequalities. The original idea of a short, surgical purge of "chaos, communism, and corruption" gave way to a program of national development and integration.

Under Costa e Silva, links with the United States were loosened as both sides backed off in irritation. U.S. officials, embarrassed by the tales of arbitrary arrest and torture, cut back on projects of the U.S. Agency for International Development (USAID) and held up loans. The Brazilians asserted themselves by refusing to sign the nuclear Nonproliferation Treaty, renouncing advocacy of an inter-American peace force, demanding entry into the United States of Brazilian instant coffee, and joining other Latin American countries in demands for U.S. trade concessions.[43]

Censorship hid the growing coldness between the two governments from the Brazilian people. The left failed to exploit U.S. disenchantment with the revolution and contributed to the cycle of violence and repression. In 1968 a U.S. army captain studying at the Universidade de São Paulo was gunned down in front of his home and in 1969 Ambassador C. Burke Elbrick was kidnapped. Rather than demonstrating U.S.-Brazilian solidarity in the face of such guerrilla tactics, his ransoming caused further irritation in military circles.

Garrastazu Médici in effect expanded Brazil internally by launching the trans-Amazon highway project to open the sparsely settled region and externally by claiming a 200-mile maritime zone. He led his countrymen in rejoicing in Brazil's victory in the 1969 World Cup soccer matches—encounters that some Brazilian army officers saw as a substitute for war. The number of cannon a country had would no longer determine its prestige, they argued, while teasingly inquiring how many World Cups the United States had won. Médici's government

opened relations with East Germany, moved toward recognition of
China, and intensified trade with the Soviet Union. Though President
Richard Nixon acknowledged Brazilian preeminence in Latin America
during Médici's 1971 visit to Washington, the old closeness had faded.

Ernesto Geisel's (1974–1980) administration, building upon earlier initiatives, exchanged ambassadors with Peking, formed a nuclear alliance
with West Germany, shifted Brazil's support to the Arabs in the Middle
East, recognized the Movimento Popular de Libertação de Angola
(MPLA) in Angola, and broke the military alliance with the United
States. This last move in 1977 emphasized the degree to which Brazil's
military, especially the army, had freed itself from arms dependence on
the United States. Indeed, Brazil was becoming an arms exporter. The
1976 Kissinger-Silveira consultive agreement had been an attempt on
Brazil's part to have a relationship, as Foreign Minister Antônio Francisco Azeredo da Silveira noted, "without any sense of dependency." But
he also warned that "very cordial relations are not enough . . . if
American participation in Brazilian development does not accelerate in
the future, Brazil will seek other options."[44] Geisel pointedly avoided
visiting Washington, while finding the time to make state visits to West
Germany, France, Great Britain, Japan, and Mexico. It was President
Jimmy Carter who in 1978 flew to Brazil in an unsuccessful attempt to
soothe Brazilian irritation with Washington's human rights pronouncements and U.S. interference in the atomic agreement with the
Germans. The U.S. president had to suffer the embarrassment of hearing
Foreign Minister Silveira observe that Carter had not been invited, while
the Brazilians enjoyed Carter's references to Brazil as a major power.

As the 1980s opened, Geisel's hand-picked successor João Baptista de
Figueiredo, who had served with Castello, Médici, and Geisel, moved to
strengthen trade ties with Africa, the Arab countries, and Brazil's
neighbors. In what may turn out to be the single most important event in
Brazilian diplomacy since World War II, he visited Argentina with a
large delegation in May 1980. By itself this would have been an important event—only two other presidents had made such a visit, Manuel
Campos Sales in 1900 and Getúlio Vargas in 1935—but the result may be
an economic union between the two former rivals. This is startling when
one considers that as recently as July 1977 military forces on both sides of
the frontier went on alert in readiness for possible attack. Now the two
countries have agreed to lower tariffs and to hold bimonthly meetings to
discuss economic integration. Presidents Figueiredo and Jorge Rafael
Videla and their top aides exchanged private telephone numbers and
promised to call often. More significantly, they pledged themselves to
nuclear cooperation.[45] Already the Brazilian military has stopped

development of its medium-range Piranha self-propelled missile as a gesture.[46]

Certainly if Brazil and Argentina combine their economic might it will affect the power balance of South America and create a South Atlantic power center of the first order. However, old antagonisms may be slow to die in some sectors. And the question that the Buenos Aires magazine *Cabildo* raised will only be answered in time: Does all this imply integration *with* Brazil or *into* Brazil? The implications for Paraguay and Uruguay are especially great.[47]

On balance, Brazilian diplomacy has served as a protective device and as a support for Brazilian development throughout the century. Rio Branco's dreams now seem less grandiose as they have taken more solid form. Pragmatically, Brazilians have sought foreign aid, advice, and even protection when necessary. But their diplomacy has tended to maintain a deliberate flexibility in the face of the circumstances of the moment, always with an eye to the future, to the establishment of new relationships based upon new international realities.[48] When looked at over nearly a century, their diplomacy has been more consistent than not and one can only expect that with its firm institutionalization, it will continue to serve as a means of expanding Brazilian influence.

Notes

1. Quoted in J. O. de Meira Penna, *Política Externa, Segurança e Desenvolvimento* (Rio de Janeiro, 1967), p. 91.

2. J. H. Rodrigues, *Interêsse Nacional e Política Externa* (Rio de Janeiro, 1966), pp. 51–60.

3. Ibid. José Honório calls this mental trait *caiação*, literally "whitewashing." For a full discussion see Thomas Skidmore, *Black Into White* (New York, 1974).

4. Estado-Maior do Exército, *Documentos relativos à tese XII da 5ª Conferência Panamericana de Santiago do Chile* (Abril e Maio de 1923), Primeira Parte (Rio de Janeiro, 1924), pp. 19, 47.

5. Maj. F. L. Whitley, Memorandum for the Chargé d'Affaires, Rio de Janeiro, 22 July 1922, Record Group (RG)-165, 2006-60, General Staff, War Department, Old Navy & Army Branch, National Archives (NA), Washington, D.C.

6. Based on Arthur Bernardes's 1926 report to Congress, Câmara dos Deputados, *Mensagens Presidenciais (1923–1926) Arthur Bernardes*, Documentos Parlamentares 83 (Brasília, 1978), p. 634.

7. Ibid., p. 535.

8. Ibid., p. 426.

9. Jayme de Barros, *A Política Exterior do Brasil, 1930-1940* (Rio de Janeiro, 1941), pp. 33–37. The important Itamaraty historical archive and library were organized in this era.

10. Ibid., p. 40.

11. Gen. Francisco Ramos de Andrade Neves (Chief of General Staff), Rio de Janeiro, 3 August 1934, *Exame da Situação Militar do Brasil* (Rio de Janeiro: Imprensa do Estado-Maior do Exército, 1934), p. 66. Copy in Centro de Documentação do Exército, Brasília.

12. Ibid., pp. 5–8.

13. John D. Wirth, *The Politics of Brazilian Development* (Stanford, Calif., 1970); Frank D. McCann, *The Brazilian-American Alliance, 1937–1945* (Princeton, N.J., 1973); and Stanley E. Hilton, *Brazil and the Great Powers, 1930–1939* (Austin, Tex., 1975).

14. Oswaldo Aranha to Getúlio Vargas, Rio de Janeiro, 24 January 1943, Oswaldo Aranha Archive (OAA), Centro de Pesquisa e Documentação da História Contemporânea do Brasil (CPDOC), Fundação Getúlio Vargas (FGV), Rio de Janeiro.

15. See, for example, *A Manhã*, Rio de Janeiro, 27 February 1945.

16. Luiz Augusto de Rego Monteiro, "Relatório sôbre os problemas sociais do Argentina, do Chile, e do Uruguai," 12 February 1944, OAA, CPDOC, FGV-Rio de Janeiro.

17. Robert T. Daland, *Brazilian Planning, Development, Politics, and Administration* (Chapel Hill, 1967), p. 27.

18. José Teixeira de Oliveira, *O Govêrno Dutra* (Rio de Janeiro, 1964), p.28.

19. Ibid., p. 29.

20. Ibid., pp. 24, 124–125; and Reynold E. Carlson, "Brazil's Role in International Trade," in T. Lynn Smith and Alexander Marchant (eds.), *Brazil, Portrait of Half a Continent* (New York, 1951), pp. 281–289.

21. Getúlio Vargas, "Mensagem ao Congresso Nacional—1951," in G. Vargas, *O Govêrno Trabalhista do Brasil*, Vol. 1 (Rio de Janeiro, 1952), p. 81.

22. G. Vargas, "Mensagem ao Congresso Nacional, Rio, 7 February 1952," in G. Vargas, *O Govêrno Trabalhista do Brasil*, Vol. 3 (1951–1953) (Rio de Janeiro, 1969), p. 100.

23. Getúlio Vargas, "Mensagem ao Congresso Nacional—1951," p. 82.

24. Ibid., pp. 81, 84, 85.

25. Ronald M. Schneider, *Brazil, Foreign Policy of a Future World Power* (Boulder, Colo., 1976), p. 87.

26. Getúlio Vargas, *O Govêrno Trabalhista do Brasil*, Vol. 2 (Rio de Janeiro, 1954), p. 114.

27. Ibid., pp. 117, 118.

28. Ibid., pp. 126–127, and Vol. 3 (1951–1953), "Mensagem ao Congresso Nacional . . . 15 de Março de 1953," pp. 282–283.

29. Ibid., Vol. 3, p. 284; Vol. 4 (1953–1954) (Rio de Janeiro, 1969), pp. 143–146.

30. Lourival Fontes & Glauco Carneiro, *A Face Final de Vargas (Os Bilhetes de Getúlio)* (Rio de Janeiro, 1966), pp. 69–72.

31. From $644 million to $1,345 million. U.S. Senate, Committee on Foreign Relations, *United States-Latin American Relations*, Study No. 4, "United States

Business and Labor in Latin America" (Doc. 125, 86 Congress, 2nd Session), p. 296.

32. Moniz Bandeira, *Presença dos Estados Unidos no Brasil* (Rio de Janeiro, 1973), p. 392.

33. José Honório Rodrigues, *Brasil e África, Outro Horizonte* (Rio de Janeiro, 1964), 2, pp. 372–373.

34. Fontes and Carneiro, *A Face Final de Vargas*, p. 76.

35. Bureau of Intelligence and Research, Department of State, "Nationalism in Brazil," 24 July 1959, No. 8002, RG-59, NA.

36. Moniz Bandeira, *Presença dos Estados Unidos*, p. 397.

37. Text of speech, in Irving L. Horowitz, *Revolution in Brazil, Politics and Society in a Developing Nation* (New York, 1964), pp. 361–365.

38. Francisco de San Tiago Dantas, *Política Externa Independente* (Rio de Janeiro, 1962), p. 6.

39. Quoted in *Newsweek*, 11 March 1963, p. 56.

40. See Riordan Roett, *The Politics of Foreign Aid in the Brazilian Northeast* (Nashville, Tenn., 1972); Jan K. Black, *United States Penetration of Brazil* (Philadelphia, 1977); and Phyllis R. Parker, *Brazil and the Quiet Intervention, 1964* (Austin, Tex., 1979).

41. As quoted in Luís Viana Filho, *O Govêrno Castelo Branco* (Rio de Janeiro, 1975), 2, p. 438.

42. See ibid., p. 451.

43. For a summary account see Peter D. Bell, "Brazilian-American Relations," in Riordan Roett (ed.), *Brazil in the Sixties* (Nashville, Tenn., 1972), pp. 77–102.

44. *Veja* (São Paulo), 25 February 1976, p. 18.

45. In 1975 Argentine General Juan Guglielmelli had proposed in *Estratégia* that negotiations with Brazil seek an atomic accord and the "possible fabrication of explosive devices." *Veja* (São Paulo), 14 May 1975, p. 21.

46. *Veja* (São Paulo), 28 May 1980, p. 28.

47. *Veja* (São Paulo), 21 May 1980, pp. 16–19; *Isto É* (São Paulo), pp. 22–23; *Latin American Weekly Report* (London), 23 May 1980 (WR-80-20), p. 3.

48. Ronaldo Mota Sardenberg, "A Política Externa do Brasil num Mundo em Mudança," *A Defesa Nacional*, Ano 67 (January-February 1980), No. 687, pp. 19–29.

2
Brazil in the World: A Ranking Analysis of Capability and Status Measures

Wayne A. Selcher

International relations specialists conventionally consider Brazil as a typical, if large, non-petroleum-exporting Latin American country with consequently marginal relevance in global, and perhaps even regional, issues. It is cited much more frequently as an object of influence than as a wielder of influence. With this image, and in spite of general acceptance of the theory of diffusion of international influence (the principle of multipolarity), the broader field was initially inattentive or skeptical when presented by some Brazilianists with the "Brazil as a candidate for major power status" thesis, which appeared about 1974. Even more discordant with previous interpretations was the position of Brazil as number 6 in the first two editions of Cline's *World Power Assessment*, the only thorough attempt to rank all of the states of the world according to "perceived power" in its tangible and intangible components.[1]

Within the Carter administration, despite the difficulties in carrying out the original consultative intent of the 1976 "Memorandum of Understanding" with Brasília, there was official recognition of Brazil's greater weight in the world, even if it was not widely publicized.[2] President Carter himself, during his visit to Brasília, referred to Brazil as a "world power."[3] Zbigniew Brzezinski, at a White House press briefing at that time, included Brazil on the roster of "new influentials," noting that

I would like to thank both the Fulbright Faculty Research Abroad Program (U.S. Office of Education) and Elizabethtown College for research support granted for this chapter. In addition to written sources, this study makes use of extensive interviews in Brazil, given on a nonattributable basis. To these many helpful individuals I also express my appreciation.

it is "emerging as a very powerful country."[4] Former Assistant Secretary of State for Inter-American Affairs Terence Todman referred to Brazil as a "world power."[5] Assistant Secretary of the Treasury C. Fred Bergsten commented on Brazil's "new world role" and asserted that "Today Brazil is clearly one of the most important participants in the international economic system," adding that it "is clearly moving into the front ranks of the world's economic powers."[6] Luigi Einaudi, of the State Department's policy planning staff, stated that "Brazil is no longer an emerging nation, it is already an economic and political power."[7] By the late 1970s Brazil was receiving greater attention, principally as a member of several categories of states that were making themselves felt in the international system: the "advanced developing countries," the "upper-middle income countries," the "newly industrializing countries," and the "emerging middle powers."

Even while acknowledging that relations with Brazil are not a central concern of U.S. foreign policy, it would be going too far to insist that such increasingly common official assessments (along with similar ones made by leaders of other major powers) can be dismissed as mere gratuitous diplomatic pleasantries. Brazil's candidacy for major power status is now being taken seriously by government officials, businessmen, and academicians on several continents. There appears to be a consensus among specialists that Brazil is growing in global significance and is likely to continue to do so, even with its severe economic problems.

Methodology

Although some works on Brazil's significance support this contention with the time-honored references to the country's land mass, population, and gross national product (GNP), none have gone empirically and comparatively beyond use of these indicators as a base for more abstract speculation on Brazil's actual or potential capabilities. At this stage in the development of the literature, therefore, it would be appropriate to make use of the national capability measures and stratification theory of international relations to do an across-the-board assessment of just how large Brazil bulks in the world, that quality that former Foreign Minister Azeredo da Silveira termed its "pêso específico no mundo." If such an exercise is done in a global rather than in a solely hemispheric, less developed country (LDC), or middle power context, it can shed some light on Brazil's position in the international hierarchy on a broad range of measures relevant to national capabilities, significance, and (more indirectly) status in a really comparative setting.[8] A ranking approach over a time span, with percentages as applicable, is particularly suitable to this purpose because it reveals changes in either capabilities or status relative to all other states and therefore measures "objective" changes in hierarchical position, a term that itself implies ranking. The intent of an analysis of this type is not to determine definitively whether Brazil is "really" number 6 or 12 or 15 overall in capabilities among the nations of the world, but to find where it stands on a variety of indicators, general and detailed, and whether its overall competitive position is strengthening or weakening; in short, whether it is in a general way climbing the capabilities and status hierarchies or not and how it fares in a rough capabilities and status comparison with the states now generally considered to be major powers. Such a macro approach over time allows year-to-year fluctuations or discontinuities in any one sector to be evaluated only as relevant to longer-term trends in what Brazil has already accomplished. As the rise of the current major powers and superpowers demonstrated, the ascension of a state toward the upper levels of the international hierarchy is an involved process requiring decades. The point-in-time quality of this essay limits us to consideration of relatively short-term factors of the 1970s and cautions against unwarranted extrapolation beyond the period under examination.

Some distinctions of terminology must be made to establish just what is being tapped and how this empirical approach fits into the conceptualizations of national power current in the international relations field. As central as the concept is to political science, there is a diversity of theory on what constitutes "power," and numerous attempts have been made to define its components, nature, and effects in a measurable and comparative way. None of them is accepted without substantial reservations, but some conventions of usage have been widely acknowledged. Following those established practices, those resources of a state upon which is based its ability to attain its national goals will be termed its "political potential," inherent in all those tangible (mainly "quantitative") and intangible (mainly "qualitative") elements upon which it can draw to affect events beyond its borders. Political potential has three modes of implementation: power (coercion, deprivation, or the threat or actual use of force), influence (noncoercive and often cooperative effects on others, such as bargaining, persuasion, advice, rewards, or foreign aid), and prestige (status, deriving from respect or a reputation for importance, success, or excellence). In practice, all three modes rest on the same general resource bases, and differences in utilization of resources (different bases for different situations) account for the differences of terminology.

Because of the methodological difficulties of such a comprehensive operationalization, both in general and in specific issue areas or events, theorists attempting to rank states by political potential have avoided trying to measure such problematical concepts as actual influence on the system or national effectiveness in foreign policy (i.e., relative success in goal attainment). Instead, for quantitative comparisons they fall back upon measures of the tangible bases or resources of power, influence, and status, to the extent that the list of tangible elements regarded as central has become rather standardized. It is that inventory that is employed here, without a justification of each item, but with an assessment as well of some intangible (i.e., nonmeasurable) factors of Brazil's political potential across a broad range of interactions. The statistics are from standard and reliable sources for 1970 to 1976. (See Statistical Source Codes at end of chapter for sources.) Rankings given do not include any microstates (such as Malta or Oman), colonies, or trusteeships, to make the per capita measures more significant. Only cross-nationally comparable data were used.

A capabilities analysis, it must be noted, is not the same as an analysis of Brazil's actual effects on the rest of the world, because the relational variables intervening between national capabilities and either bilateral or multilateral outcomes are too numerous in a given situation to allow an easy correspondence.[9] Thus Klaus Knorr distinguished conceptually between *putative* power as a somewhat abstract means or stock that states can accumulate and hold to call upon in foreign policy and *actualized* power as the actual effect that a state can achieve on a situation.[10] (My usage would substitute "political potential" for "power.") James Rosenau drew a similar distinction between *capabilities* as "attributes or resources possessed" and *control* or *influence* as "the relational dimension of power," or what is actually accomplished vis-à-vis another state or states.[11] Influence, then, is a property of an interaction relationship, defined in terms of results achieved. Within these definitions, Brazil's stock of attributes or capabilities (principally but not exclusively the material resources) will be ranked and evaluated relative to those of other states to inform discussion of its present and probable future significance in the broad range of international interactions, particularly regarding levels of influence and prestige in political and economic issue areas rather than in strictly bilateral relationships. But national political potential in practice is not the sum total of tangible capabilities. As the analytical frame of reference is refocused from abstract capabilities to concrete influence toward a goal (for example, moving from Brazil's position as a rising steel producer to possible future competition with the United States in the Latin American steel market), more case-specific interaction information has to be brought to bear and more situational variables regarding strategies and objectives must be introduced.

Given these caveats, and the noncontinuous nature of orders of magnitude, it is important to avoid too literal an interpretation of each of Brazil's capability rankings. The overall intent is to produce a comprehensive ranking configuration relevant in the abstract to the full range of its foreign relations. In drawing such a political-potential profile of strengths and weaknesses, patterns and trends are more significant than single years or sectors. Whether these resources are used for foreign relations purposes, how efficiently and autonomously they are used, against what countervailing resources, and to what effect are questions that must be answered in a series of actual circumstances. The outcomes of those circumstances, not the raw capabilities in themselves, will determine whether Brazil will be deemed to be of greater consequence and perhaps eventually conceded the degree of attention and respect by others that constitutes effective major power status. Yet, in a fundamental way, the comparative level and quality of those attributes possessed will either hinder or facilitate Brazil's actualized political potential and achievement of higher status. Conceptually, they represent the quantitative base that must inform qualitative analysis, such as that of Katzman in Chapter 4.

Agricultural Production

Brazil is clearly one of the major agricultural nations of the world, so much so that, according to a U.S. Department of Agriculture (U.S.D.A.) report, "No other country in the world produces a wider variety of agricultural products in significant quantities."[12] Brazil is at the same time a mildly food-deficit nation and a major factor in international agricultural trade. A world food supply-and-demand assessment noted, however, that, unlike the situation in most middle-income food-deficit nations, food production and consumption in Brazil are projected to be in approximate balance by 1990, especially if the shift toward cereal production continues.[13] Unusually poor weather was the chief reason Brazil was unable to achieve general self-sufficiency in food production in the late 1970s.

Brazil has been following a long-established pattern of using agricultural exports to gain foreign exchange for development projects, a strategy that was reaffirmed by the Third National Development Plan (1980–1985). In early 1978, Brazil became the second most important exporter of farm products, surpassed only by the United States. While this advance gained considerable recognition in world agricultural trade, it detracted from more equitable incentives for and distribution of food

TABLE 2.1
Brazil's Rank among all States in Measures of Unprocessed Agricultural
Production, 1970-76

Commmodity	70	71	72	73	74	75	76	1976 as a Percent of World Total	Source Code[+]	Note
Sisal	1	1	1	1	1	1*	1*	39.2%	J	1
Coffee Beans	1	1	1	1	1	1	1	15.2	J	2
Roundwood-broadleaf	1	1	1	1	1	1	1	10.0	A	
Castor Beans	1	1	1	1	1*	1*	2*	35.3	J	3
Cocoa Beans	3	4	3	4	4	2	2	17.1	A	
Soybeans	3	3	3	3	3	3	3	18.1	A	
Palm Kernels	2	2	2	2	2	3	3	15.4	A	
Corn	3	3	3	3	3	3	3	5.3	A	
Oranges, Tangerines	6	3	3	3	2	3*		13.0	J	3
Cattle	4	4	4	4	4	4	4	7.8	A	
Swine	4	4	4	4	4	4	4	5.5	A	
Tobacco	5	5	5	5	5	5	6	5.3	A	
Cottonseed	6	6	6	6	6	6*		3.4	J	3
Cotton (lint)	5	8	6	6	7	5	7	3.2	A	
Cow's Milk	11	11	11	11	10	8	7	2.7	A	
Roundwood-coniferous	7	7	7	7	7	6	7	2.2	A	
Rough or Paddy Rice	9	9	9	9	9	8	8	2.7	A	4
Peanuts	6	6	4	6	9	9	9	2.9	A	
Sheep	11	10	11	11	11	10	10	2.4	A	
Hen Eggs	10	10	10	9	9	10	10	2.2	A	
Wool	12	11	11	11	12	11	11	1.4	A	
Natural Rubber	10	10	9	9	11	11	11	0.6	A	
Fish Catch - fresh and salt	22	23	24	24	24	19	19	1.3	A	
Potatoes	24	24	22	24	24	20	20	0.6	A	
Wheat	26	23	35	25	23	28	22	0.8	A	

Notes: Most of the 1976 statistics of source "A" are estimates.
*Ranking based on statistical estimates or preliminary figures.

1. Percent is 1976 estimate
2. Tied with Colombia in 1976
3. Percent is 1975 estimate
4. Largest outside Asia

Brazil is generally considered to be the largest producer of bananas,
manioc, papaya, and dry beans, but practically all of this production
is consumed domestically.

+ Source codes are listed at the end of this chapter.

production internally. Investments flowed toward coffee, soybeans, sugarcane, cocoa, and citrus for export to the detriment of staple crops for national use; most pointedly, the domestic price of black beans was driven sharply upward when large quantities of this staple in the diet of the poor had to be imported from Mexico and Chile because acreage formerly devoted to its production was diverted to soybeans for export. During 1978–1979, government policy showed signs of turning more attention toward problems of production and supply in the domestic staples market to correct some distortions, even at the risk of promoting inflation.

Table 2.1 ranks Brazil's raw agricultural production against that of all other states on principal products, showing that it scores high on most of them, but that, with the important exceptions of citrus and milk, no notable advances in rank were made after the late 1960s, when the country suddenly broke from obscurity into the front ranks of the soybean producers. There have characteristically been substantial yearly increases in both planted area and output. Among food grains, the wheat harvests have been especially poor and erratic, usually because of climatic conditions hostile to current varieties, diseases, and pests, so Brazil has had to import large quantities of the grain annually to meet a rapidly growing demand that was stimulated by price subsidies. Wheat self-sufficiency targets have become more elusive, as the costs of growing wheat in Brazil are very high. By mid-1978, for example, the Minister of Agriculture recognized the impossiblity of self-sufficiency by the earlier goal of 1979–1980 and predicted that ten to fifteen more years might be required.[14]

Much arable land remains (according to many, more than in any other country), as only about 8 percent of the national territory is now being cultivated. Progress is being made in cultivating the extensive *cerrado* savannahs. About 90 percent of the agricultural production gains of the 1970s came from increased acreage rather than yield improvement, but most experts agree that continuation of current improvements in seed, fertilizer, and pesticide use will increase general yield per acre as well. In international comparisons of yield per acre, Brazil fares well in soybeans, oranges, and irrigated rice, but has poor showings in all other major crops. To achieve higher productivity, much more in the way of research, support systems, and extension services will be required.

Relative to other sectors of the economy, the growth of agriculture has generally lagged, so the respectable increases in productivity achieved during the 1970s are small relative to the potential, as the impressive surge in the dairy industry demonstrates. Corn, a major world food grain, is the next likely candidate for modernization, as soybeans, rice, and wheat are already well mechanized. A chief policy dilemma of the management of agriculture as it affects national political potential will continue to be to strike a judicious balance between lucrative export crops with minimal nutritional value and production and distribution of major domestic staples, the latter a social necessity that has been pushed aside by the drive for foreign exchange to repay the national debt and to import petroleum. Brazil thus faces a dual challenge, to provide sufficient nutrition for all levels of its own population and to produce larger quantities of food for the expanding world market. Should both of these goals be met, Brazil's political potential in a food-short world will be greatly augmented; Japan and West Germany have shown serious investment interest in Brazil's role as a food supplier and processor. In sum, the greatest strengths in this sector are diversity, quantity, growth rate, and potential of production; the greatest weaknesses are inefficiencies, a food-grain deficiency, and inadequate systems for production and distribution of staples for domestic consumption.

Industrial Production and Consumption

The size and sophistication of a state's industrial plant are most commonly taken as the primary measure of national might. Further, according to Organski, differential industrialization among nations has been the key to understanding shifts in international power relationships in this and the last century, because during a period of successful industrialization, a stage of transitional growth in power occurs that moves the industrializing state rapidly toward the level of political potential possessed by industrialized states of similar size. He referred to this period as the "power transition" of a state. The internal changes occurring in an intermediately industrialized nation (such as Brazil) are qualitative and, said Organski, bring great increases in the ability of that nation to affect the behavior of other nations. The greater the speed of industrialization and the larger the industrial plant, the more rapid the rise of the capabilities of the aspiring major power relative to those of the top-dog states and to those of states beneath it.[15]

In 1979, Brazil's industrial output value stood 13th in the world, above any other LDC, with a 1970–1976 average annual growth rate of 11.6 percent, one of the most rapid of any major nation. The fact that 39 percent of the gross domestic product (GDP) originated in industry in 1976 would seem to class Brazil as an industrial nation, yet only 11.0 percent of its labor force was employed in industry at the time, ranking it close to Syria and Honduras and only number 62 among the nations on this variable. It is, then, because of the sheer size and scope of Brazil's in-

TABLE 2.2
Brazil's Rank among all States in Measures of Agricultural Industry, 1970-76

Item	70	71	72	73	74	75	76	1976 as a Percent of World Total	Source Code	Notes
Industrial Molasses	3	2	3	2	1	2	1*	10.2%	J	
Raw Centrifugal Sugar	4	3	2	2	2	3	2	8.4	A	
Beef	5	4	4	4	4	4	4	4.7	A	
Cattle Hides	4	4	4	3	4*			NA	J	
Phosphate Fertilizer Consumpt.	14	13	9	9	7	6	5	4.6	A	
Broadleaf Sawnwood	6	6	7	7	6	5	5	4.5	A	
Tobacco Cigarettes	7	8	7	6	6	6	6	3.5	A	1
Potash Fertilizer Consumption	11	10	10	9	10	10	6	3.0	A	
Meat	7	6	6	6	6	5	7	3.2	A	
Wood Pulp, Chem.	12	12	10	9	8	8	7	1.6	A	
Lard	5	6	6	6	7*			3.0	J	2
Margarine	17	17	14	13	13	13	10	2.5	A	3
Wheat Flour	12	18	18	16	14	13	13	1.8	A	4
Pork	8	9	11	11	14	12	13	1.8	A	
Paper & Cardboard	14	14	14	14	13	13	13	1.5	A	
Coniferous Sawnwood	12	12	11	11	12	13	13	0.9	A	
Tractors in Use	16	13	13	13	13	13	14	1.5	A	
Harvester-Threshers In Use	16	16	16	16	16	15	15	1.1	A	
Newsprint	21	21	21	20	20	20	20	0.6	A	
Nitrogenous Fertilizer Consumpt.	24	26	17	25	20	23	21	1.0	A	
Butter	25	23	24	23	21	21	21	NA	A	
Wood Pulp, Mech.	17	18	16	15	24	27	24	0.5	A	
Cheese	33	33	33	33	34	35	32	NA	A	

Notes: Most of the 1976 statistics of source "A" are estimates.
*Ranking based on statistical estimates or preliminary figures.

1. Excludes North Korea and China
2. Percent is 1974 estimate
3. Excludes China and India
4. Excludes China and Pakistan

dustrial economy that the level, complexity, and progress of its industrial development compared to that of other major nations is the single most important element in analysis of its capabilities.

The key statistics on this indicator are presented in Tables 2.2 and 2.3. In agricultural industry, significant gains were made in refined sugar, in which Brazil surpassed the USSR to take first place for the season of

1976-1977, according to the U.S.D.A. Beyond foreign exchange uses, this quantity of production is expected to contribute greatly to the distillation of fuel alcohol to decrease dependence on imported petroleum. A long-term depression in world prices starting in the late 1970s facilitated this outlet for productive capacity. With its huge forest reserves under development, at a time when more LDCs are becoming wood-poor, Brazil is emerging as a chief world source of lumber, pulp, cellulose, plywood, and paper products and can be expected to rise in rank on those items, based on recent growth rates and conservation-minded projects now underway. With the world's third largest cattle herd (if India's is excluded), Brazil could become a major source of beef, but much progress is needed in management and marketing for this to occur. Current beef production suffers from dry-season losses, disease, poor breeding, and improper feeding practices. As a countercase, great progress has been made in modernization in a short time by the poultry industry.

Agricultural industry has been hindered by insufficient chemical fertilizers and low levels of mechanization, so attacks on both bottlenecks were made during the 1970s, most recently with a governmental shift of emphasis toward making up for previous neglect of the agricultural sector relative to the industrial sector. Because of the agricultural boom, consumption of phosphate and potash fertilizers rose dramatically, with corresponding increases in ranking, as previously uncultivated soils with nutrient deficiencies were brought into production. Discoveries of large raw materials deposits and new factories coming on line increased production to the extent that self-sufficiency is expected soon in nitrogenous fertilizers and possibly in phosphates as well, although not in potash. Fertilizer use per hectare, however, still remains at a level much lower than that of countries with more modernized agriculture; Brazil ranked only 38th worldwide in 1976 on this item. In the utilization of tractors and combine harvesters, Brazil made little progress in rank (51st in tractors per hectare in 1976) and is suffering from investment and buyer credit binds. In both types of equipment and their implements, Brazil's production is sufficient for domestic demand plus modest exports, while locally designed airplanes for agricultural use are being turned out for national and foreign markets.

Of essential significance to a national capabilities analysis are measures of basic and heavy industry (see Table 2.3), in which Brazil shows a clear pattern of advance relative to other economies on most items; several are within or approaching "top ten" status, and almost all are well above the output of other developing countries. Advances in production of reclaimed rubber, tin, iron, and steel are especially

TABLE 2.3
Brazil's Rank among all States in Measures of Basic Industrial Production
and Consumption, 1970-76

(All items are productivity rankings unless otherwise noted.)

Item	70	71	72	73	74	75	76	1976 as a Percent of World Total	Source Code	Notes
Reclaimed Rubber	7	6	5	4	4	4	3	7.5%	A	
Magnesium (Consumpt.)	10	5	5	5	5	5	5	4.1	B	
Commercial Vehicles	8	8	8	8	7	6	6	4.4	A	1
Primary Tin	11	11	10	9	9	7	6	3.7	A	2
Cotton (Industrial Consumption)	7	7	7	7	7	7	6	3.3	A	
Phosphate Fertilizers	29	21	20	20	17	10	6	3.0	A	
Production of TV Receivers	8	8	8	8	8	8	8	NA	A	1
Tires	10	10	10	10	8	8	8	NA	A	1
Rayon & Acetate Continuous Filaments	10	11	9	9	11	10	9	2.9	A	
Synthetic Rubber	10	10	10	10	9	10	9	2.7	A	3
Non-cellulosic Continuous Filaments	11	14	13	11	10	11	9	2.3	A	4
Cement	12	13	12	12	11	11	10	2.6	A	
Passenger Cars	12	11	10	10	10	10	10	1.9	A	1
Refined Copper (Consumption)	17	14	14	14	11	11	11	2.1	B	
Tin (Consumption)	18	15	17	15	16	16	11	1.9	B	
Primary Aluminum (Consumption)	20	18	14	13	13	11	12	1.6	B	
Zinc (Consumption)	17	15	15	14	14	13	13	1.7	B	
Pig Iron and Ferro-alloys	17	16	16	17	17	15	13	1.6	A	
Non-cellulosic Discontinuous Fibers	16	17	15	13	14	13	13	1.4	A	4
Raw Steel (Consumption)	17	15	16	13	11	11	13	NA	A	
Raw Steel	20	17	17	16	16	15	16	1.4	K	
Merchant Ship Tonnage	19	18	16	19	20	17	16	1.2	I	
Coke Oven Coke	20	20	19	20	20	20	17	0.8	A	
Refined Lead (Consumption)	29	23	26	18	18	19	19	1.2	B	
Primary Lead	27	25	27	21	22	21	20	1.2	A	
Primary Aluminum	26	27	25	19	22	18	20	1.0	A	
Rayon & Acetate Discontinuous Fibers	22	22	22	22	23	22	21	1.0%	A	
Primary Zinc	27	26	27	25	25	25	22	0.8	A	
Refined Copper	28	25	25	26	24	24	24	0.4	A	5
Smelter Copper	31	31	31	31	31	31	32	NA	A	
Nitrogenous Fertilizers	53	41	41	37	35	36	34	0.4	A	
Raw Steel Consumption Per Capita	45	43	46	47	44	47	47		A	

Notes: Most of the 1976 statistics of source "A" are estimates.

1.   Excludes China
2.   Excludes China, U.S.S.R., Vietnam, and GDR
3.   Excludes U.S.S.R. and China
4.   Nylon, orlon, etc.
5.   Primary and secondary production

noteworthy, while levels for lead, aluminum, zinc, and copper are much lower. Brazil is now self-sufficient in manufactured consumer goods and is concentrating on greater self-sufficiency in capital goods and basic inputs. Because of its central role in industrial (and, by implication, military) capacity, a number of capabilities theorists consider raw steel production perhaps the single most important measure of national economic, political, and military strength.[16] The steel industry in a modern economy is fundamental to a wide variety of processing and consuming industries. The speed of advance of the Brazilian steel industry has been remarkable, despite fluctuations. Ranking only number 23 worldwide in 1965, within eleven years the country had climbed to number 16, reaching number 14 in 1977 and number 13 in 1979, by International Iron and Steel Institute estimates.

The figure for 1979, 13.9 million tons, places Brazil well above any other LDC, 1.8 million tons above Spain, 0.8 million tons above Belgium, and 2.1 million tons below Canada. Among Western nations, Brazil ranked 8th in 1979. The only developing country with production remotely approaching Brazil's is India. In 1970 Brazil's production was 85.9 percent of India's; 1972 saw Brazil surpass Indian output; and by 1979 Brazil produced 1.38 times as much steel as India. Mexico, the third most important LDC producer, turned out only 50.4 percent of Brazil's output in 1979, while Argentina, often cited as a rival for influence in South America, produced a mere 23 percent of Brazil's figure.[17] In 1977, when steel output in the LDCs rose by 11.6 percent, half of the tonnage increase was accounted for by Brazil, which produced 26.8 percent of all steel manufactured in the LDCs that year.[18] It is notable in a trend context that Brazil is already a supplier of iron and steel technology to other LDCs.

Part of Brazil's rise in rank, while buoyed by its own expanding production, was aided by relative immunity from the international steel recession in the Western countries, which began in the mid-1970s. Brazil's mills could, and did, run closer to capacity than those of West European middle steel powers, in which capacity increasingly outstripped demand after about 1973. Brazil's industry has continued at full stride, and steel production can be expected to grow at a rate greater than that of the GNP. National steel output expanded by 62.4 percent between 1974 and 1978, a rate surpassed only by the remarkable cases of Taiwan and South Korea. Under the assumption of continued growth in demand, major priority projects are going forward to build additional large-scale mills and related infrastructure, including a steel railway.

By 1979, Brazil had become self-sufficient in steel products, although not in steel plant equipment. Based on projects under way, official estimates of the Steel and Non-Ferrous Metals Council (CONSIDER) in 1979 predicted production of 22 million tons in 1984, equal to the 1979 production of the United Kingdom. General international uncertainties in steel, as well as domestic organizational and investment problems in the largely state-run industry, make hazardous any comparative predictions about Brazil's future rank, particularly regarding the competitive viability of plans to boost considerably its now modest exports of pig iron and alloys in the early 1980s, vis-à-vis Japan, West Germany, and South Korea as rivals in the trade. In 1979, the field around 13th place was crowded enough on either side that Brazil's entry into the top ten in the early 1980s is possible, but not a foregone conclusion. For example, 10th place was held by Canada, which had a substantial lead over Brazil, with 16.0 million tons and a moderately expanding output. In addition, for the next several years at least, Brazil will need considerable advanced foreign technological assistance and financing in its steelworks. At the operational level of steelmaking, Brazil's technological absorption has been good, but, according to CONSIDER officials, only 10 to 15 percent of the technology in steel plant heavy equipment production in the country is really Brazilian.

In spite of its ranking surge in gross production and consumption of steel, Brazil's per capita consumption rank remained low, largely as a result of its regionally and socially uneven development. Per capita consumption was 98 kilograms in 1976, well under the levels of Spain (305 kg.) and Italy (389 kg.)[19] Similarly low per capita rankings occur in Brazil's consumption of nonferrous metals.

Along with steel has grown the automobile industry, now in the world's top ten, yet of relatively recent initiation. The first Brazilian-manufactured trucks left the factories in 1957; the first cars left in the following year. By 1966, 99 percent of the components were produced in Brazil; 1978 was the first year in which one million cars were turned out, a figure recently surpassed by only eight Western industrial states and the USSR. Future production figures are not expected to show such a rate of growth (13 percent in 1978), because of governmental economic deceleration policies and the cost of fuel. Some growth can be expected in the pattern of exports of vehicles and components to a large number of Western and Third World countries, an indication of the international acceptance of the products' quality and of Brazil's competitiveness in sophisticated manufactures.

In a similar case, the national shipyards were not put into operation in a serious manner until 1959 and received strong government support and greater foreign investment only after 1967, stemming from a decision to carry a higher percentage of national trade in national vessels. Brazil's shipyards are now the largest in the Southern Hemisphere and among the most modern and best equipped in the world; only South Korea's industry has a greater output among the LDCs, while those of all the other LDCs fall far below Brazil's tonnage completed yearly. Brazil's shipyards are outfitted to build up to very large-size vessels (including supertankers) and by late 1978 were second in the world in tonnage under order, behind only Japan, according to Lloyd's Register, with contracts from major foreign shipping companies and several countries.[20] As in steel, a worldwide recession in shipbuilding in the late 1970s tended to work to Brazil's advantage relative to its developed country (DC) competitors, which increased its ranking markedly after 1977, as its shipyards worked at full capacity and tonnage tripled between 1977 and 1979.

Energy Production, Consumption, and Reserves

National capabilities theorists consider total energy produced and total energy consumed to be key measures of political potential because of their relationship to industrialization, mechanization, and transportation. Energy-use levels increase with advancing industrialization and rising per capita income, both in total consumption and in consumption per capita. The standard unit of measure used is metric tons of coal equivalent. Brazil's standings on all the indicators for this energy variable are presented in Table 2.4. They reflect the facts that energy supplies are a severe constraint on national development and that slowness in energy-use transition is one of the principal hindrances to increased political potential for Brazil.[21] Because these are macroeconomic indicators of diffuse and long-term impact, it would be helpful in evaluating the global proportionality of each one to keep in mind that in 1975 Brazil stood 5th in territorial size, 7th in population, and 10th in GNP in the world.

Although demonstrating a tendency to rise slowly in rank in total consumption and production of energy over the period, Brazil fell well below even the industrial economies of countries with much smaller populations (such as Czechoslovakia and East Germany) because of the regionally and socially uneven nature of energy use and sharply reduced levels of electrification and mechanization outside the urban centers. Energy use has not been economically efficient, as it has been rising more rapidly than GNP, partly as a function of filling in the uneven areas of energy availability to the public. Over the long run, Brazil's rates of energy production have not been spectacular; in average annual growth rate of energy production from 1960 to 1975 it stood only 50th. The gap

TABLE 2.4
Brazil's Rank among all States in Measures of Energy Production,
Consumption, and Reserves, 1970-76

Measure	70	71	72	73	74	75	76	1976 as a Percent of World Total	Source Codes	Notes
Gasoline Production	9	9	8	8	8	8	8	2.0%	G	1
Imports of Crude Oil	12	12	12	12	11	10	9	2.6	G	2
Domestic Demand for Refined Products	13	11	10	9	8	8	9	1.7	G	2
Uranium Reserves							10	1.2	A	1*
Output of Refined Products	15	14	13	12	11	9	11	2.1	G	1
Petroleum Refinery Distillation Capacity	15	16	8	10	10	11	12	1.6	A	(1)
Electrical Energy, Installed Capacity	16	16	16	15	14	14	12		A	(2)
Electricity Production	15	15	15	15	13	14	14	1.3	A	(2)
Energy Consumption	22	21	20	20	20	19	19	1.0	A	(3)
Coal Reserves							21	0.02	L	
Coal Production	26	26	25	25	23	23	23	0.1	A	
Crude Oil Production	23	22	24	26	26	27	30	0.28	A	
Oil Reserves							32	0.15	A	
Energy Production	38	36	35	34	33	33	36	0.3	A	(3)
Natural Gas Production	42	NA	43	43	40	41	43	0.06	A	(4)
Natural Gas Reserves							50	0.04	A	
Energy Consumption Per Capita	68	70	72	71	67	69	64		A	(3)

Notes: Most of the 1976 rankings in source "A" are estimates.
*As of 1/1/77

1. Neither rank nor percentage include Sino-Soviet area, minus Cuba.
2. Ranking does not include Sino-Soviet area minus Cuba, but 1976
    percentage does include these countries.

(1) Excludes China, USSR
(2) Excludes China
(3) In coal equivalent
(4) In teracalories

between energy consumed and energy produced, in either rankings or percentages, is quite large, and both consumption and production are well below the relative size of Brazil's economy in the world. On the other hand, electricity production is more in line with the economy's size, although installed capacity rankings have risen quickly and can be expected to rise further when hydroelectric complexes now under construction are completed.

The presence of smaller states with higher consumption levels has the effect of driving Brazil's per capita energy consumption ranking down, but in comparison with the industrial states of any size it still fares very poorly. In 1976 Brazil's per capita energy consumption was only 17.0 percent of Western Europe's, 12.3 percent of West Germany's, 16.7 percent of France's, 22.3 percent of Italy's, and 30.5 percent of Spain's; within Latin America, Brazil's rate was 59.6 percent of Mexico's and 40.5 percent of Argentina's. It was about equal with the rates for Turkey, Algeria, Iraq, and Syria, none of them serious candidates for industrialized status.[22] In consumption of electrical energy per capita, in 1975 Brazil stood 58th, on a par with Mexico and Saudi Arabia.

Brazil has become a major importer of petroleum, to cover about 87 percent of the approximately 1.1 million barrels a day it needs (as of late 1979), for a 1979 cost of about $7 billion, or approximately 50 percent of export earnings. Because of scant coal deposits and primary reliance on motor vehicles rather than railroad or water transportation, petroleum is the source of about 52 percent of all the energy consumed in the country. This percentage is higher than in most industrial nations and constiututes the driving force behind Brazil's surge and high rankings in imports of crude oil, gasoline production, domestic demand for and output of refined products, and refinery capacity. (Brazil is a major producer of petrochemicals, but not a significant importer or exporter of refined products.) According to Petrobrás, the full extent of national reserves will not be known until at least 1981, but the known reserves as of 1979 were meager relative to national needs and world reserves. Although small discoveries are being made from time to time, few impartial observers see any reason to expect more than a moderate reduction in foreign dependency. Brazil has been slipping in absolute volume and in rank in crude oil production even as the domestic demand for refined products rose at a brisk rate and entered the top ten outside the Sino-Soviet area. The percentage of consumption accounted for by domestic crude production fell from 30 percent in 1971 to 15 percent in 1978. After five years of declining domestic crude production, only in 1979 did production show a slight increase—only 3 percent relative to 1978, a year when Brazil ranked only 32nd worldwide. Again, the per capita rankings on the refined products indicator are low, as in the country's 48th ranking in 1976 in per capita consumption of gasoline.

Among the other fossil fuels, natural gas production, use, and reserves are minuscule, while coal reserves are limited and of poor quality. Coking coal is in especially short supply. Should it ever become economically feasible to exploit shale oil, Brazil has an advantage, with the second largest deposits in the world. Two noncarbon sources show considerable promise and are being developed in major projects that have aroused domestic and international controversy: hydroelectric energy and nuclear power, as symbolized in the Itaipu Dam disputes and the nuclear pact with West Germany. Although comparable statistics on the subject are hard to find, it is commonly said that Brazil has one of the greatest undeveloped hydroelectric potentials in the world. Much of it, however, is prohibitively far from coastal population centers. In January 1977 it stood 10th outside the Sino-Soviet area in known reserves of uranium. Recent major discoveries since then have raised its position, not only guaranteeing sufficient material for its own increasingly curtailed nuclear power plans but also contributing a strategic element to the resource base. One of the attractions, and increasingly a justification, of the nuclear agreement with West Germany has been acquisition of plants and technology to allow Brazil to become an exporter of enriched as well as unprocessed uranium. Brazil also has large reserves of thorium. Energy conversion plans are now concentrating particularly on more hydroelectricity (at the investment expense of nuclear power) and sophisticated use of biomass to distill fuel alcohol, both several years or more from coming to significant levels of contribution to solving the energy requirements problem.

Brazil's energy balance has been considered a problem of the highest priority as a national security issue, because of the crimp on industrialization that insufficient energy supplies or rationing would cause, the outflow of capital required to import such large quantities of petroleum, the immense costs of the transition to other sources, and the immediate weakening of political potential that lessened fuel autonomy has already brought in foreign policy. Brazil will be one of the most negatively affected and vulnerable countries in the oil price and availability squeeze of the 1980s, because of its continued level of foreign dependence for supplies, the size of its foreign debt, and its hopes for an economic lift by boosting exports in what promises to be a world economy twisted by general economic and political difficulties of energy transition. Even in the best of circumstances it appears that petroleum is probably the only energy source from which Brazil will be able to derive the largest single share of its energy needs for the 1980s. Yet if the serious short-run hazards can be attenuated and the necessary investment made, in the longer run Brazil has one of the greatest ranges of energy options in the world and may well be in a position to suggest solutions, such as fuel alcohol, to other nations undergoing their own energy transitions.

Mineral Production

Although poor in fossil fuels, Brazil is widely described as one of the most mineral-rich countries in a wide range of basic and special-purpose metals and clays. The mining sector is still poorly developed, with the exception of iron ore and manganese, and contributes only 2 percent of GNP, with a growth rate lagging behind that of industry. The full extent of national reserves is yet to be determined for most nonfuel minerals, and enough major discoveries are being made in places such as Carajás in the Amazon that any ranking assessment now of the country's position in world mineral deposits and production must be considered incomplete. Given the territorial extension involved, the amount yet to be prospected, and the relatively low level of utilization of many of the mineral deposits already known, Brazil's rankings in reserves and production are certain to increase on most items.

Table 2.5 sets out Brazil's production rank on major minerals. According to Cline, five nonfuel minerals are particularly vital to modern industry and therefore to national political potential: iron, copper, bauxite, chromium, and uranium.[23] Brazil is well situated in reserves for all except copper, which in view of its cost could be substituted for by aluminum in many uses. On the basis of recent finds in the Carajás region, Rio Grande do Norte, and Minas Gerais, Brazil is among the world leaders in quantity and quality of iron ore, bauxite, and (to a lesser extent) uranium; because the full dimensions of the discoveries are not yet known, any rankings would be premature. Although there is no current or anticipated world shortage of or political significance to iron ore or bauxite, Brazil's own industrialization and export plans are at least assured an abundant supply. Most of these new-found deposits are so distant from the present points of final processing, however, that an expensive transportation and local processing infrastructure must be set up, which will take years before exploitation is feasible and markets sufficient to justify exploitation costs are assured.

Brazil's advance in production of iron ore in the 1970s was related to both the domestic steel industry and growing exports. Linked with local availability of a number of common ferroalloys, the resource situation regarding steelmaking can be said to be highly favorable, the only principal drawbacks being shortage of nickel and coking-quality coal.

TABLE 2.5
Brazil's Rank among all States in Measures of Mineral Production,
1970-76

Commodity	70	71	72	73	74	75	76	1976 as a Percent of World Total	Source Codes	Notes
Iron Ore	5	6	4	4	2	3	2	11.8%	A	
Manganese Ore	2	3	3	3	4	4	4	9.2	A	
Magnesite	11	11	9	9	9	9	7	3.6	A	1
Tin Ore	10	10	10	9	10	8*	8*	2.6	J	
Asbestos	12	11	10	8	8	8		1.8	A	2
Chromium Ore	11	9	6	8	8			4.8	A	3
Tungsten Concentrates	13	13	13	13	11	11	11	3.0	A	
Bauxite	18	19	17	17	15	15	14	1.3	A	
Gold	11	12	9	11	12	13	14	0.5	A	4
Nickel	13	13	13	14	15	16	16	0.4	A	
Phosphate Rock	18	19	18	20	21	21	18	0.4	A	
Zinc Ore	26	28	29	26	26	23	21	1.1	A	5
Lead Ore	24	25	24	24	23	25	26	0.7	A	
Silver	36	34	37	37	36	39	37	0.1	A	
Copper Ore	36	35	37	38	39	43	40	0.03	A	

Notes: Most of the 1976 statistics of source "A" are estimates.
*Ranking based on statistical estimates or preliminary figures.

1. Excludes U.S., Canada
2. Percent is for 1975
3. Percent is for 1974
4. Excludes USSR, China
5. Excludes Czechoslovakia, Romania, Vietnam

Brazil's combination of huge bauxite deposits in the Amazon and great accessible (if remote) hydroelectric potential to exploit them should also be noted in relation to the longer-run development of its industrial potential and probable status as a major factor in world production of aluminum by the 1990s.

The major metals in which Brazil is short relative to national needs are copper, zinc, lead, nickel, gold, and silver; the first two rank with aluminum in the "big three" in volume in nonferrous world consumption and Brazilian importation patterns and would cause continued but not onerous foreign dependency if greater progress is not made in prospecting. Brazil is expected to experience an intense growth in copper consumption by the late 1980s. It is a significant producer of the ores of manganese, magnesium, tin, asbestos, and tungsten, in addition to a number of more specialized minerals: kaolin, mica, cadmium, antimony, columbium, tantalum, beryllium, niobium, industrial diamonds, lime, lithium, and monazite.

With the present exceptions of iron ore and manganese and the future cases of aluminum and perhaps tin and nickel, because of the projected increase in national demand, government planners are thinking of national mineral resources in terms more of self-sufficiency than of foreign sales. The relatively low level of national metallurgy generally and the amount of foreign capital needed to exploit the large deposits will delay the use of many of these resources for some time. Unlike other LDCs, Brazil is both a large producer and a large consumer of minerals, with a rather small proportion of excess for export and, hence, impact on the world market across the sector. No international influence or special market advantage accrues to the minerals it exports, so its mining sector must be interpreted primarily as a support for the broader kind of political potential inherent in industrialization rather than as a significant direct contribution to national political potential in its own right. Further, if we were to make a broad-brush resource appraisal of all fuel and nonfuel minerals, Brazil would be seen to have a severe current deficit in the sector. Petroleum, natural gas, coal, iron, aluminum, and copper make up two-thirds of global consumption by value in this combined category, but Brazil has strengths only in iron (also widely found elsewhere) and aluminum.

Social Welfare and Integration

Even while acceding to the idea that "populous is not necessarily powerful," customary forms of capability analysis present a serious flaw in considering sheer population size without comparison of the level of contribution that inhabitants of the nations being compared can make to the national effort. Such a practice comes up with quite distorted results in the case of Brazil, which has a population equal to that of Japan; yet the average Brazilian is much less capable of participation in the economic and political life of the nation than the average Japanese. Beyond mere population size, other measures of the quality of human resources available to a state must be included in a capabilities assessment, as suggestive of the physical and mental capacity of the population, the extent of societal integration, and the degree of achievement of effective national community. Quality of life or distribution of economic benefits statistics are appropriate to evaluating this dimension of the national political potential base because they provide an insight into the human potential available for mobilization toward modernization and international activities. Measures of income, health, nutrition, education, and communications are particularly useful as indicators of modernization and therefore international competitiveness on a per capita basis. The higher a state scores on these indicators, the more effectively it can utilize its material resources and the more influential it can become, should its leadership so choose. Conversely, a state suffering from persistently low rankings on these indicators labors under not only loss of influence (which sheer numbers may not be able to overcome), but also loss in the prestige element of political potential.

Brazil's rankings on standard societal welfare measures, given in Table 2.6, show a set of indicators nearly all of which fall between numbers 50 and 70 out of 140 countries in 1976, placing a great burden on the country's chances for major power status. Although Brazil is an upper-middle-income country, considerable portions of the population remain outside the benefits of economic growth because emphasis on production was followed to the near-exclusion of concerns about distribution. It is ironic, for example, that Brazil is the 3rd largest producer of soybeans and 4th of cattle, yet a high percentage of the population suffers from malnutrition and the nation stands 69th in protein supply per capita. Nor has much apparent progress been made in societal welfare measures over the period relative to other nations, even at the GNP per capita level. The only appreciable exception is in school-age population per teacher, which does not imply an even distribution of teachers or school attendance by region or social class.

The most widely accepted composite indexes to measure the level of general welfare in a developing country are Sivard's "Socio-economic Standing" and the "Physical Quality of Life Index" (PQLI) of the Overseas Development Council, on which Brazil ranks 54th and 69th respectively, among all states. Both indexes are designed to summarize, from slightly different perspectives, distribution of the provision for minimal and basic human needs—GNP per capita, education, and health in the case of Sivard's index and life expectancy, infant mortality, and literacy in the case of PQLI.[24] Sivard's index measures both input of national effort and actual results, but the PQLI measures only results, especially those affecting the most elemental needs of the poorest, which accounts for much of the difference in rank. Over the long run, the PQLI shows that Brazil is making some, albeit slow, progress in general social welfare: Brazil's PQLI *rating* (not ranking) during the 1950s was 54, climbing to 63 during the 1960s and to 68 in the 1970s.[25] Yet national income is becoming more unevenly distributed by region and by social class.[26]

In view of the uneven development experienced until now, the currently low level of social expenditures, the age distribution of the popula-

TABLE 2.6
Brazil's Rank among all States in Social Welfare and Integration
Measures, 1970-75

Measure	70	71	72	73	74	75	1975 as a Percent of World Total	Source Code	Notes
Population	8	7	7	7	7	7	2.74%	E	
GNP	13	11	11	10	10	10	1.81	E	1
Percentage of Dwellings with Electricity						42		L	
GNP per Capita	51	49	46	45	46	47		E	1
School-age Population Per Teacher				56	54	49		F	
Dwellings with Piped Water						50		L	
Domestic Mail Per Capita						52		L	1976
Newsprint Consumption per Capita	48	56	57	49	51	53		A	
Socio-economic Standing						54		F	2
Population per Hospital Bed				54	56	54		F	
Population per Physician			51	51	53	54		F	
Life Expectancy				55	55	58		F	
Percentage of Required Calories per Capita					59	59		F	
Calories per Capita				45	58	60		F	
Telephones in Use per Capita	57	57	58	59	61	61		A	
Per Capita Public Expenditures on Education			63	63	57	61		F	
Literacy			61	62	60	62		F	
Infant Mortality			76	65	64	66		F	
Daily Newspaper Circulation per Capita						66		L	Mid-1970s
Per Capita Public Expenditures on Health Care			86	87	100	68		F	
Protein per Capita			61			69		F	
Physical Quality of Life Index						69		N	
School-age Population in School				72	73	79		F	

1. Market prices
2. Average of all rankings on GNP per capita, education, and health,
   according to Sivard
3. Brazil's PQLI score = 68

tion, and the speed of urbanization, rapid provision of adequate social services to the deprived, and particularly to pre-adults, will be mandatory for longer-term national development to be successful, let alone equitable according to Western standards. The problem of abandoned children, rapidly growing with no solution in sight, is illustrative of the antisocial threats to the future national potential posed by the current low level of attention to social questions in a country in which the dependency ratio by age (economically dependent ÷ economically active) is 1.6, 23rd highest in the world in the mid-1970s.

Although Brazil's rise to greater international significance could well be achieved in the first decade or so largely due to the activities of the better-off sectors of the population and regions of the country, sustained growth in actual influence will necessitate expansion of benefits to broaden the social base to take in larger proportions of the population. This is true for reasons of internal political stability and broader-based economic growth as well as for advancement of international influence, political acceptability, and prestige; a position as "great power and tropical slum" is a precarious one not likely to attract great international confidence.[27] The negative economic and political aspects of the Brazilian model of development were a cause of attrition in relations with Western allies and the World Bank in the mid-1970s, hindering closer political ties with major West European countries in a way reminiscent of the difficulties of Franco's Spain in reaching rapprochement with the European Economic Community. The "trickle down" theory of benefits has been amply debated, but the extent to which greater social equity can continue to be ignored or retarded while still advancing the nation's political potential toward major power status in the longer run has yet to be thoroughly examined. On the face of it, the prospects for success in carrying unbalanced development and a restricted internal market to that level do not appear promising, either in the long run or during periods of economic downturn. Neither is low civic consciousness characteristic of a major power.

Brazil's current level of social deficiencies hinders its political potential in various consequential ways relevant to poor use of human resources resultant from narrow and shallow development. Deficiencies in health and literacy have already caused shortages in skilled manpower, especially at the technical level important to economic and business activities, as middle- and lower-level managers and support and paraprofessional personnel are available in insufficient numbers to maintain the full hierarchy of skills and organization optimally required by the developed sector of the economy.[28] There is a notable weakness in the links or commonalities between the international-caliber technological and managerial elites, public and private, on the one hand, and the general public on the other, a dualism that extends to the minutiae of daily urban life and reduces the social cohesion necessary to advancement of the modern sector. The educational system hinders the general absorption of technology and the production of sufficient scientists and engineers to help the country become more technologically and scientifically innovative and competitive. The result is continued dependence on imported foreign technology and consequently diminished political potential. The relatively reduced level of Brazil's scientific effort is apparent from the following rankings:[29]

	Rank	Value	Period
Contribution to world scientific authorship, by number of articles	31	0.16%	early 1970s
Professional and technical workers as percentage of economically active population	52	4.8%	1976
Expenditure on scientific R&D as percentage of GNP	57	0.2%	mid-1970s
Percentage of national scientists engaged in basic research	57	0.8%	mid-1970s

Even in the best of circumstances (which the country cannot count on in the 1980s), with such a backlog and the rate of population growth and in view of the lead time necessary for any significant improvements, the social welfare and integration factor will continue to be one of the most serious vulnerabilities in the national capabilities equation.

Military Effort

Even though some theorists of trends forecast a declining utility for military power in future international relations, the inclusion of military capability measures remains de rigueur among national capabilities theorists. In the recent past, in a more force-oriented paradigm, it was commonly asserted that military might was one of the most accurate, if not the best, measures of national political strength. This came to be widely accepted because in the modern international system no state became recognized as a "major power" without a sizable military establishment, which served to demonstrate, symbolically or in battle, that the state was a force to be reckoned with in its own right, could make significant alliances, and could lend military aid. It may well be that future major powers will not be expected to possess large military forces, but it will remain true that a state with a credible military force has the option to threaten to or attempt to impose its will when the government deems it necessary, a tactic denied to a militarily weak state when its vital interests are threatened. Conversely, a militarily strong state is better able to resist imposition of unacceptable political solutions on itself. This capability to resort to force, or the perceptions of others that the state *might* resort to force, falls within the definition of "power" as the coercive component of political potential and is therefore integral to a comprehensive analysis of national capabilities. This is so even though the vast majority of international political relationships are carried out through the modes of influence and prestige rather than by imposition. A thorough discussion of Brazil's military significance is developed by Manwaring in Chapter 3, but the power element of the political-potential theme of this essay necessitates some consideration of the topic here.

A number of conventional but rough measures are used to compare states' performance in putative or potential military power, as a quantitative base for further qualitative analysis. The bulk measures are total forces in being and total military expenditures (measures of size of effort), and these two on a per capita basis and expenditures divided by GNP provide an indication of the proportion of national human and economic resources devoted to military purposes (a measure of intensity of effort). Brazil's rankings on these variables are presented in Table 2.7. It should be noted that the forces statistics of the U.S. Arms Control and Disarmament Agency (ACDA) include Brazil's paramilitary forces (largely public security forces) on the supposition that they have received sufficient military-equivalent training, weapons, or mission or are so organized as to be considered as regular forces. (This judgment is made, incidentally, for few other states). The International Institute for Strategic Studies (IISS) does not so regard Brazil's paramilitary units. For 1976, the ACDA interpretation yields a force size of 450,000, and the IISS a size of 257,200. Neither source includes reserve units for Brazil, so these rankings involve only active-duty personnel.

Over the period, Brazil's rank in armed forces size rose significantly, but its armed forces, excluding paramilitary, did not go over 1.0 percent of the world total. Brazil was surpassed by a number of LDCs and ranked at the bottom of the top twenty worldwide, ten places below its 7th rank in population. Rank in total expenditures remained steady until dropping out of the top twenty in 1976, when the value was less than half of one percent of world expenditures. Over the longer run, in total

TABLE 2.7
Brazil's Rank among all States in Measures of Military Effort,
1970-76.

Measure	70	71	72	73	74	75	76	1976 as a Percent of World Total	Source Code
Armed Forces Size (including paramilitary)	16	15	14	15	15	13	13	1.71%	D
Armed Forces Size (excluding paramilitary)		21	21	20	22	17	17	0.98	M, D
Arms Exports	76	79	79	31	81	22	17	0.64	D
Arms Imports	47	29	35	18	32	32	25	1.26	D
Military Expenditures	19	21	20	20	19	19	27	0.41	D
Military Expenditures per Soldier			30	31	35	43	42		F
Military Expenditures per Capita	66	64	66	63	65	63	64		D
Armed Forces per 1000 Population (including paramilitary)	73	76	74	76	76	76	80		D
Armed Forces per 1000 Population (excluding paramilitary)*		101	107	101	104	99	100		M, D
Military Expenditures as Percent of GNP	71	75	82	81	84	84	100		D

*Calculated using IISS armed forces statistics and ACDA population
statistics for Brazil.

military expenditures from 1960–1976, Brazil ranked 22nd, surpassed by
Iran, India, Egypt, and Saudi Arabia among the LDCs, equal to Belgium
at $15 billion, and surpassing Turkey at $13 billion and Yugoslavia at
$12 billion.[30] On either of the bulk or mass indicators, therefore, Brazil
does not show up as a major military power in the world context, even
less so when it is considered that an unusually high proportion of those
expenditures is directed toward personnel costs rather than equipment.

The measures of intensity of effort strengthen this conclusion. In
forces per capita, Brazil comes in extremely low, about 100th when
paramilitary units are discounted, showing a minute percentage of the
human resources devoted to military service relative to other nations.
The rank on military expenditures per capita remained steady at about

number 65, but standings on expenditures as a percentage of GNP and expenditures per soldier declined rapidly. In both policy and results, government decisions have given priority to developmental and social spending above spending for military purposes, nor is military force considered as a useful foreign policy instrument by a significant number of policymakers.

Mere quantitative measures, of course, do not take into account crucial intangibles such as organizational skills, quality of training, physical stamina of the troops, sophistication of equipment, will to use military force, mobilization ability, and other subjective factors necessary to evaluate military effectiveness. Even less do they allow prediction of conflict outcomes. What assessments do exist of the qualitative variables for Brazil indicate considerable weaknesses beyond the ones implied by the numbers alone.[31] These weaknesses, nevertheless, should not be taken as seriously diminishing the future political significance of Brazil's status as the most prominent military power of South America and perhaps of Latin America, depending upon how the capabilities of Cuba are evaluated.

A Measure of Diplomatic Status

Discussion of the more "objective" national capabilities measures of Brazil's political potential compared with that of other states, which in stratification and interaction terminology is referred to as *achieved* status, has just been completed. What is now of interest is its *ascribed* status, the "subjective" level of international deference or prestige accorded to Brazil by the other states of the international system, based on their collective evaluation of its significance or consequence in the world. It then remains to compare the ascribed status with the achieved status to see the degrees of discrepancies on various measures.

The standard measure of ascribed status or attributed diplomatic importance in the international system in its broadest (i.e., non-issue-specific) sense has been developed by Singer and Small for the Correlates of War Project. The diplomatic status rank assigned to a state equals its ranking against all other states in terms of the absolute number of diplomatic missions received by each. The state receiving the most missions is designated as having the highest status, the next highest becomes number 2, and so on down the list, in a sort of sociogram of formal political exchange that measures routine official interaction.[32] With this status conceptualization of exchange of missions, and a second, which involves total number of diplomats exchanged, world rankings in receiving and sending categories were run on the global diplomatic exchange

TABLE 2.8
Brazil's Rank among all States in Measures of Diplomatic Exchange,
1973-77

	1973	1974	1975	1976	1977	Period Mean
Missions Sent by Brazil						
Number	66	65	72	74	76	70.6
Rank among all States	17	17	13	13	14	14.8
Brazil's Missions Sent as Percent of Total Sent by Highest Ranked State	54.5%	54.2%	60.5%	61.2%	60.8%	58.2%
Missions Received by Brazil						
Number	62	68	69	69	68	67.2
Rank among all States	17	13	13	16	17	15.2
Brazil's Missions Received As Percent of Total Received by Highest Ranked State	52.1%	59.1%	57.0%	58.5%	57.6%	56.9%
Brazil's Diplomats Abroad						
Number	451.5	463.0	502.2	528.4	573.3	503.7
Rank among all States	25	25	23	24	22	23.8
Percent of World Total	1.05%	1.05%	1.10%	1.10%	1.15%	1.09%
Brazil's Total as Percent of Total Sent by Top Ten States	3.20%	3.17%	3.34%	3.38%	3.55%	3.33%
Diplomats Received by Brazil						
Number	441.7	437.7	456.6	475.4	494.3	461.1
Rank among all States	24	28	28	27	26	26.6
Percent of World Total	1.02%	0.99%	0.99%	0.99%	0.99%	1.00%
Brazil's Total as Percent of Total Received by Top Ten States	3.99%	3.80%	3.75%	3.79%	3.82%	3.83%

Source: USNA Foreign Affairs Theory, Operations, and Monitoring (Project
         FATHOM). This data bank includes 207 actors, with major IGOs,
         the PLO, and some few other non-state entities, but with
         negligible results for global ranking purposes. Missions sent
         and received include only bilateral transactions and are
         calculated on the basis of ambassadors in residence, providing
         figures very close to the actual number of missions. In the
         diplomats abroad and diplomats received categories, total
         figures are obtained using the following scoring system:

              Each fully accredited diplomat = 1.0
              Dual representative to OAS and host state = 0.5
              Cumulative representation = 0.2
              Relations listing but no exchange = 0.1

         All figures were derived from official diplomatic receiving
         lists worldwide.

data bank of the U.S. Naval Academy's Foreign Affairs Theory, Operations, and Monitoring (FATHOM) Project, for the years 1973 through 1977.[33] The results for Brazil are presented in Table 2.8.

A five-year span is too short to indicate major changes in status, and there is enough yearly fluctuation in our variable of primary interest, ranks on missions received, that it would be more valid to average the number of missions for each state over the period and to rank states on the basis of that result. The top twenty states in diplomatic rank for 1973–1977 then appear as:

Rank	State	Average Missions Received, 1973–1977
1	France	116.0
2	United States	113.8
3	United Kingdom	112.8
4	Federal Republic of Germany	106.8
5	USSR	93.6
6	Egypt	92.6
7	Italy	92.2
8	Belgium	87.2
9	Japan	79.6
10	India	75.4
11	China	75.2
12	Canada	75.0
13	Sweden	67.6
14	Brazil	67.2
15	Spain	66.4
16	Yugoslavia	66.2
17	Nigeria	64.2
18	Switzerland	63.6
19	Iran	62.8
20	Algeria	62.6

Using either system, the only LDCs above Brazil for the entire period were Egypt and India, although, in figures taken yearly, Algeria surpassed Brazil slightly in 1975 and 1976 and Iran ranked higher in 1976 and 1977, as did Nigeria in 1977. The rise in the rankings of Iran and Nigeria, as regional oil, political, and military powers, is quite brisk even during this brief five-year span.

A second receiving measure, not used by Singer and Small but following a similar logic, is the total number of diplomats received by a country. This would be a way of ranking the portion of the total "international diplomatic workload" taken up by each state, something different from measuring a simple exchange of representatives, because it is sensitive principally to the sizes of the missions rather than only to the existence of an embassy. On this measure over the period, Brazil drops about 14 points in rank to number 28 in average diplomats received per year, which lowers it toward the bottom of the middle powers, and close to Mexico, the Netherlands, Romania, Sweden, Switzerland, and Turkey. A number of LDCs consistently outranked Brazil, and the list is one of local influentials with some regional and/or global significance: Argentina, Egypt, and India for the whole period; Indonesia (after 1973), Iran (after 1974), Lebanon (1973–1976), Thailand (1973–1975), and Algeria and Nigeria (1977 only). Among middle powers for the period as a whole, Brazil ranked close to Mexico, the Netherlands, Sweden, and Switzerland. This considerable discrepancy in rank between missions received and diplomats received implies that Brazil's average mission size is significantly lower than those of the middle-sized and smaller states that rank below it in missions received. Several reasons for this can be advanced. Although Brasília is the site of several LDC missions accredited to other South American countries as well, it is definitely not a regional diplomatic or business center like Mexico City, Buenos Aires (for the Southern Cone), Cairo, Brussels, Lagos, or (for a time) Beirut. The vigorous and assertive Third World leadership attempts of several countries in recent periods tended to attract more diplomats, as in the cases of Algeria, Iran, Nigeria, and India, but Brazil had deliberately avoided such offensives in favor of a low-profile and cautious diplomatic style. Further, Brazil's geopolitical position far from world tension centers and the main flow of   international affairs negatively affects the diplomatic workload assigned to it, much as is the case with Australia. In a more mundane vein, demand for the post among foreign diplomats sharply dropped when the capital was moved from more glamorous Rio de Janeiro to Brasília, which also offers fewer attractions than Buenos Aires or Mexico City.

A National Capabilities and Diplomatic Status Profile

To gain an overview of the ranking profile of the main tangible measures of Brazil's achieved political potential and how these compare with its ascribed status, Table 2.9 was drawn up to show change over a ten-year period. A decade is, to be certain, a short period in the path of a nation's progress, and some of the rankings fluctuated slightly from year to year. Nevertheless, Brazil's rise in relation to other states from 1965 to

TABLE 2.9
Brazil's Rank among all States in Standard Measures of National
Capability and Diplomatic Status, 1975 and 1965

Measure	1975 Rank	1965 Rank	Data Source
Area	5	5	
Population	7	8	World Bank
GNP	10	14	World Bank
Diplomatic Missions Received	13		USNA FATHOM
Armed Forces Size (including paramilitary)	13	16	U.S. ACDA
Imports	13	35	USNA FATHOM; UN Statistical Yearbook
Raw Steel Production	15	23	Iron Age
Exports	17	22	USNA FATHOM; UN Statistical Yearbook
Armed Forces Size (excluding paramilitary)	17	NA	International Institute for Strategic Studies
Energy Consumption	19	23	UN Statistical Yearbook
Military Expenditures	19	25	U.S. ACDA
Size of Merchant Fleet	19	18	U.S. Department of Commerce
Diplomats Received	28		USNA FATHOM
Energy Production	33	38	UN Statistical Yearbook
GNP per Capita	47	65	World Bank
GNP per Capita	54	55	U.S. ACDA
Energy Consumption per Capita	69	69	UN Statistical Yearbook
Military Manpower per 1000 Population (including paramilitary)	76	65	U.S. ACDA
Military Expenditures as percent of GNP	84	61	U.S. ACDA
Military Manpower per 1000 Population (excluding paramilitary)	99	NA	International Institute For Strategic Studies and U.S. ACDA

1975 on almost all "bulk" tangible measures of national political potential is striking, and, from the major indicators beyond 1975 examined earlier, appears to be continuing. On the other hand, progress relative to other states on the developmental per capita or "quality" indicators is either slight or nonexistent. It is, of course, the states that are high on both size and development measures that can more consistently be effective in international affairs.

Diplomatic status measured by missions received falls at number 13 (or number 14, using the 1973–1977 average)—about in the middle of the 11 measures running from number 5 to number 19 in rank (perhaps as the result of an attraction to the potential represented by area, population, and GNP), about even in level with imports and steel, and higher than energy consumption and military force size and expenditures. Because no single figure or composite index is used and we are dealing with a single case, it is impossible to ascertain definitively whether there is any significant discrepancy between Brazil's achieved status and its ascribed status as assigned by the usual measures. Its rank in missions received, however, does not appear to be out of keeping with what would be expected as normal. Its 28th rank in total diplomats received does appear to be inordinately low, particularly in view of some of the states ranking higher on this measure than Brazil. In Brazil's case, it would appear that the above-mentioned factors other than those tangible capabilities considered here are at work to drive down its ranking on total diplomats received. It could also be reasoned that although Brazil's rank in total diplomats received (share of the world's current diplomatic workload) is low, its rank in missions received (ongoing routine contacts) is high as a form of "anticipatory status" or "attributed future influence" based upon the credit given today for the level of development and weight in the world that the national actors of the system expect it to have tomorrow.

More empirical systemic research would be necessary on correlations between achieved status and ascribed status, using many states and several time periods to establish patterns, before such an assertion of face validity in this particular case could be more adequately tested. To summarize, though, without taking single-number ranks too literally, it would appear reasonable to conclude that in the mid-1970s Brazil ranked somewhere between number 10 and number 15 in achieved status, the tangible elements of national political potential (particularly considering the centrality of steel production), and that its ascribed status rank of about number 14–15 reflected the achieved status rather closely.[34]

Although Brazil appears to be increasing in the attributes of political potential relative to other states, it has a long way to go to achieve major power status in capabilities, even without considering the influence on other states that actually confers that status. According to Steven Spiegel, during the 1970s the international hierarchy was broken down into a number of levels. The superpowers were two, the United States and the USSR. The secondary or major powers were Japan, the Federal Republic of Germany, China, France, and the United Kingdom. These seven collectively are the great powers. The third level of middle powers comprised seventeen regional powers, including Brazil.[35] Within this widely accepted terminology, a "major power" can be defined as a state with sufficient capabilities across a wide range to be influential in a considerable variety of international matters and to affect in a substantial way the behavior of other states at various levels in the hierarchy and beyond its own region. A "world power," then, can exercise this influence on a global scale, although a strict application of the term would require worldwide capability to exert military or punitive power as well as the more frequent political and economic influence and prestige.

To gauge the distance in the mid-1970s between Brazil and the five major powers in regard to tangible capabilities and status, Table 2.10 was constructed. It demonstrates that, overall, huge capabilities and status gaps lie between Brazil and the major powers on the average values of all variables except population. Qualitative assessments do not show that Brazil exercises any influence beyond what its tangible capabilities imply; its actual influence appears to be less than its tangible attributes, not more, but this assessment remains a matter of subjective judgment and cannot be measured empirically.

Because Brazil has no resources that will be critical or "political" in the foreseeable future, and in fact lacks sufficient petroleum, it cannot claim the special rapid elevation in status that was bestowed upon Mexico, Venezuela, Saudi Arabia, Iran, and Nigeria in recent years. Ironically, although the type of diversified industrial development and diversified trade (in partners and commodities) that Brazil has been undergoing is the most conducive to stable and growing long-run influence, its effect on other nations and the international system in the short run is so diffuse and gradual that it appears to be tantamount to obscurity when contrasted with impressions created by smaller states making more narrow impacts in dramatic areas such as petroleum and international conflict. On most key measures examined, Brazil accounted for between 1 percent and 3 percent of world consumption or production; combined with a GNP that was only about 2 percent of the total world product in 1978, the country has a claim to greater significance but lacks a resource base for strong influence on more than several issues beyond its region. Its advances in rankings have been notably uneven. At this point, possible changes in the future aside, it is premature, perhaps fanciful, to speak of contemporary Brazil as a "major power" or, even more so, a "world power," as the terms are now understood. To have considerable spot influence on certain issues, even to be of world significance in these matters, does not in itself make a state a world power. Much less so does having a mere stake in global affairs confer this designation, which is one of political potential actualized at a high level across issues and regions.

At present there is a quantum jump between middle power status and major power status, many aspects of which have not been discussed here, such as a strong currency, large amounts of exportable investment capital, and innovative high technology, all of which Brazil lacks. Given current problems, it is unlikely that Brazil will be able to cross that

TABLE 2.10

Comparison between Brazil and the Major Powers on Principal National Capability and Status Measures, 1975 (Absolute Values)

Measure	Brazil	FRG	Japan	France	United Kingdom	China*	Source Code
Population (millions)	107	61.8	111.6	52.8	55.9	822.8	E
GNP ($ U.S. billions)	110.1	412.5	496.3	314.1	211.7	315.3	E
GNP per capita ($ U.S.)	1030	6670	4450	5950	3780	380	E
Physical Quality of Life Index	68	95	98	97	97	59	N
Armed Forces Size (thousands)	254.5	495.0	236.0	502.5	345.1	3250.0	M
Military Expenditures ($ billions)	2.4	15.3	4.7	13.1	11.5	32.7	D
Energy Consumption (million metric tons of coal equivalent)	73.3	330.5	403.7	208.4	297.2	564.0	A
Energy Production (million metric tons of coal equivalent)	25.1	165.9	37.4	47.6	184.0	589.5	A
Energy Consumption per capita (kg. of coal equivalent)	670	5345	3622	3944	5265	693	A
Raw Steel Production (thousands of metric tons)	8.4	40.4	102.3	21.5	19.8	26.0	K
Exports ($ U.S. billions)	8.6	89.8	53.0	51.6	43.7	5.7	C
Imports ($ U.S. billions)	13.6	74.7	57.6	53.6	53.2	6.5	C
Diplomatic Missions Received	69	106	82	115	117	68	C
Diplomats Received	456.6	1293.1	885.3	1597.6	1912.4	777.4	C

*Many of the statistics for China are estimates.

capabilities and power-of-decision gap in this century. Nevertheless, it is safe to say that Brazil is clearly becoming a more significant actor and more important middle power, and that it has the strong potential through the 1980s to be one of the most important middle powers, to be taken more seriously by more nations in this decade. Among LDCs, only India can compare with Brazil in broad capabilities, and the U.S. penchant for considering Brazil in the same rather amorphous class with Mexico and Argentina, or, lately, newly industrialized countries such as Hong Kong and South Korea, is far out of line with reality.

The international system is evolving as new forms of influence appear and the seven great powers find their established patterns of influence weakened by diffusion of capabilities. We are still waiting for new paradigms of the international system of the 1980s to emerge from the unexpected discontinuties of the 1970s, and it is certain that a scheme such as Spiegel's already requires revision of conceptualizaton and terminology. Some of the new perspectives are so transnational as to frontally challenge the continued validity of the state-centered view of international relations and therefore the whole concept of national capabilities itself. Even with these reinterpretations of the nature and evolution of the international system, and the cautious reluctance to extrapolate into the future, Brazil's opportunities for influence in the long run do seem to be greater than those of other middle powers such as Canada, Australia, Spain, Italy, and Belgium. Yet during the 1980s it is most likely to find itself in similar (and probably frustrated) straits with them with respect to its general lack of ability to shape international outcomes and to initiate changes across a range of issues beyond its own region. Ultimately, it will be the amount of power, influence, and prestige that it can actually bring to bear on specific issues, not its raw political potential, that will determine whether it will become a major power by century's end or will be considered just a large country.

Notes

1. Ray S. Cline, *World Power Assessment, 1977* (Boulder, Colo: Westview Press, 1977). The first edition was dated 1975. The third edition (1980) ranked Brazil 3rd, behind only the Soviet Union and the United States.

2. A good overview of the subject of U.S.-Brazil relations is Albert Fishlow, "Flying Down to Rio: Perspectives on U.S.-Brazil Relations," *Foreign Affairs* 57 (Winter 1978-1979):387–405.

3. Daniel Southerland, "Carter Successful 'Walking on Eggshells' in Brazil," *Christian Science Monitor* (March 31, 1978):26.

4. Nathan Haverstock, "Brzezinsky Speaks," *Times of the Americas* (Feb-

ruary 15, 1978).

5. Winthrop P. Carty, "Civil Rights Guarantee for All Rights—Todman," *Times of the Americas* (April 26, 1978):7.

6. C. Fred Bergsten, "Brazil and the United States in the World Economy: A New Mode of Relations," *Vital Speeches of the Day* (February 15, 1978):261–264.

7. "The Newest Superstate," *Newsweek* (April 10, 1978):54.

8. Wayne A. Selcher, *Brazil's Multilateral Relations: Between First and Third Worlds* (Boulder, Colo.: Westview Press, 1978) uses a similar approach adapted to multilateral issues to analyze Brazil's policy, strategy, and tactics (diplomatic style) as a function of its interests and position in the international hierarchies.

9. As a sequel to this chapter, the qualitative factors that inhibit Brazil's exercise of actual influence and explain the discrepancy between its achieved political potential in terms of resources and its actual effect on events beyond its borders are analyzed in Wayne A. Selcher, "Brazil in the Global Power Systems," Occasional Papers Series, Center of Brazilian Studies, School of Advanced International Studies, Johns Hopkins University, Washington, D.C., 1980.

10. Klaus Knorr, *The Power of Nations* (New York: Basic Books, 1975), p. 9.

11. James N. Rosenau, "Capabilities and Control in an Interdependent World," *International Security* 1 (1976):36.

12. Leon G. Mears, "Farm Output, Trade Boom Still Continues in Brazil," *Foreign Agriculture* (March 14, 1977):12.

13. *Food Needs of Developing Countries: Projections of Production and Consumption to 1990* (Washington, D.C.: International Food Policy Research Institute, 1977), pp. 105–106.

14. "Brazil's Wheat Goal and Wheat-Soybean Connection," *Foreign Agriculture* (August 14, 1978):10.

15. A.F.K. Organski, *World Politics*, 2nd ed. (New York: Alfred A. Knopf, 1968), p. 345.

16. These include the Correlates of War Project at the University of Michigan. Ray Cline (*World Power Assessment, 1977*, p. 69) says, "The gross magnitude of national steel production is one of the most appropriate measures of the strength of an industrial nation."

17. *Iron Age* (January 4, 1968, and January 7, 1980).

18. "Steel," *Bank of London and South America Review* (June 1978):333.

19. United Nations, Department of Internal Economic and Social Affairs, Statistical Office, *Statistical Yearbook, 1977* (New York: United Nations, 1978), pp. 634–635.

20. Brazilian Embassy, Washington, D.C., "Boletim Especial" (December 27, 1978), and "Naval Construction: The Big Shipyards of Brazil," *Brazil Trade and Industry* (March 1979):32–35.

21. An overview of the topic by a prominent Brazilian scientist is J. Goldemberg, "Brazil: Energy Options and Current Outlook," *Science* 200 (April 14, 1978):158–164.

22. United Nations, *Statistical Yearbook, 1977*, pp. 385 and 387.

23. Cline, *World Power Assessment, 1977*, p. 66.

24. For an explanation of the indexes, see Ruth Leger Sivard, *World Military*

and Social Expenditures (Leesburg, Va.:WMSE Publications, 1974, 1976, 1977, and 1978); Martin L. McLaughlin, ed., *The United States and World Development—Agenda 1979* (New York: Praeger Publishers, 1979); and Morris David Morris, *Measuring the Condition of the World's Poor* (New York: Pergamon Press, 1979).

25. James P. Grant, "Targeting Progress in Meeting Basic Needs," in *Partners in Tomorrow: Strategies for a New International Order*, ed. by Anthony J. Dolman and Jan van Ettinger (New York: E. P. Dutton, 1978), p. 172.

26. The most thorough study of the impact of human resources on Brazil's development is *Brazil: Human Resources Special Report* (Washington, D.C.: World Bank, 1979).

27. The suggestive designation is adopted in terms of alternative prospects ("Great Power or Tropical Slum") by Philip Raine in *Brazil: Awakening Giant* (Washington, D.C.: Public Affairs Press, 1974), p. 222.

28. See, for example, the series on Brazil's human resources problems and the business climate in *Business Latin America* (Second Quarter, 1979). This publication estimates that 40 to 50 percent of the population is subsisting outside the economy (February 8, 1978:42).

29. George Thomas Kurian, *The Book of World Rankings* (New York: Facts on File, 1979), pp. 218–219, 332–335.

30. Sivard, *World Military and Social Expenditures, 1978*, p. 8.

31. Cline's assessment of combat capabilities of Brazil in comparison to those of European neutrals and some Latin Americans is done in ways comparable to rankings assigned several other LDC powers (*World Power Assessment, 1977*, p. 121). Limitations on Brazil's combat readiness are cited by Thomas E. Skidmore, "Brazil's Changing Role in the International System: Implications for U.S. Policy," in *Brazil in the Seventies*, ed. by Riordan Roett (Washington, D.C.: American Enterprise Institute for Public Policy Research, 1976), pp. 25–28.

32. The justification of the system and 1950–1970 country rankings are given in Melvin Small and J. David Singer, "The Diplomatic Importance of States, 1816–1970: An Extension and Refinement of the Indicator," *World Politics* 25 (July 1973):577–599.

33. A special note of appreciation goes to U.S.N.A. political science professors John Hutchins, who collects the data and meticulously compiles it, and Rodney Tomlinson, who designed and ran this program. The data base used by FATHOM, all yearly receiving lists checked against most sending lists, is more comprehensive and sensitive to changes over time than that of Singer and Small, which is the *Europa Year-Book, Statesman's Yearbook*, and the *Code Diplomatique*, supplemented by inquiries to some foreign ministries. Therefore, the rankings produced with FATHOM statistics differ from Singer and Small's, but I am satisfied that they have a high degree of accuracy because of their global inclusiveness from primary official sources rather than secondary compilations. Although these rankings are useful measures, it would be advisable not to take small variations between years or countries too seriously.

34. Cline's composite and weighted total for the tangible or "concrete" elements of Brazil's political potential, before national strategy and will to pursue

national strategy were applied as multipliers, ranked Brazil 10th in the world in 1977, at the top of the 10–15 range in achieved status suggested here, and only 4 points above our averaged 1973–1977 ascribed status rank. Cline considered Brazil's strong points to be territorial extension, population size, GNP, nonfuel minerals, steel production, and trade volume. It was downgraded regarding energy dependence and a small military establishment. On the other hand, it was assigned one of the highest national strategy and national will scores of any state. See *World Power Assessment, 1977*, pp. 173–174.

35. Steven L. Spiegel, *Dominance and Diversity: The International Hierarchy* (Boston: Little, Brown and Co., 1972), pp. 93–94.

Statistical Source Codes
Referred to in the Tables of Chapter 2

Code	Source
A	United Nations. Department of Internal Economic and Social Affairs. Statistical Office. *Statistical Yearbook*. New York: United Nations. Principally the 1977 Yearbook. Most 1976 statistics are estimates.
B	Metallgesellschaft Aktiengesellschaft. *Metal Statistics, 1967–1977*. 65th ed. Frankfurt am Main: Metallgesellschaft AG, 1978.
C	U.S. Naval Academy's Foreign Affairs Theory, Operations, and Monitoring data bank (Project FATHOM), with the assistance of Professors Rodney Tomlinson and John Hutchins, Department of Political Science, U.S.N.A.
D	U.S. Arms Control and Disarmament Agency. *World Military Expenditures and Arms Transfers, 1967–1976*. Washington D.C.: ACDA, 1978.
E	World Bank. *World Bank Atlas: Population, Per Capita Product, and Growth Rates*. Washington, D.C.: World Bank, 1972 through 1977 editions.
F	Ruth Leger Sivard. *World Military and Social Expenditures*. Leesburg, Va.: WMSE Publications, 1974, 1976, 1977, and 1978 editions.
G	U.S. Department of Energy. Energy Information Administration. *International Petroleum Annual*. Washington, D.C.: U.S. Department of Energy, 1970 through 1976 editions.
H	U.S. Department of Commerce. Maritime Administration. *Merchant Fleets of the World*. Washington D.C.: U.S. Department of Commerce, 1970 through 1976 editions.
I	Lloyd's. *Lloyd's Register Annual Summary of Merchant Ships Completed in the World*. London: Lloyd's, 1970 through 1977 editions.
J	Commodity Research Bureau. *Commodity Year Book, 1978*. New York: Commodity Research Bureau, 1978.

K   *Iron Age*, January 7, 1980, p. 87, and January 4, 1968, p. 119.
L   George Thomas Kurian. *The Book of World Rankings*. New York: Facts on File, 1979.
M   International Institute for Strategic Studies. *The Military Balance*. Boulder, Colo.: Westview Press, yearly.
N   Martin M. McLaughlin, ed. *The United States and World Development—Agenda 1979*. New York: Praeger Publishers, 1979.

3

Brazilian Military Power: A Capability Analysis

Max G. Manwaring

Military capability analysis is generally considered important for manifold reasons. The historical record does not support the notion that international coercion is declining. In this connection, it is hard to see the increasing number of nuclear arsenals and the extraordinary amount of military spending throughout the world as benign.[1] Governments must expect international military conflict, direct and indirect foreign intervention, and wars of national liberation to continue at a high level.[2] The international system is an anarchy in which national military forces can be used for threatening or making war. They can be employed coercively in order to influence the behavior of opponents or to alter or preserve the status quo by simple attack or defense. Moreover, military forces can be politically effective even when doing nothing. For example, Country A may not choose or even consider a policy that might prompt a military response from Country B.[3] Consequently, given a global context of limited chaos, capability analysis can be an important tool in assessing the relative position of a state vis-à-vis possible enemies and friends.

Some recent work on the analysis of world power status suggests the direction for this chapter.[4] We propose to expand on some of these and other ideas and methods and apply them to a Brazilian context.[5] Consequently, this chapter has one primary and three secondary objectives. The major purpose is to determine Brazil's relative military capability. The secondary objectives are: (1) to determine where the military capability of Brazil ranks in relation to that of twenty-nine other selected countries in the world and twelve other Latin American nations; (2) to determine the direction in which Brazil seems to be going in relative military capability over the past ten years as compared to other selected countries; and (3) to contribute further to a theoretical-empirical elucidation of one aspect of the overall phenomenon of power—military capability. Through the accomplishment of these goals, we can better understand the realities of military power in the contemporary world and begin to determine Brazil's military significance in the hemisphere and in the world.

Assumptions

Two basic assumptions underlie this examination of Brazilian military power in the regional and world context. First, it is our position that military power is no longer, by itself, the guarantor of political authority in the world. The power equation has been drastically altered as the international system has become multipolar and more interdependent. Nevertheless, the ability to project military force abroad remains an important element in assisting a government to accomplish foreign policy goals. Second, the results of any capability analysis at the macro level must inevitably be uncertain. One cannot be sure of what types of crisis might be generated, what kind of domestic or foreign support might exist, the location and characteristics of a theater of operations, the capabilities available to an opponent, or the amount of time that might be available for preparation. Therefore, there can be no precise answer to the questions: "Capability for what?" or "In what context?" The best we can suggest is that we are analyzing the capability to develop pressures across the entire spectrum of conflict—from traditional mobilization, to movement of forces and maneuvers, to low-intensity warfare, all the way to nuclear holocaust.

Military Capability

This notion is more than a quantitative and qualitative evaluation of military forces in being. As a result, the elements that might constitute military power capabilities are numerous.[6] However, in the interests of parsimony and manageability it is necessary to determine which indicator-variables are the best. I chose to empirically identify the variables most closely related to military power capability, rather than determine them a priori. Consequently, I submitted sixteen variables to the SPSS (Statistical Package for the Social Sciences) Factor Analysis.[7] Instead of a clear-cut, single military capability factor emerging, the principal components analysis indicated that military capability consists of the ability to sustain and increase military strength, the ability to project force over long distances, and actual military forces. Interestingly, Knorr's "putative" military capability concept is very similar.[8]

More specifically, the factor analysis indicates the following. First the principal component called *Armed Forces Strength* is best explained by two variables: (1) the number of armed forces personnel in a given country (AFT) and (2) the theoretical capacity to produce a given number of 20-kiloton (KT) bombs per year (NUC). These indicators represent projectable power. Second, the factor identified as *Reach* is also best explained by two indicator-variables: (1) the merchant marine (RE1) and (2) the number of passengers flown on domestic airlines per year (RE2). Although the airlines and sea transport of a given country are not part of the regular military structure, they constitute an extremely important set of assets that could and would be used in any military exigency. Third, the component called *Infrastructure* is composed of three variables : (1) defense expenditure per capita (DEP), (2) arms exports (AEX), and (3) government revenue per capita (GRP). These indicators not only measure the ability of a state to sustain and increase armed forces strength and reach, but each one suggests something more. For example, the capacity to produce armaments for export can be channeled immediately for national requirements, provides an important dimension for projection and staying power in international security matters, and can contribute favorably to the balance of payments and general economic health and progress of a country. Moreover, DEP measures the amount of resources a government makes available to the military and, thus, the level of commitment to the armed forces. Finally, GRP is an indicator of administrative control and what Organski and Kugler called "political development."[9]

Graphically, the model is as follows:

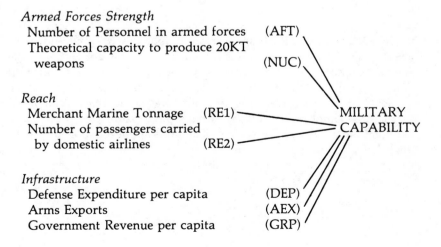

Armed Forces Strength
Number of Personnel in armed forces (AFT)
Theoretical capacity to produce 20KT
  weapons (NUC)

Reach
Merchant Marine Tonnage (RE1)
Number of passengers carried
  by domestic airlines (RE2)

Infrastructure
Defense Expenditure per capita (DEP)
Arms Exports (AEX)
Government Revenue per capita (GRP)

MILITARY
CAPABILITY

Methodology

After the factor analysis compressed the original sixteen variables into seven that best explain a three-component military capability, it remained to devise a suitable technique for aggregating the data and producing a single index for a given point in time. As a preliminary step, each country's score on each variable was rescaled and expressed as a percentage of the sum of the scores on that respective variable for all the nation-states examined. This was done in order to establish a single basis from which to measure and compare relative standings and to eliminate the problem of measuring inflation. With the data rescaled, the indicators were combined into a single index.

Common sense and factor analysis suggest some sort of weighting of the variables. Consequently, weights were assigned to the variables on the basis of the factor loading scores that resulted from the factor analysis. [10] These figures were squared and multiplied by 100. The resulting numbers were set to equal to unity, and the total number of units was set at one million. Then each nation-state's Relative Military Capability (RMC) score was computed according to the following equation:

$$RMC = (^PAFT_{aw} - {}^PNUC_{aw}) \times (^PRE1_{aw} - {}^PRE2_{aw}) \times (^PDEP_{aw} - {}^PAEX_{aw} - {}^PGRP_{aw})$$

RMC = Relative Military Capability
p = Percentage
aw = Adjusted Weight

Finally, each country's RMC score was multiplied by one million to produce the final score, which allows for ranking and categorization of the countries examined. Each factor was multiplied because multiplication implies nonsubstitutability. That is to say, a country with a relatively high level of armed forces strength, but little or no reach and/or infrastructure cannot be considered to have the capability to project and sustain military force over distances. The same applies to a country with a high level of infrastructure and reach, but a small number of armed forces. Thus, a viable military capability requires relatively high scores in all three principal components.

Accordingly, the model was applied quantitatively to identify and clarify the military capabilities of the Brazilian state in relation to a sample of Latin American and other states. The sample of Latin American countries includes twelve: Argentina, Bolivia, Chile, Colombia, Cuba, Ecuador, Guyana, Mexico, Paraguay, Peru, Uruguay, and Venezuela. The twenty-nine countries representing the rest of the world are the top fifteen in terms of population, territory, and GNP. They also include those twenty-two states to which Cline's world power assessment gave ten or more total weighted units of perceived power.[11] Finally, these countries represent all major geographic regions of the world.

In addition to establishing a contemporary ranking of Brazil with other powers and with all but the smallest Latin American countries, we have compared Brazil to a few selected countries (Nigeria, Turkey, South Korea, and Argentina) over the 1968–1977 time frame. These states represent all the major geographic regions of the world, they have a wide range of military-strategic defense requirements, and, importantly, they represent the large cluster of "lesser powers" or "emerging powers" out of which Brazil appears to be moving. As noted above, the purpose of the ranking analysis was to measure Brazil's relative position in the Latin American region and in the wider world arena. The purpose of the trend comparison was simply to examine the relative direction in which Brazil appears to have been going over the past several years. Patterns examined lead to the general conclusion that Brazil is in the process of steadily and significantly increasing its relative military capability.

Findings

General

At first glance it appears that Brazil is in a middle position between powers such as the United States, the Soviet Union, Britain, France, and West Germany, and the "lesser" military powers such as Nigeria, South Africa, Libya, Sudan, and Zaire. However, a closer examination of the data suggests (see Chart 3.1) that there are large gaps between the various clusters of countries. (See Table 3.1.) Ranking, per se, means very little in this kind of analysis. What is important is the number of RMC points one nation has as compared to another. For example, the United States has 7533 RMC points to Brazil's 1.889. Consequently, even though Brazil is ranked number 16 of thirty countries examined, the gulf between Brazil and those ranked in the top ten is enormous. At the same time, Brazil is slightly ahead of the large cluster of states that have less than

CHART 3.1
Final relative position of world sample countries, in terms of RMC points

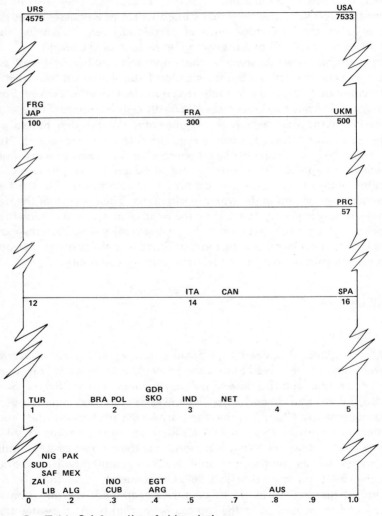

See Table 3.1 for a list of abbreviations.

one RMC point. In some contrast to the world arena, the analysis places Brazil as a kind of "super power" within the Latin American region. (See Table 3.1A.)

The longitudinal part of this analysis reveals that recent governments have, in fact, been steadily and significantly increasing Brazilian military capability. (See Chart 3.2.) The data show that over the period 1968–1977 (1) the size of the armed forces has increased, (2) there has been an increase of potential in nuclear energy production and war making, (3) there has been a vast increase in the ability of the country to project power on the regional and international levels in terms of airlift and sealift capacity and arms exports, and (4) the infrastructure has been improved somewhat. Finally, a trend comparison involving Brazil and four other countries representing the lower part of the scale (shown in Table 3.1 and Chart 3.1) indicates that Brazil is increasing its RMC faster than all but the most defense-oriented states.

Armed Forces Strength (AFT)

This indicator records the number of soldiers, sailors, and airmen who are immediately available for engaging in military hostilities. War, regardless of the level of intensity, must be fought with people. Territory, airspace, and critical sea lanes must be physically controlled. As a rule, the more individuals in the armed forces of a given state, the better that state's fighting capability in relation to that of another. However, numbers alone cannot show a complete picture. What will be attempted here is a brief description of the missions, tactical organization and location, and major weapons of the Brazilian armed forces in conjunction with the results of the analysis. (See Tables 3.2 and 3.2A.)

In addition to that of defense, the Brazilian armed forces have been given several other missions by law. Politically, the armed forces are the guardians of the constitution and other political institutions of the country. Economically and socially, the military has the responsibility of expanding its participation in civic action programs, public works projects, and the building of the nation's industrial base. Consequent activities include such things as literacy and manual-labor training projects; road, railroad, and airfield building; and the initiation of the armaments industry, aircraft production, and naval construction. Moreover, military research and development is to be coordinated and applied to the civil sector as a part of the national development plan.[12] In the various roles the armed forces have been called on to perform, they have shown aggressiveness, professionalism, and competence. However, if the government is not careful, the military could become a marginal organization incapable of performing its primary defense mission.

TABLE 3.1
Final Relative Position of World Sample Countries

Rank	Country	RMC Scores
1	USA	7,533.000
2	URS (USSR)	4,575.000
3	UKM (United Kingdom)	558.000
4	FRA (France)	320.000
5	FRG (Fed Rep of Germany)	100.000
6	JAP (Japan)	99.000
7	PRC (People Rep of China)	57.000
8	SPA (Spain)	16.376
9	CAN (Canada)	14.584
10	ITA (Italy)	13.981
11	NET (Netherlands)	3.506
12	IND (India)	3.493
13	GDR (German Dem Rep)	3.069
14	SKO (South Korea)	2.727
15	POL (Poland)	2.128
16	BRAZIL	1.889
17	TUR (Turkey)	1.230
18	AUS (Australia)	.796
19	ARG (Argentina)	.417
20	EGT (Egypt)	.363
21	INO (Indonesia)	.335
22	CUB (Cuba)	.284
23	PAK (Pakistan)	.227
24	MEX (Mexico)	.171
25	ALG (Algeria)	.147
26	NIG (Nigeria)	.117
27	SAF (South Africa)	.106
28	LIB (Libya)	.102
29	SUD (Sudan)	.024
30	ZAI (Zaire)	.003

TABLE 3.1A
Final Relative Position of Latin American Countries

Rank	Country	RMC Score
1	BRAZIL	13,406
2	ARG (Argentina)	2,021
3	CUB (Cuba)	1,039
4	MEX (Mexico)	918
5	PER (Peru)	185
6	VEN (Venezuela)	140
7	CHI (Chile)	77
8	COL (Colombia)	45
9	ECU (Ecuador)	19
10	URU (Uruguay)	11
11	BOL (Bolivia)	4
12	PAR (Paraguay)	0
13	GUY (Guyana)	0

CHART 3.2—TREND COMPARISON

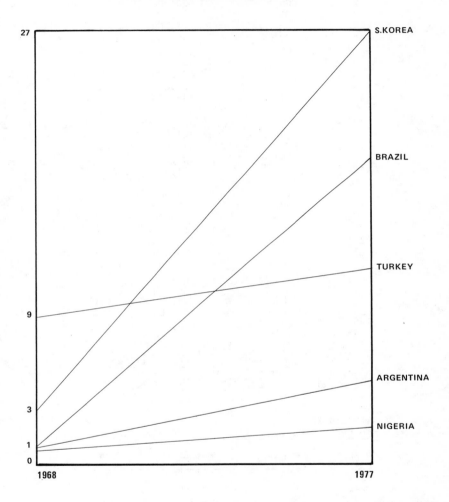

The Army. The past few years have been characterized by a profound transformation in the organization and location of the regular army, the creation of new units, the deactivation of units considered obsolete, and a renewed attempt to create a viable reserve.

In 1970, the army had a strength of 120,000.[13] The major concentration of force was located along the Argentine and Uruguayan frontiers and near important coastal cities. The principal tactical units included twelve and one-third divisions—seven infantry, four cavalry, one ar-

TABLE 3.2
Numbers in World Sample Armed Forces, 1979

Rank	Country	Number	$P_{AFT_{aw}}$
1	PRC	4,360,000	.1136
2	URS	3,658,000	.0953
3	USA	2,022,000	.0527
4	IND	1,096,000	.0285
5	SKO	619,000	.0161
6	TUR	566,000	.0147
7	FRA	509,000	.0133
8	FRG	495,000	.0129
9	PAK	429,000	.0117
10	EGT	395,000	.0103
11	ITA	365,000	.0095
12	UKM	323,000	.0084
13	SPA	321,000	.0083
14	POL	317,000	.0082
15	BRAZIL	281,000	.0073
16	JAP	241,000	.0063
17	INO	239,000	.0062
18	NIG	193,000	.0051
19	CUB	189,000	.0049
20	GDR	159,000	.0041
21	ARG	133,000	.0034
22	NET	115,000	.0030
23	MEX	100,000	.0026
24	ALG	89,000	.0023
25	CAN	80,000	.0021
26	AUS	70,000	.0018
27	SAF	63,000	.0016
28	SUD	63,000	.0016
29	LIB	42,000	.0011
30	ZAI	21,000	.0005

Source: The Military Balance, 1979-1980 (London: IISS, 1979), pp. 96-97., and World Military Expenditures and Arms Transfers, 1968-1977 (Washington, D.C.: USACDA, 1979, pp. 70-112.)

TABLE 3.2A
Numbers in Latin American Armed Forces, 1979

Rank	Country	Number	$P_{AFT_{aw}}$
1	BRAZIL	281,000	.1174
2	CUB	189,000	.0790
3	ARG	133,000	.0556
4	MEX	100,000	.0418
5	PER	92,000	.0384
6	CHI	85,000	.0355
7	COL	68,000	.0284
8	VEN	42,000	.0176
9	ECU	33,000	.0138
10	URU	28,000	.0117
11	BOL	23,000	.0096
12	PAR	16,000	.0067
13	GUY	5,000	.0021

Source: The Military Balance, 1979-1980 (London: IISS, 1979), pp. 75-83.

mored, and an airborne brigade. By 1979, the size of the army had increased to 182,000.[14] New and reorganized units were located in the Amazon, in industrial areas and important cities in the interior, and within easy reach of other neighboring countries. The major tactical units were reduced to seven infantry divisions and one transport division. Each infantry division contains up to four armored, mechanized, or motorized infantry brigades. In addition to these divisions, there are three independent infantry brigades, one independent jungle brigade, five jungle battalions, and two infantry battalions. Antiaircraft units, located in Rio Grande do Sul, São Paulo, and Rio de Janeiro are also a part of the recently reorganized Brazilian army.[15]

This army is equipped with approximately 60 medium tanks, 550 light tanks, 150 armored cars, 600 armored personnel carrriers, 155mm, 105mm, and 90mm artillery, Cobra antitank weapons, Roland suface-to-air missiles, and Oerlikon antiaircraft guns.[16] Moreover, during the 1974–1978 period, the army acquired approximately 5,000 trucks, 250 additional armored vehicles, and large quantities of communication equipment and light weapons from the Brazilian arms industry.[17] Finally, during the same period, some 12,000 cadets began training for commissions in the reserve.[18] In the past, officers came exclusively from the Military Academy. Clearly, the Brazilian army has begun a process of strengthening, reorganization, relocation, and modernization.

The Navy. The navy is the senior service. Brazil's population and industry have been concentrated along the 4,598-mile Atlantic coastline. International trade has been and continues to be largely across the Atlantic Ocean. Consequently, Brazil's international orientation has always been to the ocean and the navy has been the primary instrument for external defense and for foreign policy. Today, the Brazilian navy continues to stress its traditional defense and foreign policy roles through an active building program and through almost continuous interaction with the U.S., British, French, Dutch, Canadian, and other fleets in the Atlantic Ocean.[19]

The navy's manpower strength in 1970 was 44,000.[20] The principal ships included one aircraft carrier, two cruisers, seventeen destroyers and corvettes, and two submarines. Transports and other auxiliary craft rounded out the fleet. (The presence of transports in the navy reflects the fact that there is a small naval infantry [marine] force within that organization.) By 1979, the size of the navy had come up to 49,000.[21] The quality, if not the quantity, of ships had also increased. The aircraft carrier has undergone a major modernization and some of the older ships, including the cruisers and two submarines, have been deactivated. Under the building program of the navy, five new frigates and two relatively new submarines have replaced some of the old destroyers and other vessels.[22] As a result, the principal ships of the navy now include one aircraft carrier, nineteen frigates, and eight submarines. In addition, one more frigate—the *Union*—is near completion, along with two transport ships, each of which is capable of carrying 2,000 troops.[23]

It appears that the fleet has been modernized, even though it has not significantly increased its size. At the same time—and perhaps most importantly—Brazilian shipyards are now producing first-rate vessels such as the Niteroi class frigates.[24] Finally, this modernization also applies to the naval infantry, which has been receiving new Brazilian-built armored vehicles, artillery, and amphibious equipment.[25]

The Air Force. This is the newest branch of the Brazilian armed forces. Nevertheless, the air force was bloodied in Italy in World War II, has made a magnificent contribution to the development of the interior of the country, and has developed the same pride and esprit de corps of the other services.

In 1970, the air force had a strength of 30,000 and an inventory of virtually all kinds of aircraft, from jet fighters to light bombers to transports.[26] At that time, the air force inventory was totally imported. However, since then, the air force has grown to 50,000 and Brazilian industry supplies about 60 per cent of its airframes.[27] Foreign-made aircraft, however, are still an important part of the service. They include the Mirage interceptors, F-5 fighter-bombers, the large transports and tanker aircraft, and the helicopters. Brazilian-made aircraft are primarily light and medium transports and reconnaissance planes. At present, there are one interceptor squadron, two tactical air squadrons, one antisubmarine warfare squadron, one maritime reconnaissance squadron, four search-and-rescue squadrons, eight counterinsurgency squadrons, and twelve transport squadrons.[28] The relatively large number of counterinsurgency and transport squadrons reflects an important capability to move troops and supplies quickly over the long distances of Brazil. In this connection, the air force has recently acquired two KC-130s and now can refuel, and thus increase the range of, aircraft in flight.[29]

Data Summary and Conclusions. The data show that Brazilian AFT has increased from 195,000 in 1970 to 281,000 in 1979. These forces significantly outnumber those of any other Latin American country. The super powers and the major powers, of course, maintain superior numbers of armed forces personnel. In the context of the thirty-nation sample, Egypt, India, South Korea, Pakistan, and Turkey are the only countries in Africa and Asia that maintain larger force structures than does Brazil. It must be noted that each of these countries perceives significant external threats. Simple observation of the trends showing the

AFT variable for five selected countries suggests that whatever advantage Brazil may have in this area is likely to be maintained. (See Chart 3.3.) It might be added that, with a population of over 120 million, Brazil also has recourse to a manpower pool that is among the largest in the entire world.

Shortly after taking control of the government in 1964, General Humberto Castelo Branco made it clear that one of the purely military tasks of the "revolution" would be to reorganize and professionalize the armed forces into a modern force, capable of assisting the state to take its rightful place at the highest levels of international security affairs. Castelo Branco and the succeeding military governments appear to have been working toward these ends.[30]

Brazil's Nuclear Capacity (NUC). Because of the seriousness of even the possibility of the use of nuclear weapons, this indicator measures the amount of electric power currently produced by nuclear plants and suggests the total theoretical capacity for 20 KT atomic bomb production in 1980. As a rule, the greater the capacity to produce energy by means of nuclear reactors, the greater the ability to make nuclear weapons, and the greater the capacity to make and deliver nuclear weapons, the greater a state's capability and influence in relation to that of another.

The Brazilian nuclear program has been in progress for some time,[31] but it did not move quickly until 1972 when construction was begun on the nuclear power plant at Angra dos Reis. The 1973 oil crisis and subsequent quadrupling of oil prices brought the Brazilian "economic miracle" to an untimely halt. Under these circumstances the government responded with a commitment to a massive and diversified program for the development of internal energy resources—including nuclear energy. At the same time, the United States made it clear that no new contracts would be let for the supply of enriched uranium and that existing agreements with Brazil were subject to review. This motivated the Geisel administration to seek nuclear technology elsewhere. Consequently, a $5 billion agreement was signed with the Federal Republic of Germany on June 27, 1975, to provide Brazil with a full nuclear cycle and eight reactors. Subsequent agreements have been made with the United States, Britain, the Netherlands, and France for additional nuclear fuels and technology.[32]

In November 1978, the nuclear facility at Angra dos Reis was completed and is to be producing 626 million watts in 1980. It had been estimated that with two other (Angra II and Angra III) nuclear power plants currently under construction, Brazil would be producing 3116 million watts of nuclear energy by 1984.[33] However, delays have slowed the development of the program and recent estimates suggest that the

CHART 3.3—AFT, 1970—1980

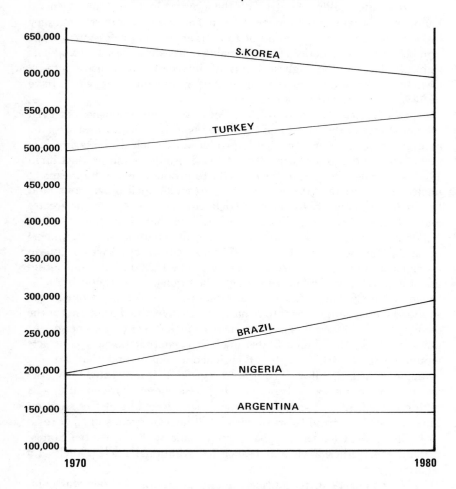

Sources: The Military Balance, 1970 - 1971, and
The Military Balance, 1979 - 1980

CHART 3.4–Nuclear Power Production
Projected to 1984 (in M W (net))

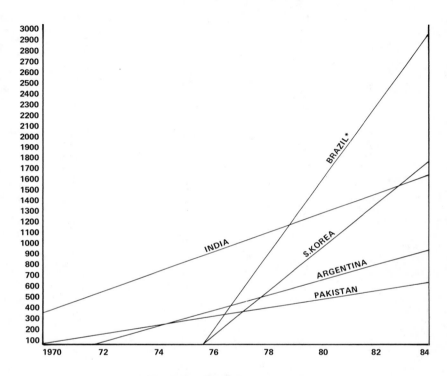

Source: SIPRI Yearbook, World Armaments and Disarmament
(Stockholm: SIPRI, 1977), pp. 38 - 39.
*probably delayed until 1986

nuclear energy output slated for 1984 will not be forthcoming until at least 1986.[34] In terms of percentage of projected increase over the period from 1981 to 1984, Brazil is only matched by two other countries—Italy and Pakistan. All the others, including the United States and the Soviet Union, range from no increase in nuclear power production to slightly more than twice their 1981 figures.[35] These projections, then, suggest that Brazil, Italy, and Pakistan are increasing their nuclear power production at a rate more than twice as great as any other country in the world. Nevertheless, percentage of increase does not indicate the reality of the situation as clearly as Chart 3.4. Even with its late start and slowed development, Brazil has a nuclear power production capability greater

TABLE 3.3
Theoretical Capacity of World Sample for 20 KT
Atomic Bomb Production, 1980 (Bombs per year)

Rank	Country	Number	$P_{NUC_{aw}}$
1	USA	999	.0914
2	URS	999	.0914
3	FRA	999	.0914
4	UKM	999	.0914
5	PRC	500	.0457
6	JAP	450	.0412
7	FRG	330	.0302
8	SPA	210	.0192
9	CAN	200	.0183
10	GDR	45	.0041
11	SKO	45	.0041
12	ITA	35	.0032
13	IND	30	.0027
14	MEX	30	.0027
15	ARG	25	.0023
16	BRAZIL	15	.0014
17	NET	12	.0011
18	PAK	3	.0003
19	ALG	0	.0000
20	AUS	0	.0000
21	CUB	0	.0000
22	EGT	0	.0000
23	INO	0	.0000
24	LIB	0	.0000
25	NIG	0	.0000
26	POL	0	.0000
27	SAF	0	.0000
28	SUD	0	.0000
29	TUR	0	.0000
30	ZAI	0	.0000

Source: The Evolving Strategic Environment (Carlisle Bks, PA: Strategic Studies Institute, US Army War College, 1979), p. 17.

TABLE 3.3A
Theoretical Capacity for 20 KT Atomic Bomb Production
in Latin America, 1980 (Bombs per year)

Rank	Country	Number	$P_{NUC_{aw}}$
1	MEX	30	.2325
2	ARG	25	.1937
3	BRAZIL	15	.1163

Source: The Evolving Strategic Environment (Carlisle Bks, PA: Strategic Studies Institute, US Army War College, 1979), p. 17.

than those of such celebrated nuclear powers as India and Pakistan.

Moreover, at its 1980 production rate, Brazil is theoretically capable of producing fifteen 20 KT weapons a year. (See Tables 3.3 and 3.3A). Consequently, the expected increase in nuclear power production capacity by 1986 represents an important step toward a serious nuclear weapons production capability. This limited capability is complemented by the additional ability to deliver nuclear weapons. In this connection, Brazil has a dual delivery capability, the appropriate aircraft and a recently demonstrated missile delivery system.[36]

If the capability of producing nuclear weapons, coupled with the ability to deliver them is, in fact, a basis for inclusion in the deliberations and activities of the major powers, the implications for Brazil are clear: the possibility of growing influence and escalating involvement in hemispheric and world affairs.

Reach (RE1 and RE2)

The size, and even quality, of an armed force may have little significance in the context of world affairs. The indicators labeled RE1 and RE2 are intended to measure a country's capability to project and sustain its armed forces into international security affairs. In this connection, the airlift capacity of a state, in terms of numbers of passengers carried on domestic and international routes in a given year by its airlines, and the capacity of a country to move bulk cargo, in terms of the tonnage of its merchant marine, are examined. Civil air and sea transport are used as indicators of reach simply because they are considered an integral part of the military infrastructure of virtually all the countries of the world and would be employed to supplement military and naval capacity to move and support troops and equipment. Moreover, small numbers of aircraft and troops can be deployed to most parts of the world within hours of notification, given a secure airbase and adequate fuel. Sustaining even a small force over a period of time, however, is complex and cumbersome. The most readily identifiable means of accomplishing the tasks associated with projection and sustaining of power over long distances is airlift and sealift. Again, the greater the capacity, the greater the relative advantage.

In terms of airlift and sealift capability as measured by our indicators, Brazil is ranked 10th and 12th respectively, in our world sample. (See Tables 3.4 and 3.5.) It is somewhat above the other less developed countries, but considerably below those in the modern, industrial world. Brazil tripled its airlift capacity and doubled its sealift capacity during the periods 1970–1977 and 1969–1978, respectively. However, while Brazil was achieving these increases, countries such as France were doing

TABLE 3.4
Merchant Marine in World Sample, 1978 (in
thousands of gross reg. tons)

Rank	Country	Number	$P_{RE1_{aw}}$
1	JAP	39.2	.0988
2	UKM	30.8	.0776
3	URS	22.3	.0562
4	USA	16.1	.0405
5	FRA	12.1	.0307
6	ITA	11.4	.0287
7	FRG	9.7	.0244
8	SPA	8.0	.0202
9	PRC	6.7	.0189
10	IND	5.7	.0144
11	NET	5.1	.0128
12	BRAZIL	3.7	.0093
13	POL	3.5	.0088
14	CAN	3.0	.0076
15	SKO	3.0	.0076
16	ARG	2.0	.0050
17	AUS	1.5	.0038
18	GDR	1.5	.0038
19	TUR	1.4	.0035
20	INO	1.2	.0030
21	ALG	1.1	.0028
22	LIB	.9	.0022
23	CUB	.8	.0020
24	MEX	.7	.0018
25	SAF	.7	.0018
26	EGT	.5	.0013
27	PAK	.4	.0010
28	SUD	.4	.0010
29	NIG	.3	.0007
30	ZAI	.1	.0003

Source: Statistical Yearbook, 1978 (New York:
United Nations Organization, 1979), pp. 552-553.

TABLE 3.4A
Merchant Marine in Latin America, 1978 (in
thousands of gross reg. tons)

Rank	Country	Number	$P_{RE1_{aw}}$
1	BRAZIL	3,702	.1858
2	ARG	2,001	.1005
3	VEN	824	.0414
4	CUB	779	.0391
5	MEX	727	.0365
6	PER	575	.0289
7	CHI	466	.0234
8	COL	272	.0137
9	ECU	201	.0101
10	URU	174	.0087
11	BOL	0	.0000
12	GUY	0	.0000
13	PAR	0	.0000

Source: Statistical Yearbook, 1978 (New York:
United Nations Organization, 1979), pp. 552-553.

TABLE 3.5
Civil Aviation in World Sample, 1977 (millions
of passengers carried in domestic airlines.)

Rank	Country	Number	P_{RE2} $\overline{aw}$
1	USA	241.2	.2315
2	URS	93.0	.0893
3	JAP	36.1	.0346
4	UKM	19.4	.0186
5	CAN	17.5	.0168
6	FRA	15.4	.0148
7	SPA	13.3	.0127
8	AUS	11.3	.0108
9	FRG	10.9	.0105
10	BRAZIL	9.5	.0091
11	ITA	9.4	.0090
12	MEX	8.1	.0077
13	GDR	6.0*	.0057
14	PRC	6.0*	.0057
15	IND	5.1	.0049
16	NET	4.4	.0042
17	ARG	3.9	.0037
18	INO	3.8	.0036
19	SAF	3.1	.0030
20	TUR	2.8	.0027
21	SKO	2.5	.0024
22	PAK	2.3	.0022
23	ALG	2.0	.0019
24	POL	1.6	.0015
25	EGT	1.2	.0012
26	NIG	1.0	.0010
27	LIB	.8	.0008
28	CUB	.6	.0006
29	ZAI	.5	.0005
30	SUD	.4	.0004

Source: Statistical Yearbook, 1978 (New York:
United Nations Organization, 1979), pp. 602-604.
*Estimates

TABLE 3.5A
Civil Aviation in Latin America, 1977 (passengers
carried in domestic airlines--to include international travel.)

Rank	Country	Number	P_{RE2} $\overline{aw}$
1	BRAZIL	9,514,000	.1456
2	MEX	8,172,000	.1251
3	COL	4,117,000	.0630
4	ARG	3,884,000	.0594
5	VEN	3,409,000	.0522
6	PER	1,425,000	.0218
7	BOL	862,000	.0132
8	CUB	635,000	.0097
9	CHI	589,000	.0090
10	ECU	529,000	.0081
11	URU	290,000	.0045
12	GUY	0	.0000
13	PAR	0	.0000

Source: Statistical Yearbook, 1978 (New York:
United Nations Organization, 1979), pp. 602-604.

as well. At the same time, the LDCs appear to be falling behind and the gap is widening. (See Charts 3.5 and 3.6.) In the Latin America context, again Brazil is well ahead of the second-place countries (Argentina and Mexico), and far more significantly ahead of the rest. (See Tables 3.4A and 3.5A.) It is in the Reach factor that Brazil makes its strongest showing in comparison with the sample of world powers. No doubt these variables are indicative of the ability to project and sustain power over long distances. Consequently, it appears that, in these terms at least, Brazil is at the point of beginning to compete with the nations commonly thought to be viable powers in the contemporary world.

Defense Expenditure Per Capita (DEP)

This variable qualifies the capability of the armed forces of a given state. First, it suggests the extent of the scope of operations of a military organization. Second, and less reliably, it suggests a qualitative measure of armed forces strength. In these terms, insufficient funds imply deficiencies in training, equipment, and supplies. The size of a country's population has a great impact on this statistic. For example, the DEP for Argentina in 1977 was $28; Brazil's DEP was about half, at $13. Nevertheless, total defense expenditures in the same year were only $722 million (in constant dollars) for Argentina, and twice as much—$1536 million—for Brazil.[37] Thus, more accurately, the DEP indicator measures the degree of commitment a government has made—the priority it has given—to the quality of its armed forces. An adequate index for measuring the degree of a state's exploitation of military capability to international advantage would include this variable.

Only Pakistan, Sudan, Indonesia, Mexico, India, and Zaire spent less than Brazil in this area. All other countries included in this analysis spent from almost twice as much to over 400 times as much as Brazil in DEP. (See Table 3.6.) It is this variable, more than any of the other six, that probably explains why Brazil's level of military involvement in world affairs has been so low. AFT (Armed Forces Strength) and NUC for Brazil are respectable in relation to the rest of the world; Reach (RE1 and RE2) is more than respectable at the world level; yet Brazil is ranked 24th out of thirty in this important part of Infrastructure, DEP. Within the Latin American context, Brazil ranks 9th out of thirteen countries examined. Only Bolivia, Paraguay, Mexico, and Colombia spend less in terms of DEP than does Brazil. (See Table 3.6A.)

Over the past few years, the aggregate data show Brazil to be moving out of the cluster of African, Asian, and other Latin American countries that have the least relative military capability. In examining the individual variables, and comparing Brazil to other countries in approx-

CHART 3.5—RE 1, 1969–1978
(in thousands of gross reg. tons)

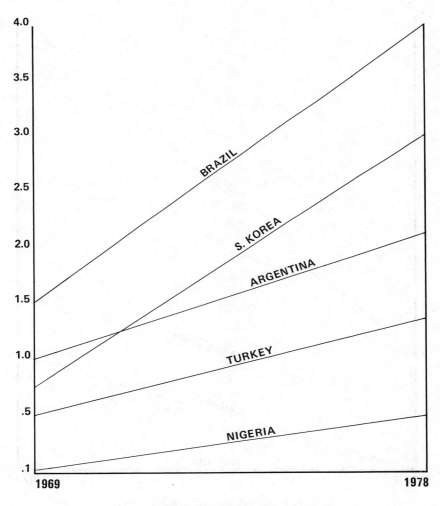

Source: Statistical Yearbook, 1978 (New York: UNO, 1979), pp. 552 - 553.

CHART 3.6—RE 2, 1970—1977
(in millions of passengers flown in domestic airlines)

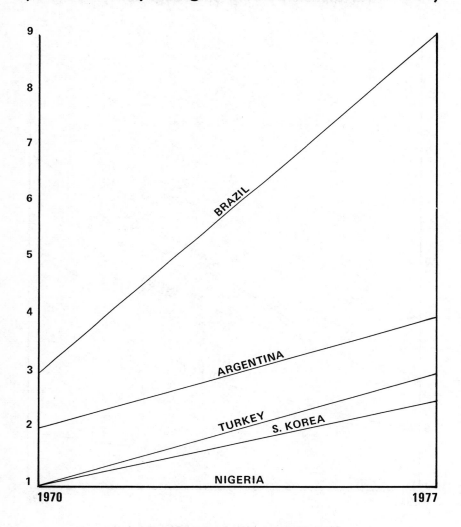

Source: Statistical Yearbook, 1978 (New York:
UNO, 1979), pp. 598 - 611.

TABLE 3.6
Defense Expenditure per capita in World Sample,
1977 (in constant dollars)

Rank	Country	Number	$P_{DEP_{aw}}$
1	URS	574	.0584
2	USA	520	.0529
3	FRG	396	.0403
4	FRA	349	.0355
5	NET	338	.0344
6	UKM	314	.0319
7	GDR	266	.0270
8	AUS	209	.0213
9	LIB	162	.0165
10	CAN	157	.0160
11	ITA	124	.0126
12	CUB	118	.0120
13	POL	99	.0101
14	SPA	90	.0092
15	JAP	87	.0089
16	SKO	85	.0086
17	SAF	76	.0077
18	TUR	58	.0059
19	ARG	56	.0057
20	EGT	54	.0055
21	PRC	46	.0047
22	ALG	32	.0032
23	NIG	25	.0025
24	BRAZIL	18	.0018
25	PAK	14	.0014
26	SUD	12	.0012
27	INO	10	.0010
28	MEX	7	.0007
29	ZAI	7	.0007
30	IND	6	.0006

Source: The Military Balance, 1979-1980 (London: IISS, 1979), pp. 94-95.

TABLE 3.6A
Defense Expenditure per capita in Latin America,
1977 (in constant dollars)

Rank	Country	Number	$P_{DEP_{aw}}$
1	PER	51	.0766
2	CUB	44	.0660
3	VEN	43	.0645
4	ARG	28	.0420
5	URU	26	.0390
6	CHI	25	.0375
7	GUY	15	.0225
8	ECU	14	.0210
9	BRAZIL	13	.0195
10	BOL	12	.0180
11	PAR	9	.0135
12	MEX	8	.0120
13	COL	4	.0060

Source: World Military Expenditures and Arms Transfers, 1968-1977 (Washington, D.C.: USACDA, 1979), pp. 75-110.

CHART 3.7—DEP, 1969—1979
(in $)

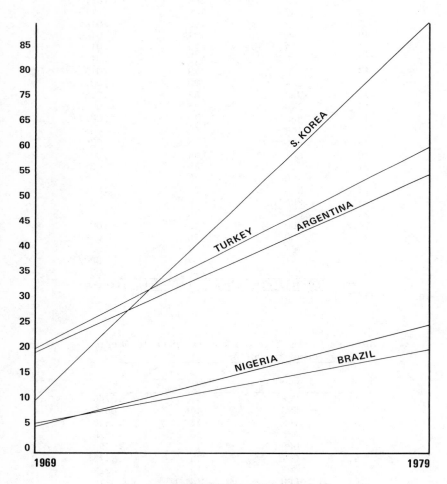

Source: The Military Balance, 1970 - 1971 and
The Military Balance 1979 - 1980 (London: IISS),
pp. 110 -111; 94 - 95.

imately the same world position, the data show clearly perceptible upward trends—except in the case of DEP. Brazil was near the bottom of the DEP scale ten years ago and remains there today. (See Chart 3.7.) If Brazil indeed has aspirations to major power status, more money will be required for armed forces training, equipment, manpower, supplies, and facilities. This need not be economically debilitating. For example, Brazil's total military expenditures for 1978 were 1.0 percent of GNP. Only Japan (0.9 percent) and Mexico (0.5 percent) were spending less.[38] Perhaps the present construction of extensive air and naval facilities on the Island of Trinidade is an indication of Brazilian resolve to expand the scope of military operations into the international arena.[39] Trinidade is located 1,200 km east of the state of Espirito Santo in a position from which Brazil could have some influence over the vital sea lanes of the South Atlantic Ocean.

Government Revenue as a Percentage of GDP (GRP)

The use of this particular indicator as an important dimension of the military capability that Knorr calls "putative power" is based on a notion suggested by him and more fully developed by Cline and by Organski and Kugler.[40] They argue that recent important miscalculations in determining a comprehensive estimate of the military capability of nations have been the result of the failure to take into account the idea of will to fight. Organski asserts that will, per se, is not the vital difference that allows one state to prevail over another in international conflict. Rather, it is the capacity to effectively penetrate a society and extract resources from it. Revenue data provide good, strong indicators that can measure that capacity. The better a government can perform in extracting resources from a society, the more successful it is in penetrating and controlling it. The better the control, the better the capability to fulfill tasks imposed by the international environment and to generate the will to sustain a fight. Thus, GRP suggests a level of capability to administer, coordinate, and sustain political and military goals across the conflict spectrum in the contemporary world.

On this variable, Brazil falls into the middle of the sample of significant countries. (See Table 3.7.) As noted above, Brazil tends toward the modern industrial states in terms of AFT, NUC, RE1 and RE2. In GRP and DEP, it appears that Brazil is much closer to those countries at the lower part of the relative power continuum. Examination of trends in the 1965–1973 time frame suggest something of an improvement with regard to this indicator. For example, during this period Brazil increased GRP from 17 to 28. This substantially improved its relative position in the world and in the hemisphere. (See Chart 3.8.) Yet, in comparison to its

TABLE 3.7
Total Government Revenue as a percent of GDP in
World Sample, 1973

Rank	Country	Number	$P_{GRP_{aw}}$
1	NET	49	.0146
2	i IB	48	.0143
3	FRG	41	.0122
4	GDR	41	.0122
5	FRA	38	.0113
6	UKM	38	.0113
7	NIG	37	.0110
8	CAN	36	.0107
9	ALG	35	.0104
10	ITA	33	.0098
11	SUD	32	.0095
12	USA	32	.0095
13	EGT	29	.0086
14	AUS	28	.0083
15	BRAZIL	28	.0083
16	PRC	26	.0077
17	CUB	26	.0077
18	POL	25	.0074
19	TUR	25	.0074
20	ZAI	25	.0074
21	SPA	23	.0069
22	JAP	22	.0066
23	URS	22	.0066
24	SAF	20	.0060
25	IND	16	.0048
26	SKO	16	.0048
27	INO	15	.0045
28	PAK	15	.0045
29	ARG	9	.0027
30	MEX	9	.0027

Source: World Tables, 1976 (Baltimore, MD: Johns
Hopkins Press for the World Bank, 1976), pp. 440-447.

TABLE 3.7A
Total Government Revenue as a percent of GDP in
Latin America, 1973

Rank	Country	Number	$P_{GRP_{aw}}$
1	URU	31	.0301
2	CHI	30	.0291
3	BRAZIL	28	.0272
4	ECU	27	.0262
5	GUY	26	.0252
6	VEN	21	.0204
7	CUB	19	.0184
8	PER	19	.0184
9	COL	15	.0145
10	BOL	14	.0136
11	PAR	10	.0097
12	ARG	9	.0087
13	MEX	9	.0087

Source: World Tables, 1976 (Baltimore, MD: Johns
Hopkins Press for the World Bank, 1970), pp. 440-447.

CHART 3.8—GRP, 1965—1973
(in $)

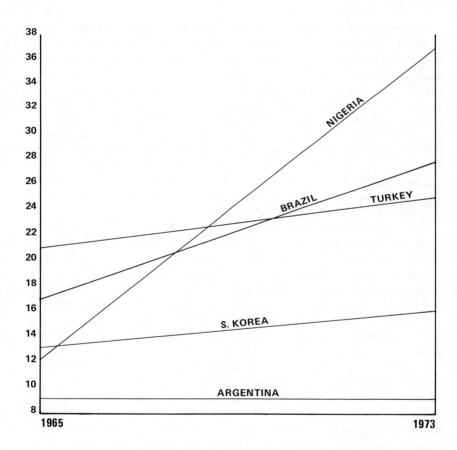

Source: World Tables, 1976 (Baltimore: The Johns
Hopkins University Press for The World Bank, 1976),
pp. 440 - 447.

hemispheric partners, Brazil is not in its usual position at the top of the list. Instead it ranks under Chile and Uruguay and just above Ecuador and Guyana. (See Table 3.7A.) It appears that Brazil is improving its relative position as far as most of the world is concerned, but it is still significantly below the countries with the highest capabilities for penetrating and managing their citizenry.

Total Arms Exports (AEX)

The capability to produce arms for export provides an important asset in the projection of influence in a world that is buying arms at record rates.[41] In addition, should the need arise, this capability can be immediately channeled to national requirements. It would also be an important asset for projection and staying power in international security matters. On the other hand, if a country must import war materials, as well as spare parts for old equipment and arms, it is dependent on the exporter or exporters and cannot project or sustain itself on the international scene any longer than its inventory and supplier will allow. Clearly, the larger the quantity of a nation's exports of nationally made armaments, the less dependent it is. In these terms, it can enjoy an independence of action that is absolutely necessary to exploit military capability for the national advantage.

The United States and the Soviet Union supply about 75 percent of the arms exported around the world. France, the Federal Republic of Germany, and the United Kingdom provide 16 percent of world arms transfers. The remaining 9 percent of world arms exports come from several other countries—including Brazil. (See Table 3.8.) This country is a relative newcomer in the business of exporting nationally produced war materials. Its growth in this field has been unusually rapid, and its motivation can be traced to a reaction to the decline of U.S. military exports to Latin America in the mid-1960s.[42]

Since the early 1970s, Brazil has reached a level of technology and production capability that has made it competitive on the world market and allowed it to cancel the military assistance agreement with the United States in March 1977. By 1976, in addition to small arms and electronics, Brazil was producing aircraft frames and aircraft engines and was beginning to assemble helicopters. At the same time, trucks, armored cars, tanks, 90mm tank guns, and guided missiles were being manufactured, along with river patrol boats and frigates of the Niteroi class.[43] Moreover, it has been claimed that submarines will be constructed in Brazilian shipyards in the near future.[44]

Thirty-two countries have purchased arms made in Brazil.[45] The main customers are Middle Eastern and African countries, but Brazil is aiming

TABLE 3.8
Total Arms Exported, World Sample, 1976 (in millions of constant dollars)

Rank	Country	Number	$P_{AEX_{aw}}$
1	USA	5900	.1298
2	URS	4700	.1034
3	FRA	925	.0203
4	UKM	675	.0149
5	FRG	650	.0143
6	POL	350	.0077
7	ITA	300	.0068
8	CAN	120	.0026
9	CUB	120	.0026
10	PRC	100	.0022
11	SPA	90	.0020
12	BRAZIL	80	.0017
13	NET	60	.0013
14	AUS	30	.0007
15	IND	20	.0004
16	GDR	10	.0002
17	JAP	10	.0002
18	TUR	10	.0002
19	SKO	5	.0001
20	SAF	5	.0001
21	ALG	0	.0000
22	ARG	0	.0000
23	INO	0	.0000
24	MEX	0	.0000
25	PAK	0	.0000
26	SUD	0	.0000
27	AUS	0	.0000
28	LIB	0	.0000
29	TUR	0	.0000
30	ZAI	0	.0000

Source: World Military Expenditures and Arms
Transfers, 1968-1977 (Washington, D.C.: USACDA,
1979), pp. 118-153.

CHART 3.9 —AEX,1968—1977
(in millions of constant $)

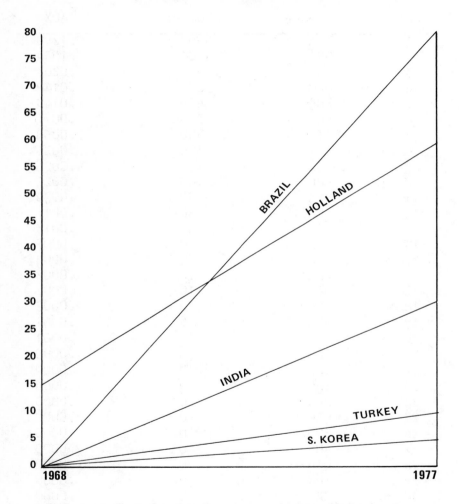

Source: World Military Expenditures and Arms
Transfers, 1968 - 1977 (Washington, DC: USACDA,
1979), pp. 119 - 150.

for a larger share of the market throughout the entire world. It has been reported that Iraq is negotiating for some 2,000 armored cars,[46] the Soviet Union has closed a contract for the sale of 1,000 tank guns,[47] the People's Republic of China appears to be very interested in some $600 million worth of armored cars,[48] and ironically, the Brazilian aircraft corporation EMBRAER now makes some components for Northrop and the U.S. F-5 fighter.[49]

Brazil's rank in world arms exports in 1977 is likely to be only a harbinger, as the country was slated to export $500 million in war materials in 1979.[50] (See Chart 3.9.) If this level of export is maintained—and it will be, easily, if any of the Soviet or Chinese or Iraqi deals come to fruition—Brazil will have catapulted itself into a position close to that of the United Kingdom. Cuba is the only other Latin American country in the arms export business; however, these exports are generally not of Cuban manufacture.

It would seem that AEX is a major key to Brazil's emerging military capability. First, the armed forces could be completely modernized, and general qualitative Armed Forces Strength considerably enhanced. Second, the export of armaments complements Reach. Sealift and airlift capacity allows a nation to project and sustain its military force over long distances. At the same time, there must be something to lift. In this connection, Brazil would be able to project a modern, well-equipped, and well-supplied force. It would be more or less independent of any other country for sustenance, and the industrial base producing for export could be effectively turned to the immediate need. Finally, through the sale of large amounts of military goods abroad, a positive contribution may be made to the balance of payments. A generally more healthy economy would result, and the components of Infrastructure (GRP and DEP) pertinent to military capability could benefit greatly.

Recapitulation

The indicator-variables discussed above examine and measure the relative postion of a state's military capability vis-à-vis other states at a macro level. In these terms, Brazil has, first, increased the size of its armed forces, entered into a long-term modernization program, and begun to develop a technology theoretically capable of producing nuclear weapons; second, that country has substantially increased its Reach; and, third, Brazil has created an armaments industry that appears to be the basis of a discernible effort to continue to improve its military capability. Nevertheless, Brazil's financial commitment to its armed forces and capacity to extract resources from the society are well below those of many peer countries and severely limit the scope of its military capabilities. Brazil has been and appears to continue to be moving toward a capabilities position that would justify an expanding role in international security affairs. However, it has not yet made the political decision to seek such a role.

Notes

1. See SIPRI Yearbook, 1978, *World Armaments and Disarmaments* (Stockholm: Stockholm International Peace Research Institute, 1979).

2. Klaus Knorr, "Is International Coercion Waning or Rising," *International Security* (Vol. 1), Spring 1977, pp. 92–110.

3. Klaus Knorr, "On the International Uses of Military Force in the Contemporary World," *Orbis* (Vol. 21, No. 1), Spring 1977, pp. 5–27.

4. See Wayne H. Ferris, *The Power Capabilities of Nation-States* (Lexington, Mass.: D. C. Heath & Co., 1973), pp. 37–54; Ray S. Cline, *World Power Assessment: A Calculus of Strategic Drift* (Washington, D.C.: Georgetown University Center for Strategic and International Studies, 1975); and A.F.K. Organski and Jacek Kugler, "Davids and Goliaths: Predicting the Outcomes of International Wars," *Comparative Political Studies* (Vol. 11, No. 2), July 1978, pp. 141–181.

5. In addition to those noted above and below, see C. Gorman, "A Tentative Evaluation of World Power," *Journal of Conflict Resolution* (Vol. 4, No. 1), March 1960, pp. 138–144; A.F.K. Organski, *The Stages of Political Development* (New York: Alfred A. Knopf, 1965); K. Knorr, *Military Power and Potential* (Lexington, Mass.: D. C. Heath & Co., 1970); K. Heiss, K. Knorr, and O. Morgenstern, *Long-Term Projections of Political and Military Power* (Princeton, N.J.: Mathematica, 1973); D. Singer, S. Bremer, and J. Stuckey, "Capability Distribution, Uncertainty and Major Power War, 1820–1965," in B. Russett (ed.), *Peace, War and Numbers* (Beverly Hills, Calif.: Sage Publications, 1972); and K. Knorr, *The Power of Nations* (New York: Basic Books, 1975).

6. A list of a few of these indicators would include quality and quantity of supplies, equipment and training, civil and military transportation and communications facilities, morale, population, raw materials, GNP, industrial capacity, technical and administrative skills, tax revenue, capability of an intelligence service, ease of making and implementing governmental decisions, generalship, and military reputation.

7. Factor analysis is a relatively straightforward method of transforming a given set of variables into a new set of composite variables. These sixteen variables are armed forces manpower, total defense expenditure, defense expenditure per capita, defense expenditure as a percent of GNP, arms exports, GNP, territorial area, population, total foreign trade, merchant marine, domestic airlines, theoretical capability to produce 20 KT nuclear bombs, government revenue, government revenue per capita, and military reputation.

8. Klaus Knorr, "Notes on the Analysis of National Capabilities," in J.

Rosenau, V. Davis and M. East (eds.), *The Analysis of International Politics: Essays in Honor of Harold and Margaret Sprout* (New York: Free Press, 1972).

9. Organski and Kugler, "Davids and Goliaths," pp. 143–147.

10. It is assumed that variables that correlate highest (load high) with a given factor or dimension are more important than those that load lower as determinants of the phenomenon in question. The final indicators and factor loading scores are as follows:

	Factor 1	Factor 2	Factor 3
AFT	– 0.10000	– 0.00785	0.59017
NUC	0.55048	0.51582	0.64264
RE1	0.01290	0.92327	0.05480
RE2	0.09681	0.94496	– 0.18660
DEP	0.96375	0.11050	– 0.11534
AEX	0.81244	0.20081	0.34977
GRP	0.72851	– 0.04006	– 0.13266

11. Cline, *World Power Assessment*, p. 130.

12. Decree Number 70852, June 20,1972.

13. *The Military Balance, 1970–1971* (London: IISS, 1970), p. 74.

14. *The Military Balance, 1979–1980* (London: IISS, 1979), p. 77.

15. *Realizações do Govêrno Geisel (1974–1978)* (Brasília: IPEA, 1979), pp. 29–39.

16. Ibid. and *The Military Balance, 1979–1980*.

17. *The Military Balance, 1979–1980*, p. 38.

18. Ibid., p. 31.

19. Ibid., pp. 10–11.

20. *The Military Balance, 1970–1971*, p. 74.

21. *The Military Balance, 1979–1980*, p. 77.

22. The *Independência* was launched September 3, 1979.

23. *Realizações do Govêrno Geisel*, p. 20.

24. This is being done, however, with a great deal of British help.

25. *Realizações do Govêrno Geisel*, pp. 14–15.

26. *The Military Balance, 1979–1980*.

27. *Realizações do Govêrno Geisel*, p.54.

28. *The Military Balance, 1979–1980*.

29. *Strategic Survey, 1977* (London: International Institute for Strategic Studies, 1977), p. 139.

30. President Humberto Castelo Branco, speech to the Brazilian Army General Staff in Rio de Janeiro, August 25, 1964, and *Realizações do Govêrno Geisel, passim*.

31. *A Energia Nuclear no Brasil* (Rio de Janeiro: Biblioteca do Exército Editôra, 1979), p. 17.

32. "Brazil-FRG Agreement on Cooperation in the Field of Peaceful Uses of Nuclear Energy," *The Brazilian Nuclear Program* (Rio de Janeiro: Federative

Republic of Brazil, n.d.), p. 7; and *Strategic Survey 1976, Strategic Survey 1977, Strategic Survey 1978* (London: International Institute for Strategic Studies), pp. 129, 139, and 138, respectively.

33. *SIPRI Yearbook, 1977, World Armaments and Disarmaments* (Stockholm: SIPRI, 1977), pp. 38–39.

34. *O Estado de São Paulo,* October 7, 1979, p. 14.

35. *SIPRI Yearbook, 1977,* pp. 38–39.

36. Reported in *O Estado de São Paulo,* August 24, 1979, p. 14.

37. *World Military Expenditures and Arms Transfers, 1968–1977* (Washington, D.C.: U.S. Arms Control and Disarmament Agency, 1979), pp. 33, 35.

38. *The Military Balance, 1979–1980,* pp. 94–95.

39. Reported in *Jornal do Brasil,* July 13, 1979, p. 6, and *O Estado de São Paulo,* July 17, 1979, p. 5.

40. Organski and Kugler, "Davids and Goliaths," p. 175; and Cline, *World Power Assessment.*

41. *World Armaments and Disarmaments, 1978,* Part 2.

42. A comparative overview of the development of Brazil's domestic arms production is given in Jan Øberg, "Third World Armament: Domestic Arms Production in Israel, South Africa, Brazil, Argentina, and India, 1950–75," in *Instant Research on Peace and Violence* (Vol. 5), 1975, pp. 222–239; Uri Ra'anan, Robert Pfaltzgraff, and Geoffrey Kemp (eds.), *Arms Transfers to the Third World* (Boulder, Colo.: Westview Press, 1978); and Stephanie Neuman and Robert E. Harkavy (eds.), *Arms Transfers in the Modern World* (New York: Praeger Publishers, 1979).

43. This considerable success in the development of a national armaments industry is heavily supported by foreign investment and technology. For example, 45 percent of HELIBRAS, the Brazilian helicopter manufacturer, is owned by Aerospatiale, the French manufacturer of the Concorde passenger jet. *France* (The news bulletin of the French Embassy, Washington, D.C.), April 1978, p. 3.

44. *O Globo,* April 25, 1978, reported this statement by Azevedo Henning, Minister of the Navy.

45. *Jornal do Brasil,* May 27, 1979.

46. *Latin American Economic Report,* February 16, 1979, and *O Globo,* February 9, 1979.

47. *Latin American Economic Report,* May 19, 1978, and *O Estado de São Paulo,* February 4, 1979, p. 10.

48. *Veja,* March 5, 1980, p. 25.

49. *Jornal do Brasil,* May 27, 1979.

50. Ibid.

4
Translating Brazil's Economic Potential into International Influence

Martin T. Katzman

Brazil's evolution as an actor in the international arena over the last quarter century has been impressive. From a monocultural exporter, almost exclusively oriented toward the United States as a market and source of capital, Brazil has emerged as a diversified exporter of foodstuffs and manufactures with diplomatic, trade, and investment links throughout the world. Brazil's potential hegemony in South America and future major power status are seriously discussed in chancelleries throughout the hemisphere and beyond.

Brazil bases its aspirations toward major power status on its geographical size, resource base, population, and economic weight. Brazil's ability to translate these attributes into major power status will depend upon opportunities presented in the international sphere as well as its own capabilities and will. Prognosticating Brazil's future role in the international order is a precarious enterprise, as the rules of the game are in flux, as the state has been joined by transnational nongovernmental actors and multigovernmental commodity cartels as important players, and as the positive-sum game of economic interdependence draws attention away from the zero-sum game of power, prestige, and military might.

Because of these uncertainties, this chapter is speculative and future-oriented rather than cautious and hedged with the normal academic caveats. The major theme is the mechanisms for translating Brazilian economic potential into international influence at the regional and global levels. The chapter begins with presentation of a conceptual scheme for

The author thanks Brantly Womack and Robert Bradley for comments on an earlier draft.

understanding international influence. National capability theory is contrasted with the model of economic interdependence. Next, the linkages
among economic development, internal security, regional hegemony,
and world power status from the viewpoint of Brazilian strategists are
examined. Then the regional impact of Brazilian frontier settlement is
considered. Finally, two of Brazil's major bases of global influence, as a
repository of natural resources and an outlet for investment capital, are
examined.

Elements of International Power and Influence

In the terminology of international relations, power is the ability of
one actor to induce another to undertake an action that it would ordinarily not or to refrain from undertaking an action that it ordinarily
would. Some theorists distinguish between power, which derives from
the ability to punish, and influence, which derives from the ability to
reward.[1] Power and influence derive from the same bases of material
resources and organizational capacity that translate into economic and
military potential.[2]

National Capability Theory

National capability theory views international relations as consisting
primarily of interactions among power-maximizing states. Each state attempts to draw upon its capabilities to maximize its position in the international hierarchy. States in superior positions in the hierarchy
presumably can defend a larger range of their interests over a wider
geographical area and broader range of issues than states in inferior positions.[3]

National capability theorists begin with an analysis of the attributes
that a state can ultimately draw upon for military purposes. Although at
a given moment a state may choose not to devote resources to such purposes (like present-day Japan), these underlying resources, particularly
economic strength, are looked upon as fungible and hence convertible to
military ends when necessary.

The bases of economic power consist of area and location, natural
resources, population, and gross national product. Administrative
capacity and motivation affect the ability to reallocate economic
resources to various ends in the international arena. Some national
capability theorists go so far as to quantify these attributes, establish a
set of weights, and derive a single index of power by which states can be
ranked in the international hierarchy.

Area and location, a state's Cartesian geography, are seen as major influences in international power. Although the importance of area is rarely spelled out, large states presumably possess a wider range and larger quantity of natural resources and hence a greater capacity to support a large population. These are indirect effects of large area on national power, for some large states may be poorly endowed with resources and unable to sustain large agricultural populations. More directly, large area may be of military advantage in the case of invasions; the logistics of an invading army may be stretched thin, while the defending army has room for strategic retreat.

Modern national capability theory pays less attention to location than did classical geopolitical theorists like Mackinder and Mahan.[4] Location determines who a state's neighbors are, the definitiveness of its boundaries, its access to the high seas, its control of strategic airways or seaways, and the like. Brazil, for example, has relatively pacific neighbors and ample access to the high seas, but no control over a particularly strategic air or sea route. While its borders have been well defined for generations, Brazil's population has better access to its Amazonian border areas than its neighbors, many of whom are isolated from the frontier areas by the Andes. The greater population density on the Brazilian side of the border has caused Brazil's neighbors to fear that their frontier areas will be "Brazilianized" through migration and economic attraction.

Natural resources, particularly minerals and fuels, play a major role in the assessment of national capabilities. These are seen as essential inputs into military hardware and its operation. Receiving particular attention are the rate of extraction and size of reserves of iron, the most widely used industrial metal, and oil, the most versatile fuel of industrial civilization. The list of resources that can be considered by capability theorists is practically endless, as suggested in Chapters 2 and 3.

There are several difficulties with national capability theory as a conceptual scheme for analyzing international relations. First, the theoretical linkages between the various attributes and putative or actual power are not obvious. Second, weights assigned to these attributes are selected arbitrarily rather than on the basis of their contribution to behavior. Third, national capability theory is suited more to an international environment in which national security and competition are primary concerns than to an environment of interdependence. Let us consider these difficulties in turn.

The fact that the two superpowers have large land areas and plentiful natural resources suggests that these attributes contribute heavily to a state's power. There are too many exceptions to give too much weight to these factors, however. Major powers like Japan and West Germany are relatively small, while continental nations like Canada and Australia have never been seriously viewed as more than middle powers.

In large nations, much land area may be of relatively low economic value. In Brazil, the best agricultural land is confined to the Atlantic littoral and Paulista plateau, while the best hydroelectric potential is thousands of miles from the centers of population and industry, in the Amazon and Paraná River basins. The Amazonian half of Brazil has only the most meager agricultural potential under current technologies.

Furthermore, states can generally import minerals and fuels to meet economic and military needs. Thus, the Japanese steel industry can dominate world markets on the basis of imported iron and coal. Reliance on imports can subject a state to exploitation by commodity cartels or outright embargo, but in the long run a state can reduce its vulnerability at some cost as a matter of policy through recycling, conservation, or the creation of substitutes. Brazil's hydroelectric, gasohol, and nuclear power efforts are clear expressions of the search for substitutes for petroleum.

Whether large population is an asset or a liability has been the subject of debate since Malthus challenged the mercantilists. A large population is a source of military manpower, but it is also the denominator by which the gross national product is divided in order to compute living standards. Little progress has been made in determining the optimum population of states, and simple-minded cross-national comparisons of densities are uninformative. Few strategists argue that increases in the population of India or China would enhance the power of these states. In contrast, most Brazilian intellectuals and strategists view a larger population as beneficial.[5]

Ray S. Cline has provided as system for weighting the various attributes of national power. In his system, indicators of population, area, economic capacity, and military capacity are combined in an overall index of objective power. Because gross national product is a reflection of the supply of labor, capital, natural resources, and level of technology, it renders these factors of production somewhat redundant as indicators of national capability. Similarly, because sectoral patterns of output are so highly related to product per capita, these are also redundant indicators. According to this weighting scheme, the United States and the Soviet Union are at the top of the list, with about twice as much weight as China and France. Brazil ranks 8th, but not much below West Germany, Japan, and India. One suspects that the artificially high weight associated with land area puts Brazil's power only 10 percent below West Germany and only 6 percent below Japan in 1977. By multiplying these measure of economic power by arbitrary indexes of national strategy and will, Brazil becomes the 6th ranking power in the world, behind China but ahead of Japan.[6]

Not only are such rankings incredible on their face, but they provide little assistance in predicting such phenomena as the ability of a coalition of small oil-rich nations to secure massive wealth from the rest of the world. The actions of these nations, with low levels of perceived power according to Cline's rankings, have had much more impact on the domestic and foreign policies of nations higher up in the pecking order than have higher-ranked major and middle powers.

Finally, the 1970s were a decade of increasing interdependence, as international trade and investment increased absolutely and as a share of world output, particularly among advanced capitalist nations. With the reduction of Western barriers to trade and investment with Eastern and less developed nations, some theorists speculate that the older, "high" politics of international competition may be replaced by the "low" politics of commercial transactions.[7]

The Political Economy of Interdependence

While national capability theory views states as power maximizers, the new political economy of interdependence recognizes that states may pursue other goals. Surely military power may be a mechanism for facilitating economic growth, as suggested by Marxist theories of imperialism. The pursuit of power may also reduce economic growth, as resources are diverted from productive investment into military hardware; therefore, the retreat from this pursuit may enhance economic growth, as in the case of modern Japan. In the emerging world order, transnational corporations become major actors, as a larger share of international trade and investment are actually intracorporate transactions.[8]

From the interdependence perspective, events and policies of one state can affect those of another through four major channels. First, domestic economic events and policies of one nation can spill over its boundaries and affect the residents of another. Inflation or recession, or both, in a major participant in international trade can affect the price level, flow of exports, and balance of payments of its partners. Japanese policies toward investment in the domestic steel and computer industries can affect drastically the fate of these industries as well as the total balance of payments in the United States. The vagaries of domestic economic activity and policies in countries of less economic weight, like Brazil, have far less ripple effects beyond their borders.

Second, a state can affect the behavior of foreign transnational actors within its borders or its own transnational actors abroad. U.S.-based multinationals are generally subject to U.S. restrictions regarding affirmative action, bribery, and trading with the enemy while operating on foreign territory, but they generally come under foreign jurisdiction regarding taxation, collective bargaining, and antitrust. As discussed below, a nation that is an attractive location for multinational investment, like Brazil, may have considerable power to control transnational actors.

Third, a state may use its bargaining power to obtain better prices for its export commodities, tariff concessions, or special credits without essentially altering the rules of the international game. As discussed below, Brazil exports no commodity that would endow it with OPEC-like powers, although it may have some control in the grain market in the future.

Fourth, a state in coalition may be able to alter the rules of the international game in its favor. This may involve the modification of old rules, such as those allocating seats on the boards of multilateral financing agencies, or the creation of rules where ambiguity reigned before, as in the recognition of ownership of deep-sea manganese nodules.

The interdependency paradigm recognizes competitive elements in international relations, but views these as essentially secondary to mutual gains from cooperation. The objective of states is thus not to minimize dependency upon others, but to engage in mutually beneficial commercial exchanges. Notions of hierarchy, dominance, and exploitation are conspicuously absent. A large, technically advanced economy is advantageous in this view not because it places a state high in the international hierarchy, but because it reduces the state's vulnerability to business cycles emanating from other states, it increases the ability to deal with transnational actors within its own borders and to protect its own transnational actors abroad, it raises its bargaining power in commodity markets, and it enhances the likelihood of influencing the rules of the international game in its favor. In the interdependency paradigm, a convertible currency like the Swiss franc can be a far more valuable asset than millions of hectares of Amazonian forest.

Brazil's Perception of Itself as a Regional and World Power

The military regime that assumed power in 1964 has synthesized the basic themes in Brazil's foreign policy in a new doctrine that links economic development and national security, broadly defined. This dominant doctrine has been diffused to the business and technical elite under the auspices of the Escola Superior de Guerra and is widely held.

Economic development is seen as the key to internal security, regional hegemony, and major power status in the world. Economic development will thrust Brazil to the forefront of the hierarchy of nations through the mechanisms postulated in national capability theory. Effective control of Brazil's vast frontier lands is essential, since large area is viewed as a major basis of power. In the task of frontier settlement and territorial integration, Brazil's large population is seen as an asset.[9]

According to this doctrine, the major threat to Brazilian security is internal, i.e., the threat of subversion by an impoverished and discontented mass. Repression of this discontent can buy time for rapid economic development to eliminate its ultimate causes. Economic development is defined as rapid industrialization through the application of the most modern technology. Subsidiary goals are regional integration through transportation investments that will reduce disparities in income, assure sovereignty over sparsely populated frontier areas, and make new resources available for development.

The pursuit of rapid industrialization required a redefinition of Brazil's international economic relations. The expanding presence of competing industrialized powers in the developing world enhanced the options of the military regime. First, in repudiating nonalignment and symbolic declarations of independence from the United States, Brazil established security for foreign investors and actively pursued investment from a variety of countries. U.S. investment predominates, but West European and Japanese investment is growing more rapidly.

Second, the military regime encouraged the expansion of new exports, in particular new agricultural commodities and manufactures. In the mid-1970s, Brazil's bill of lading was dominated by light manufactures (half of which were exported to Latin America), soybeans, corn, cotton, animal foodstuffs, and concentrated iron ore. This aggressive new trade policy has put Brazil into some conflict with the entire industrialized world. Taking a line from the Quadros "new foreign policy," Brazil has become a leading spokesman for developing nations seeking a new international economic order.[10] In contrast to the purely symbolic gestures of earlier alliance with Afro-Asian countries, Brazil's new policy promises to bring collective benefits vis-à-vis the industrialized world of (1) a greater voice in the management of multilateral monetary and financial agencies, (2) lower barriers against imports from developing countries, and (3) supports of prices for certain primary products.

The demonstrated vulnerability of the Brazilian "miracle" to the oil embargo created a new thrust in foreign policy toward energy independence. Paradoxically, the search for long-term energy independence places Brazil in greater short-term dependency upon other nations. To assure its oil imports, Brazil swiftly dropped its pro-Israeli stance (earlier maintained in deference to U.S. interests) in favor of stronger ties with the Arab states. As in the case of Japan, another oil-deficient power, Brazil's rhetorical about-face on Middle Eastern issues was a humiliating indicator of weakness, not strength. Second, the crash program to increase the local production of oil has necessitated the granting of "risk contracts" to foreign companies, a radical departure from the principle established earlier of nationalization of all oil exploration, transportation, and refining.

Over the longer haul, Brazil may have considerable capacity to weather the energy shocks of the 1970s. Its hydroelectric potential is good, although poorly located given current technologies of electric transmission. Future innovations in high-voltage transmission or the relocation of energy-intensive industry toward the environs of dams in the Paraná and Amazon basins might change the picture. Although relatively minor, Brazil's uranium deposts have proven interesting enough to attract German capital and technology in one of the largest bilateral nuclear agreements yet concluded. Brazil demonstrated steadfastness in the face of U.S. opposition to the deal; however, West Germany's domestic politics may block its consummation, again an indicator of Brazil's vulnerability to events beyond its borders.

Brazil's gasohol program, the most advanced in the world, may be the surest guarantor of energy independence. The bold move to convert all new cars to gasohol in the early 1980s attests to the nation's seriousness of purpose and bargaining power with the transnational automobile assemblers. Brazil's comparative advantage as a sugar producer may enable its alcohol to capture a large share of markets abroad, as "backup" energy technologies become more profitable.

Brazil has outgrown its role as junior partner of the United States, and several issues have brought the two nations into conflict, such as the Brazilian positions on population control, pollution policy, human rights, the Nonproliferation Treaty, and the nuclear deal with Germany. Brazil's vulnerability to oil price increases and its frantic diplomatic reaction to these increases suggests that either the nation is far from achieving major power status, or that major power status is no insulator from economic pressures by lesser powers.

The Regional Significance of Brazilian Frontier Expansion

Of all the continental-size nations of the world, Brazil has undergone the most rapid frontier settlement in the past few decades. Initially concentrated on the Atlantic coast, Brazil began penetrating the interior for purposes of agricultural exploitation after 1860. By 1940, the Paulista plateau was effectively settled, and frontier settlement picked up pace as the nation entered the era of highways and the internal combustion engine. Through the 1950s and 1960s, Paraná and Goiás were major centers of pioneering. In the 1970s, Goiás and Mato Grosso were the major foci of frontier settlement, and ranching in Amazonia accelerated.[11]

Although the early railroads in Brazil (as in the United States) were financed by British capital, frontier expansion until recently was associated with ownership of land resources by Brazilians or recent immigrants. The production of the major export crops was well within the technological and financial capabilities of Brazilians. Although responsive to markets abroad, Brazilian frontier settlement was of largely domestic significance until recently.

Amazonian frontier settlement is now of much greater international significance. First, in attempting to control and exploit its natural resources in Amazonia, Brazil has become caught in the economic development versus dependency dilemma. On the one hand, it wishes to defend its resources against foreign pillage. On the other hand, it lacks the capability to exploit these resources without foreign technology, capital, and market organization. It was easy to tread the path of economic nationalism in Amazonia during the 1950s, when there were few known deposits to exploit and even less confidence in the ability of primary-producing countries to expand their exports, but the temptation to rely upon foreign involvement has increased as the extent of mineral resources has become better known and confidence in the ability to export has increased. Second, interest groups in the advanced nations have protested Amazonian development on grounds of adverse impacts on the atmosphere and on the aborigines.[12] Brazil is likely to remain invulnerable on these issues. Third, the westward thrust of Brazilians into Amazonia poses threats to its neighbors.

Scenarios for the Remainder of This Century

At the beginning of the last fifth of the twentieth century, a dynamic Brazilian economy is increasing its effective control over its territory. Following the borders from south to north, Brazil faces a stagnant Uruguay, an Argentina with an unsettled economic and political system, a Paraguay and a Bolivia that are becoming increasingly integrated into the Brazilian economy by transportation linkages and free-port privileges, as well as a rim of Andean nations whose presence is barely visible at the Brazilian border. In contrast, Brazil's economic dynamism in its portion of Amazonia is visible and increasing and is extending toward its borders.

Partly prompted by fear of their territories becoming integrated in the Brazilian economy, the Andean countries have enunciated goals of occupying their empty lands east of the Andes. Although all of the Andean nations have adopted fiscal incentives and colonization programs for their portions of Amazonia, these have had minimal effect. The most grandiose reaction has been the proposed construction of a highway at the eastern slopes of the Andes from Venezuela to Bolivia. Actual construction of this road has not proceeded as fast as Brazilian road building in Amazonia.[13]

In speculating about the future it is useful to distinguish between the northern Amazonian borders, which are sparsely settled on both sides, and the remaining borders, which have a relatively dense Brazilian population. The assumption underlying these speculations is that a regime committed to integrating Brazil into the international capitalist system will remain in power to the end of this century.

Paraguay as a new Paraná. The last decade has seen Paraná become well penetrated by a transportation network that has spread commercial farming throughout this state. The indirect effect of these roads is to increase the profitability of commercial agriculture on the other side of the Paraná River, beyond the feeder road network. The all-weather trunk road from Asunción through Iguaçú to Curitiba and São Paulo provides a major export corridor. At the same time, changes in the relative prices of coffee and soybeans and problems with frost have resulted in a shift of land out of labor-intensive coffee into land-intensive soybeans. This situation has created a crisis of rural overpopulation and a consequent ejection of the rural proletariat in Paraná. In response to this favorable conjunction of an excellent transportation-marketing system up to the edge of Paraguay and an abundance of land-seeking farmers, Brazilian and Paraguayan land developers have subdivided land west of the Paraná River.[14]

The likely result is the purchase of this Paraguyan land by Brazilian small-holders aiming to produce for Brazil's east coast markets. Because Paraguay's portion of the Paraná Valley is so sparsely settled, large numbers of Brazilian squatters are likely to occupy land until the companies assume effective control. The number of Brazilians in this area is likely to outnumber the Paraguayans by far. Although the vast majority of farmers are likely to be Brazilian, it is probable that some Paraguayans will share the fruits of this development as partners with Brazilians in trucking companies and mills and as civil servants regulating and taxing these activities.

The Itaipu Dam will further enhance the integration of Paraguay into the Brazilian economic orbit. The sale of Paraguay's share of the electricity to Brazil will improve the financial status of the former, but will further enhance the attractiveness of the border area to energy-intensive Brazilian industry. With such high stakes involved, it would be inconceivable that Brazil could remain indifferent to events that threatened the internal stability of Paraguay or the stability of their bilateral economic relations.

The most favorable scenario for Paraguay is the retention of sovereignty over its eastern region, but effective integration of the region into the Brazilian economic sphere. There will be great pressures to permit the free movement of workers, capital, and commodities between Paraguay and Paraná and for the acceptance of the Brazilian cruzeiro as legal tender in Paraguay.

A less favorable scenario for Paraguay would be a reaction, largely by portions of its bourgeoisie that are not sharing in the economic benefits of integration into Brazil, demanding a reassertion of national control. Such a reaction might involve the imposition of substantial export tariffs on crops moving eastward and requirements that all contracts be executed in Spanish and in Paraguayan currency or that only citizens might own land. Such actions could be interpreted by Brazilians as attempts by Paraguayans to improve the terms of the bargain, but the more nationalist press in Brazil might encourage Brazilians in Paraguay to defend their rights by force of arms if necessary. The threat of intervention of Brazilian troops to protect the interests of its nationals might have one of several results: (1) a capitulation by Paraguay on all the basic issues, making Portuguese the *de jure* language of commerce and instruction, making the cruzeiro the legal tender, and prohibiting the imposition of restrictions on movement of factors of production and commodities; (2) a local rebellion and the secession of eastern Paraguay, which would become a buffer state; or (3) a local rebellion supported by Brazilian troops, resulting in the incorporation of this region into Brazil.

The least favorable scenario involves a continuation of current trends to the end of the century as all of Paraguay becomes increasingly integrated into the Brazilian economy by the criss-crossing of transportation lines from Paraná and Mato Grosso and the movement of Brazilian ranchers into the Chaco, Brazilian farmers into the eastern portion of the nation, and Brazilian merchants and brokers into Asunción and other cities. By the end of the century, the essential culture of Paraguay will have been changed by the sheer demographic and economic dominance of the Brazilians. The entire country will have been drawn into Brazil's economic and political orbit, and annexation will be an unnecessary formality.

The absorption of lowland Bolivia. Acre, a decadent rubber region taken from Bolivia at the turn of the century, has received a major stimulus from the new interregional highways, the fiscal incentives program, and public and private colonization schemes. Corporate cattle ranchers in Acre have been clearing the rubber trees for pasture, thereby depriving the *seringueiros* (rubber collectors) of their livelihood. The growth of corporate mining in neighboring Rondônia has had a similar impact on placer miners. The displacement of the older population and the attraction of a new population drawn by the roads and the promise of land has created a substantial Brazilian presence near the Bolivian border. Although this portion of Brazil has attenuated linkages to the markets of the industrial central south, a spillover of activity across the border, similar to that on the Paraná-Paraguay border, is likely to occur. Squatters and land developers are likely to ignore the borders if the supply of land made available by the colonization schemes is substantially less than the demand. Ranchers are likely to behave in a similar fashion along the entire Bolivian-Brazilian border. Just as in Paraguay, these border regions are likely to become economically integrated into the Brazilian economy.

An additional factor in Bolivia is the existence or possible existence of petroleum and other mineral resources. To the extent that the Bolivian government discourages exploitation on the part of multinational enterprises or Brazilian state enterprises, the Brazilian government might find it convenient to support the latent secessionist tendencies of the Santa Cruz region. This possibility falls under the rubric of the next scenario.

Brazil as a stalking-horse for multinational enterprise. The active mineral exploration by multinational enterprises throughout Brazilian Amazonia is not likely to be replicated on the other side of the border. Economic nationalism and the associated political uncertainties in many of the neighboring countries, like Bolivia, Peru, and even Venezuela, are likely to discourage highly speculative ventures on the part of multinationals. In the event that a vast pool of oil is found on the Brazilian-Peruvian border or in lowland Bolivia, it is not implausible that oil-hungry Brazil would take action to insure its future supply, such as by encouraging secession or military occupation. Brazilian stewardship would be the guarantee for multinationals and Brazilian state enterprises to undertake the necessary investments.

Brazil as Colossus of the South

These scenarios suggest the plausibility of Brazil's becoming an expansionist power in South America. Frustration in achieving major power status may enhance the likelihood of such regional expansionism. Although Argentina has had a traditional interest in the Platine buffer states, it is unlikely to offer any serious competition. In the tradition of *uti possidetis*, Brazil is likely to absorb the Platine lowlands through its peasants, of which it has many more than Argentina, and extend its Amazonian boundaries through its cattle and mining companies. To the extent that Brazil remains the major safe haven for international capitalism in South America, it will receive considerable technological and financial assistance from the advanced countries in this latter endeavor.

The specter of Brazil as the hegemonic power in South America suggests an additional scenario from the pages of Gerschenkron.[15] The threat of being overtaken by Brazil may galvanize Argentina or a coalition of Spanish-speaking states into accelerated investment in natural resources, human capital, and high technology, just as European threats stimulated Japan into forced-draft industrialization. Whether Brazil can forestall such a reaction depends upon its diplomatic skills in assuaging the fears of its neighbors or at least in keeping them divided. Thus far, Brazil has been successful in this respect.

Natural Resources as a Basis of Major Power Status

It would be surprising if a nation the size of Brazil were not endowed with a wide variety of depletable and renewable natural resources. Indeed, Brazil has an impressive range of mineral resources, vegetation, and soils, although it is conspicuously lacking in fossil fuels. At issue in translating resources into a power base is the current or potential market value of those resources. This market value depends upon whether such resources are scarce or ubiquitous, whether Brazil has a near monopoly on the scarce resources, whether the cost of extracting or exploiting these resources is favorable compared to that of competing suppliers, and whether the demand and hence the price of these resources is likely to rise. The most dramatic way of posing the issue is to ask whether Brazil is likely to acquire a near-monopoly of some vital resource that will translate into power.

Depletable Resources

Brazil controls some of the richest iron and bauxite deposits in the world as well as reserves of rarer metals, with the promise of further discoveries of major mineral reserves. Although Brazilian strategists point to these reserves and potential resources as bases of future power, it appears unlikely that these would provide Brazil with much leverage to increase its wealth, to alter its position within the international order, or even to bargain favorably within the existing order.

Iron is clearly an important material in an advanced industrial economy. In value, iron is second only to petroleum as an input in the U.S. economy. Among nonfuel resources, aluminum is second to iron in value as an industrial input in industrial economies. In the world economy, the role of iron looms even larger. Nevertheless, iron and aluminum ores are fairly ubiquitous and nearly infinite in supply. Nor do price trends indicate any increasing scarcity of these two minerals.[16] Furthermore, Brazil's iron resources must compete not only with iron resources in other developing countries, but also with scrap iron generated in the consuming countries. The inaccessibility of some of Brazil's iron resources, and hence the high cost of developing them, has hindered its mineral development, as indicated by the abandonment of the Carajás project by U.S. Steel.

It may have been the unlikelihood of Brazil's developing as a mineral-based power that prompted the government to reverse its longstanding policy against direct exploration by foreign oil companies under risk contracts. It would appear unlikely that the government would need to provide fiscal incentives for foreign companies to explore for minerals, were the odds of success high. This is not to say that Brazil may not suddenly discover an oil basin as spectacular as that of Mexico in its outer continental shelf, but this would be a matter of luck rather than an inevitable result of Brazil's land area.

Renewable Resources

It is in the area of renewable resources that Brazil has had in the past and may have in the future control over vital products. Brazil, after all, produced nearly three-fourths of the world's coffee at the turn of the century. Despite its falling share of world coffee exports, Brazil plays a major role in formulating the rules of the game in the world coffee market as codified in the International Coffee Agreement (ICA). It is hard to imagine that oligopolistic power in commodities like coffee could provide much basis for Brazil's claim to major power status. To a great extent the acquiescence of the developed consuming countries in ICA rules is a quid pro quo rather than a tribute unilaterally extracted by sheer power, as is clearly the case in the oil market. The advanced countries provide the producers with some stability of expectations and somewhat higher prices in exchange for good behavior in other spheres.

Perhaps the most important renewable resource Brazil controls is potentially agricultural land. Largely as a result of an energetic campaign to improve the highway network and marketing system, Brazil has brought millions of hectares into cultivation in the past three or four decades. The country has already outstripped great exporting countries like Canada, Australia, and Argentina in area under cultivation and there is room for further expansion. Barriers of climate and soil hinder the extensive growth of the area under cultivation in these other countries.

The central Brazilian savanna quite possible comprises the "largest remaining unlocked soilbank in the world."[17] Bringing this area under exploitation requires solving technical-economic problems of acidity, aluminum toxicity, and phosphate deficiency, as well as the economic problem of long hauls to market. The problems of acidity and phosphate deficiency are solvable with mineral deposits within the region, but rising energy costs clearly inhibit long truck hauls of the regional produce. These problems aside, can Brazil parlay its command of vast food-producing potential into international power?

The linkage between agricultural area and international importance as a food exporter can be tenuous. First, land is only one input into the production process. By rapid agrobiological innovation and the application of fertilizers, insecticides, and machinery, the United States has been able to increase its output many times, with virtually no increase in area under cultivation in the past fifty years. National income accounting techniques attribute a far greater share of farm output in advanced countries to labor and capital than to land.[18] Only in less advanced countries is land the major input into agricultural production.

Second, agricultural exports depend upon the demands from the domestic market, which in turn is sensitive to economic policy. China, which has three times the area under cultivation as Brazil, is an insignificant exporter because most of its produce is consumed domestically. Canada, Australia, and Argentina have been important exporters because of their small domestic markets. Argentina's and Brazil's exports have fluctuated with economic policy. Import-substitution policies in both countries have discouraged investment in agriculture in favor of industrial expansion. While Brazil's policies through the 1960s maintained incentives for coffee exports, price controls and export embargoes on foodstuffs were imposed to reduce living costs for urban workers under the "exportable surplus doctrine."[19]

An examination of international grain markets indicates that relatively few countries consistently contribute in a major way to the international supply. The United States and Canada have been the mainstays, while Australia's contribution has fluctuated with drought conditions and Argentina's with political events. Brazil has at times been an important exporter of cotton, sugar, and cacao, but not a significant exporter of food (other than coffee) until the 1970s.

The most portentous phenomenon in agricultural markets has been the rise of Brazil to the position of the world's 2nd soybean producer and 2nd food exporter. In order of importance value of world trade in 1967–1972, Brazil ranked 4th in corn exports (with less than 1 percent of the market share), 1st in coffee (33 percent), 2nd in animal feedstuffs (about 5 percent), and 3rd in cotton (5 percent). Current agricultural exports are dominated by soybeans, coffee, sugar, and orange concentrate, with lesser exports of corn, cacao, and rice.[20]

Brazil has considerable experience in centralized control of exports and participation in commodity agreements, but there is only modest likelihood that this experience can result in significant international market power. First, Brazil's shares in these commodity markets (except coffee) are too small to affect supply significantly. Second, Third World–based international commodity agreements are unlikely to help Brazil much because its potential lies in temperate-zone crops, such as soybeans, where advanced nations are major producers. Third, underlying conditions of supply and demand elasticity in the food markets in which Brazil participates are not conducive to OPEC-like organization. Fourth, there are no agricultural commodities whose quadrupling in price in OPEC style would raise Brazil's wealth commensurately.[21] After all, coffee is second only to oil in value of international trade, and rises in coffee prices have not made Brazil rich on an OPEC scale.

Finally, it is not a foregone conclusion that Brazil will continue to expand its role as an agricultural exporter. Many tropical exporters exhibit the paradox of domestic malnutrition in the face of huge agricultural exports. The simple explanation for this paradox is that those suffering from hunger do not always own the land that produces the export crops or do not legislate the incentives for growers. Brazil's export surge in the 1970s reflects a policy directed at raising export earnings, not the incomes or nutritional levels of the poorest citizens. The acknowledgment that the Brazilian model of economic development has helped this segment but little may induce decision makers to institute policies that could raise domestic demand for basic foodstuffs and hence reduce incentives to export. Although a return to the old exportable surplus doctrine is unlikely, income redistribution schemes such as land reform would have similar effects on food exports.

Several other categories of Brazil's renewable resources have so far proven disappointing. Attempts to found a great cattle empire in the Amazon region failed, seemingly because of the difficulty of sustaining nutritious grasses. This apparently results from the lack of calcium in the soil.[22] Nutrient deficiencies may be remedied by specific dosages, but they do attenuate the apparent advantage of Brazil's open space.

Brazil's timber resources have yet to provide the nation with much of a domestic economic contribution, much less a decisive international role. Forestry is generally a residual use of land on which it is not worthwhile to farm or build cities. The forestry industry has proven itself technologically flexible enough to vary its input requirements with the availability of various types of wood on the market. This reduces its dependence upon particular wood species, such as those in which Brazil might conceivably have a comparative advantage.

General Issues of Resources and Economic Development

Mainstream currents of thought dating from classical political economy hold that natural resource staples, at least in temperate zones, may be the engine of industrial development. In contrast to the optimistic staple theory of economic development is the revisionist dependency theory. This latter holds that natural resource exploitation, at least in the tropics, is the road to underdevelopment.[23] The exceptions to these theoretical generalizations are few—the Center-South of Brazil that emerged from the São Paulo coffee frontier, perhaps West Malaysia emerging from a rubber and tin export base, and potentially some of the oil-rich nations (Venezuela being the most conspicuous example).

Although the shocking rise in the prices of oil and other raw materials in the 1970s has popularized neo-Malthusian notions of resource scarcity, the wealth and power of modern industrial nations is little dependent upon the resource base. First, the share of national income going to owners of natural resources declines rapidly in the course of economic development. In modern industrial nations, only about 5 percent of the national income is attributed to natural resources, while 75–80 percent is attributed to the quantity and quality of the labor force.[24] Indeed, economic development is almost tautologically defined as the increase in the role of human and physical capital and the reduction in the role of nature. One reason is that the demand for food and fiber (for clothing) on the part of consumers rises rather more slowly than income (the well-known Engel's Law). Another is that in industrial societies, goods are more complex, deriving their value from the application of skilled labor, high technology, and reproducible capital rather than from raw materials. Second, despite the law of diminishing returns, the costs of raw materials and food have not risen relative to the price of manufactures. This is because of rapid technological change in mining and agriculture, as well as investments in transportation sufficient to extend the resource frontiers, which currently include the seas. These latter forces have been strong enough to prompt dependency theorists to declare that the terms of trade of raw materials versus manufactures chronically deteriorate. The recent spurt in oil prices was not a result of reaching the limits of supply, but of political organization of the market, and, even here, oil markets may prove to be exceptional. Third, advanced countries are entering a new "age of substitutability" in which a wide range of substitutes for specific minerals will emerge.[25]

The point of the above analysis is that Brazil is unlikely to achieve major power status on the basis of its mineral or agricultural resources. On the contrary, its resource balance sheet evinces glaring liabilities. Brazil's deficit in fossil fuels resulted in major changes in its foreign and domestic policies and is likely to be a source of chronic vulnerability. Until it can exploit its hydrological, nuclear, and biomass resources more thoroughly, Brazil will continue to be victimized by events in international fuel markets, much like Japan.

Brazil as a Favored Outlet for Capital Investment

Venerable theories of imperialism assign great importance to less advanced countries as outlets for capital and manufactures of the advanced countries. The function of these outlets is to forestall the decline in the profitability of investment as domestic markets become saturated in the advanced countries. Although more subtle and modern variants of such theories recognize that direct rule is not necessary, they presume that the foreign policies of advanced countries are aimed at maintaining in the less developed areas regimes open to inflows of capital.[26]

As the anticolonial tide rises in the less developed world, fewer and fewer of these countries may welcome foreign investment. Those that do may place great restrictions on foreign equity participation, the sectors in which investment can occur, and repatriation of profits. In such an international environment, a highly attractive less developed country that was receptive to foreign investment might be able to exact enormously favorable concessions. In providing a safe haven for foreign investment in an increasingly hostile world, such a country could make economically advanced countries dependent upon *it* and enhance its own power.

For the advanced nations of the First World, Brazil stands out as an outlet for capital investment. If one scans the world for countries that possess both a favorable climate for private investment and a large, protected internal market, Mexico and Brazil in Latin America, Nigeria in Africa, and Saudi Arabia and Indonesia in Asia stand out. If this list had been compiled a decade ago, perhaps South Africa and Iran would have been included, and a decade hence perhaps China will be. As indicated by gross national product, Brazil heads the list, with Mexico close behind. The prospects for mass markets in a wide range of products are rather thin now in Nigeria and Indonesia because of the low per capita income and in Saudi Arabia because of the small population. In long-term rate of growth of gross national product, Brazil surpasses Mexico; however, the latter's new oil wealth may alter this relationship. Brazil and Mexico have similar access to Latin American markets, but Mexico has superior access to the North American market. In openness to foreign equity participation, Brazil appears far more flexible.[27] To what extent can Brazil translate its role as a safe haven for foreign capital into increased power?

The role of nations like Brazil in international investment has both supply and demand sides. On the supply side, the cost of production in advanced regions is high because wages are high (some advanced nations have wages higher than those in the United States), because of congestion, taxes, environmental regulations, etc. As suggested by the product-cycle model, the innovative stages of manufacture occur in the advanced nations.[28] For routinized production, less advanced regions, with lower labor costs, become increasingly attractive. By the process of "filtration," manufacturing moves from the most advanced, highest-wage areas down the hierarchy. This process can be vividly illustrated by the movement of textile production from New England (the cradle of U.S. industrialization) to the southern United States (formerly a backward region) to East Asia. On the demand side, as particular industries saturate regional markets, either product diversification or branching to new regions occurs. A developing country with a growing market proves particularly attractive.

The role of Brazil as an outlet for surplus capital may extend beyond its own market. As a member of the Latin American Common Market, Brazil provides multinationals with potential access to third markets where direct foreign investment may not be so welcome. Indeed, most of Brazil's manufactured exports are to the region. These third markets might be less accessible to multinationals were the exports to originate in the advanced home country.

Contrary to the expectations of early writers on imperialism, the lion's share of the overseas investment stock of all advanced nations is in other advanced nations. Moreover, the concentration of direct overseas investment in the advanced nations of Europe, North America, and Oceania has been rising in the past twenty years or so.[29] The sheer size of the market, similarity of consumer tastes, and availability of infrastructure and suppliers makes other advanced nations attractive.

Brazil is perhaps less attractive to direct foreign investment by Americans than to investment by corporations of other advanced countries. Of the total stock of U.S. investment abroad, Brazil's share has remained at about 3 percent over the past twenty years, hardly a decisive figure. In recent years, the annual flow of U.S. investment to Brazil has approached the flow to Australia and France, but remains far behind that to Canada, Britain, and West Germany. Brazil's share of the stock of U.S. investment in the developing world has risen from less than 9 percent to more than 13 percent in the past fifteen years.[30]

Brazil, a resource-rich and capital-poor nation, is highly attractive to investors from Japan, a resource-poor and capital-rich nation. The complementarity of the resource endowments of the two nations explains Brazil's absorption of about one-third of Japan's total investment abroad. Japan's financing of Brazil's rise to the position of the world's number 2 exporter of soybeans, in response to the Nixon shocks in the early 1970s, may portend the formation of a solid Tokyo-Brasília economic axis.[31]

Investment by European corporations is also growing faster than U.S. investment in Brazil. This attractiveness has encouraged Brazilian policymakers to place new conditions on investors that would maximize technology transfer and the stimulus to Brazilian high-technology suppliers. It seems unlikely that Brazil's attractiveness is so great that it could significantly alter the rules of the game. Furthermore, Brazil would lose its uniqueness as an outlet should either China or India open its doors to massive direct investment. Should Japan and the Soviet Union resolve their residual conflicts from World War II, Japanese investment may be diverted from Brazil to resource-rich Siberia.

In addition to absorbing direct foreign investment, Brazil is a favored outlet for financial investment. Since the late 1960s, the bulk of the capital inflow to Brazil was in the form of financial capital from private institutions and multilateral agencies.[32] Brazil, then, may be important to international capitalism as an outlet of indirect rather than direct capital investment, as one of the largest debtors in the world. Although Brazil's large debt indicates its creditworthiness in the eyes of financial investors, few Brazilians argue that the nation's position as a key debtor enhances its power. On the contrary, most Brazilian strategists view this debt as at best a necessary evil, at worst a sign of weakness and dependency.

Conclusion

As the century draws to a close, Brazil is likely to be the dominant power in South America, with no rival in sight. Its very success in exploiting its own natural resources will encourage it to exploit those of its weaker neighbors, who will increasingly be drawn into its economic orbit. As the paramount power on the continent, Brazil will most certainly attempt to control events in the three Platine buffer states and influence events elsewhere. Rather than merely serving as subdominant gendarme for the interests of the United States, Brazil will try to exert regional power on its own account.

Beyond the confines of South America, Brazil is not likely to play a major role in world affairs. First, the distribution of power in the world has changed such that few nations can exercise their will decisively beyond their own region or alter the international economic order unilaterally. Second, Brazil's lack of uniqueness as a source of raw materials or a safe haven for private investment suggests that the nation's power will be proportional to its economic size (as a supplier and demander of goods in world markets) or its will to utilize its economy for purposes of influencing other nations.

With a rapid growth rate of 6 percent per annum, Brazil's gross national product would surpass by the year 2000 those of Britain, Italy, and Canada (growing more slowly at 3 percent to 4 percent per annum) and approach that of France. In its striving to move into the circle of the seven largest national economies, Brazil will be competing with oil-exporting Mexico. Room at the top will become more crowded if the economies of India and China accelerate. On sheer economic weight, then, Brazil might hope for the international status of middle powers like Canada or Italy, which is modest at best.

Notes

1. Stanley Hoffman, "Notes on the Elusiveness of Modern Power," *International Journal* 30 (Spring 1975):183–206; Susan Strange, "What is Economic Power, and Who Has It?" *International Journal* 30 (Spring 1975):207–224; and Klaus Knorr, *Power and Wealth: The Political Economy of International Power* (New York: Basic Books, 1973), Chap. 1.

2. A third dimension of international standing identified in Knorr, *Power and Wealth*, prestige, has a weaker relationship to economic power than to its ideological clothing. Although the bases of prestige have been subject to less analysis than the bases of power and influence, one suspects that in the dominant United Nations circles Brazil's avowed ideologies (but not unfailing practice) of capitalism and alignment with the West are liabilities; its protestations of racial democracy and born-again anti-Zionism, assets. Accusations of police-state practices and authoritarianism cause Brazil little loss of prestige in these circles. Paraphrasing one wag, I suspect that Brazil's prestige would soar if it merely *declared* itself a democratic people's socialist republic. See Daniel P. Moynihan, "The United States in Opposition," *Commentary* 59 (March 1975):31–44.

3. Knorr, *Power and Wealth*; Stephen L. Spiegel, *Dominance and Diversity: The International Hierarchy* (Boston: Little, Brown and Co., 1972).

4. For a brief review and application of the classics, see Carlos de Meira Mattos, *A Geopolítica e as Projeções do Poder* (Rio de Janeiro: José Olympio, 1977).

5. Herman Daly, "The Population Question in Northeast Brazil: Its Economic and Ideological Dimensions," *Economic Development and Cultural Change* 18 (July 1970):536–574.

6. See Ray S. Cline, *World Power Assessment 1977: A Calculus of Strategic Drift* (Boulder, Colo.: Westview Press, 1977). As reported in the Dallas *Times-Herald*, 29 June 1980, Cline's latest annual assessment advances Brazil to number 3.

7. An elaboration of the distinction between the old and the new international political economy is in Joan Edelman Spero, *The Politics of International Economic Relations* (New York: St. Martins, 1977); see also Hoffmann, "Notes on the Elusiveness of Modern Power," and Strange, "What is Economic Power?"

8. The concept of the transnational actor is developed in Robert O. Keohane and Joseph S. Nye, Jr. (eds.), *Transnational Relations and World Politics* (Cambridge, Mass.: Harvard University Press, 1970); see also Robert Gilpin, *U.S. Power and the Multinational Corporation: The Political Economy of Direct Investment* (New York: Basic Books, 1975); Raymond Vernon, *Storm Over the Multinationals: The Real Issues* (Cambridge, Mass.: Harvard University Press, 1977).

9. *Revista Brasileria de Estudos Políticos* 21 (July 1966) (Special issue on national security); Wayne A. Selcher, *The National Security Doctrine and the Policies of the Brazilian Government*, Strategic Studies Institute, U.S. Army War College, Carlisle Barracks, Pa., ACN 77027 (15 July 1977); Roger W. Fontaine, *Brazil and the United States: Toward a Mature Relationship* (Washington, D.C., and Stanford, Calif.: American Enterprise Institute and Hoover Institution, 1974), Chap. 3; Carlos de Meira Mattos, *Brasil: Geopolítica e Destino* (Rio de Janeiro: José Olympio, 1975) and *A Geopolítica e as Projeções do Poder* (Rio de Janeiro: José Olympio, 1977).

10. Ronald M. Schneider, *Brazil: The Foreign Policy of a Future World Power* (Boulder, Colo.: Westview Press, 1976); William R. Cline, "Brazil's Emerging International Economic Role," in Riordan Roett (ed.), *Brazil in the Seventies* (Washington, D.C.: American Enterprise Institute, 1976), pp. 63–88.

11. Martin T. Katzman, *Cities and Frontiers in Brazil: Regional Dimensions of Economic Development* (Cambridge, Mass.: Harvard University Press, 1977), Chaps. 3–5.

12. William N. Denevan, "Development and the Imminent Demise of the Amazon Rain Forest," *Professional Geographer* 25 (May 1973):130–135; Shelton H. Davis, *Victims of the Miracle: Development Against the Indians of Brazil* (Cambridge: Cambridge University Press, 1977).

13. Raymond E. Crist and Charles N. Nissly, *East from the Andes: Pioneer Settlement in the South American Heartland* (Gainesville: University of Florida, 1973).

14. "Os Brasileiros no Paraguai," *Veja*, 24 September 1975, pp. 46–54.

15. Alexander Gerschenkron, *Economic Backwardness in Historical Perspec-*

tive (Cambridge, Mass.: Harvard University Press, 1962), Chap. 1.

16. H. E. Goeller, "The Age of Substitutability: A Scientific Appraisal of Natural Resource Adequacy," in V. Kerry Smith (ed.), *Scarcity and Growth Reconsidered* (Baltimore, Md.: Johns Hopkins University Press, 1979), pp. 143–159; Donald A. Brobst, "Fundamental Concepts for the Analysis of Resource Availability," in Smith, *Scarcity and Growth*, pp. 106–142; Gardner M. Brown, Jr., and Barry Field, "The Adequacy of Measures for Signaling the Scarcity of Natural Resources," in Smith, *Scarcity and Growth*, pp. 218–248.

17. Samuel O. Ruff, "Brazil's Agricultural Export Market," *Foreign Agricultural Trade of the U.S.* (April 1977):30. See also idem, "Brazil May Soon Be the World's No. 2 Agricultural Exporter," *Foreign Agriculture* 15 (October 24, 1977):2–4. United Nations Conference on Trade and Development, *Handbook of International Trade and Development Statistics* (Geneva and New York: United Nations, 1976), Table 4.4.

18. Theodore W. Schultz, "The Increasing Economic Value of Human Time," *American Journal of Agricultural Economics* 54 (December 1972):843–850.

19. Nathaniel Leff, "Export Stagnation and Autarkic Development in Brazil," *Quarterly Journal of Economics* 81 (May 1967):286–301. Cf. Carlos Diaz-Alejandro, *Essays in the Economic History of the Argentine Republic* (New Haven, Conn.: Yale University Press, 1970).

20. Ruff, "Brazil May Soon Be World's No. 2 Agricultural Exporter"; R. L. Beukenkamp, "Brazil: Agricultural Situation, 1974," U.S. Embassy, Brasília, January 20,1975; Leon G. Mears, "Farm Output, Trade Boom Still Continues in Brazil," *Foreign Agriculture* 15 (March 14, 1977):6–7.

21. Stephen Krasner, "Oil is the Exception," *Foreign Policy* 14 (Spring 1974):68–90.

22. P. A. Sanchez and S. W. Buol, "Soils of the Tropics and the World Food Crisis," *Science* 188 (May 9, 1975):598–603.

23. Melville Watkins, "A Staple Theory of Economic Growth," *Canadian Journal of Economics and Political Science* 39 (May 1963):141–158; André Gunder Frank, *Capitalism and Underdevelopment in Latin America* (New York: Monthly Review Press, 1967); George Beckford, *Persistent Poverty: Underdevelopment in Plantation Economies of the Third World* (New York: Oxford University Press, 1972). For a comparison of the two views, see Martin T. Katzman, "São Paulo and its Hinterland," *Stanford Journal of International Studies* 13 (Spring 1978):107–129. For a comparison of their policy implications, see the essays in Albert Fishlow et al., *Rich and Poor Nations in the World Economy*, 1980s Project/Council on Foreign Relations (New York: McGraw-Hill Book Co., 1978).

24. Edward F. Denison and William K. Chung, *How Japan's Economy Grew* (Washington, D.C.: Brookings Institution, 1976), pp. 26–45; Simon Kuznets, *Economic Growth of Nations* (Cambridge, Mass.: Harvard University Press, 1971), Chap. 4; Schultz, "Increasing Economic Value of Human Time."

25. Harold J. Barnett, "Scarcity and Growth Revisited," in Smith, *Scarcity and Growth*, pp. 163–217. The abrupt rise of oil prices in the 1970s has only returned them to the levels of 1950, when Middle Eastern oil began to flow to the West. See

Sam Schurr et al., *Energy in America's Future* (Baltimore, Md.: Johns Hopkins University Press, 1979), pp. 92–95; Goeller, "The Age of Substitutability," pp. 143–159.

26. Benjamin J. Cohen, *The Question of Imperialism: The Political Economy of Dominance and Dependence* (New York: Basic Books, 1973).

27. Business International Corporation, *Operating Successfuly in a Changing Brazil* (New York: Business International Corporation, 1975).

28. Vernon, *Storm Over the Multinationals,* Chapter 3.

29. Spero, *Politics of International Economic Relations,* p. 92.

30. U.S. Dept. of Commerce, *Statistical Abstract of the United States,* "Direct Foreign Investment," various years; *Survey of Current Business,* "International Investment Position," October issues, various years.

31. Herbert Goldhamer, *Foreign Powers in Latin America* (Princeton, N.J.: Princeton University Press, 1972), pp. 40–47, 223–259; Schneider, *Brazil,* p. 147; and Stefan H. Robock, *Brazil: A Study of Development Progress* (Lexington, Mass.:D. C. Heath, 1975), pp. 61–67.

32. William R. Cline, "Brazil's Emerging International Economic Role"; and Wayne A. Selcher, *Brazil's Multilateral Relations: Between First and Third Worlds* (Boulder, Colo.: Westview Press, 1978), Chap. 5.

5

Brazil's Relations with the Northern Tier Countries of South America

Robert D. Bond

Upon assuming office in March 1979, Brazil's new foreign minister, Ramiro Saraiva Guerreiro, stated that the administration of João Baptista Figueiredo (who was inaugurated in 1979 for a six-year term) would give top priority to relations with Latin America.[1] Observers of Brazilian foreign policy greeted this statement with skepticism, pointing out that President Geisel (1974–1979) had made a similar statement in his inaugural address. Historically Brazil has never attached much importance to forging constructive relations with its neighbors on the South American continent. Rather, Brazil has chosen to play a low-profile role in hemispheric affairs, in part to minimize hostility and resentment of Brazil's status as the dominant power on the continent and in part because Brazil's leaders envisioned Brazil as a future major power, not as a regional hegemon. Consequently, most analysts doubted that Latin America would receive any more attention from Brazil than that traditionally accorded it.

However, Brazil's actions toward Latin America in the first fifteen months of the Figueiredo administration have proven that Saraiva Guerreiro's remarks were more than rhetoric. In October 1979, Brazil hosted a two-day official state visit by President Francisco Morales Bermúdez of Peru. One month later, President Figueiredo traveled to Venezuela, the first official visit to Venezuela by a Brazilian head of state in this century. In January 1980, the Brazilian foreign minister signed a memorandum of understanding with the Council of Foreign Ministers of the Andean Pact countries (Bolivia, Colombia, Ecuador, Peru, and Venezuela) to promote closer political, economic, and scientific cooperation. Shortly thereafter, Saraiva Guerreiro visited Mexico to discuss possible bilateral oil and trade agreements. More important, in May 1980 President Figueiredo paid a state visit to Argentina, Brazil's long-standing rival for influence in the Southern Cone. This was the first visit by a Brazilian president to Argentina in more than thirty years, and it resulted in agreements covering nuclear cooperation, joint exploitation of hydroelectric resources, and the creation of a permanent mechanism for political consultation.[2]

This flurry of diplomatic activity is significant and perhaps signals a radical departure in Brazilian foreign policy. It also raises a number of important questions: Why has Brazil sought to expand its political and economic ties with its neighbors? What are Brazil's goals on the continent? What difficulties and obstacles will Brazil confront as it attempts to forge more constructive relations with neighboring countries? How will Brazil's apparent decision to assume a more active role in Latin America affect its overall foreign policy? To answer these and related questions, it is necessary to review the history of Brazil's relations with Latin America, to analyze the reasons for Brazil's shift of policy towards its neighbors, and to speculate about the problems Brazil will encounter as it attempts to play a more influential role in South America. It should be noted that the main focus of this essay is on Brazil's relations with the countries on the north coast of South America and that special attention is devoted to Brazil's efforts to improve relations with oil-rich Venezuela.

Brazil and Its Neighbors

Brazil looms large in any consideration of Latin American international relations. It is the fifth largest country in the world, and occupies more than 40 percent of the South American continent. It has the seventh largest population in the world (one of every three inhabitants of Latin America is Brazilian), and its 1978 gross national product of approximately $165 billion places it tenth in the world. Moreover, Brazil borders on ten other South American nations.

Yet, in spite of its central geopolitical and economic position, Brazil has traditionally remained aloof from hemispheric affairs. As one analyst of Brazilian foreign policy notes:

> Brazil has neither sought to lead Latin America through cooperative means, nor has she attempted to establish hegemony over the region through a strategy based on power politics. Indeed, Brazil's relations with her neighbors have taken a position secondary to pressing domestic issues and to such economically consequential matters as her ties with the United States and other developed nations of the Western World.[3]

Historically, then, what have been the main tenets guiding Brazil's relations with its neighbors?

One dominant theme in Brazil's relations with its neighbors has been the expansion and consolidation of its borders. This essentially security concern has taken two forms: (1) the effective occupation of its distant territories and (2) the maintenance of a balance of power in the Rio de la Plata area.

Brazil's early diplomats have been called "instinctive geopoliticians" for their efforts to populate and integrate previously vacant frontier areas into the national territory.[4] This was the orientation of Brazilian foreign policy in the empire (1822–1889) and in the Old Republic (1889–1930). In the wake of the Wars of Independence, Brazil pursued an expansionist policy, particularly with regard to the Rio de la Plata area. In addition, in the latter half of the nineteenth century Brazil added to its territory at the expense of Venezuela (1859), Bolivia (1867), Paraguay (1872), and Argentina (1895). As a result of Brazil's territorial ambitions, one of the main preoccupations of the Baron of Rio Branco, foreign minister from 1902 to 1912, was the resolution of outstanding border disputes with its Hispanic neighbors. With a few minor exceptions, Rio Branco bequeathed Brazil its present boundaries. He did not, however, put to rest the geopolitical thinking in Brazil that emphasized effective occupation of national territory. After the 1964 revolution, territorial consolidation became a key element in the Brazilian military's national security doctrine, particularly with regard to the development of the Amazon basin.

If pushing Brazil's frontiers into the heartland of South America was one security concern of traditional Brazilian foreign policy, Brazil's rulers also exhibited an intense interest in maintaining a balance of power to the south, where they felt vulnerable to the actions of Argentina. Brazil's concern for a threat from the south caused it to intervene three times in the Rio de la Plata area (1825–1828, 1850–1851, and 1865–1870) to ensure the creation of a buffer zone of neutral states (Uruguay, Paraguay, and Bolivia). Brazil's historical concern for the Rio de la Plata area still strongly influences diplomatic and military thinking. Since 1964, and especially in the 1970s, Brazil vigorously has sought to expand its economic influence in the small nation-states of Paraguay, Uruguay, and Bolivia; it was so successful that the Brazilian government achieved a position of unprecedented influence in the border states, expertly taking advantage of Argentina's political upheavals and economic weaknesses.[5] The extent of Brazil's influence in the region is perhaps best symbolized by its joint venture with Paraguay to build the giant hydroelectric project at Itaipu on the Paraná River.

A second theme that has shaped Brazil's relations with Latin America is its aspiration to achieve the status of a major power by the end of the twentieth century. Brazil's leaders view their country as a serious candidate for major power status, based on an assessment of its size, natural resources, population, level of economic development, and military potential.[6] As a result of this view of Brazil's future *grandeza*, Brazilian foreign policy increasingly has had a global rather than a regional perspective. The Brazilian conception of its potential role in international relations and the relative priority to be accorded to Latin America is well conveyed by Wayne Selcher:

> Brazil's activity is not primarily limited to Latin America, and it has acquired a considerable degree of autonomy in its foreign relations. Although the government regularly concedes top priority to Latin America in its public diplomatic value hierarchy, for Brazil the Western Hemisphere is the smaller of several IGO [Inter-Government Organizations]-relevant arenas in which it operates. Its recent initiatives have occurred outside the hemisphere. Consolidation of primacy among Latin American nations is seen by many of its foreign policy strategists as just a first step toward being taken seriously in global forums.[7]

For Brazilian policymakers, relations with Latin America have been viewed as marginal to Brazil's drive to attain major power status. Economically, Latin America simply does not have the capital, technology, and markets Brazil needs to develop its industrial base. Consequently, with the exception of the southern border states, where geopolitical and economic interests justify an active Brazilian role, the goal of Brazilian diplomacy has been to minimize its involvement in regional affairs. This orientation is reflected, for example, in Brazil's minimal participation in hemispheric organizations such as the Organization of American States (OAS), the Latin American Free Trade Association (LAFTA), and the Latin American Economic System (SELA).

The third theme in Brazil's relations with its neighbors is defensive: Brazil has sought to prevent the formation of an alliance of Spanish American nations hostile to Brazil's interest. In the past, some Spanish American states have expressed fears of a "predatory Brazil intent on spilling over the Andes and through the Amazon Basin to the Pacific Ocean."[8] These suspicions are fueled by Brazil's history of expansionism, its aspiration to achieve major power status, its growing economic influence in the southern border states, and the possibility that it might soon have the economic and military power to act decisively. In fact, Brazil has been very restrained, attempting to allay the suspicions of its neighbors. For example, part of the motivation behind the Brazilian proposal to form the Amazon Pact was precisely to quiet fears of Brazilian encroachment in the border areas. Brazil does not want to be isolated from continental developments, and it wants to maintain its influence over events in neighboring countries that might prove inimical to its interests.

To summarize, traditional Brazilian foreign policy toward Latin America has been guided by security considerations, especially the consolidation of its border areas and the maintenance of a sphere of influence in the southern border states, by an avoidance of entangling involvements with regional affairs so that it can pursue its own path toward economic development and major power status, and by a desire to avoid an alliance of Spanish American nations arrayed against it. In order to illustrate these general themes, it is instructive to examine Brazil's relations with Venezuela, a state that has recently emerged as one of the most dynamic international actors in South America.

Brazil and Venezuela, 1960–1976

During most of the nineteenth and early twentieth centuries relations between Venezuela and Brazil were remote and peaceful. The 1,300-mile boundary between the two countries was established by treaty in 1859, and although the final demarcation of the frontier was not established until the 1970s, there were no major border disputes.[9] The virtual isolation of this border area from the developed, industrialized centers of both countries, as well as the absence of people and of roads on either side of the boundary, contributed to a feeling in Venezuela and Brazil that the Amazon region itself constituted a "natural" frontier, one that did not require defense.[10]

In the early 1960s relations between the two countries worsened considerably. One source of friction was the decision by Brazil (and also by Argentina and Uruguay) to abrogate petroleum sales agreements with Venezuela in favor of importing lower-priced Middle Eastern oil. The Venezuelan government was very unhappy about the intrusion of competition into its oil market on the east coast of South America. More serious was Venezuela's decision to suspend diplomatic relations with Brazil after the 1964 military coup that deposed Brazilian President João Goulart. Under the "Betancourt Doctrine" (1958–1968), Venezuela refused to recognize de facto regimes that came to power by nondemocratic means. It was not until the election of Rafael Caldera in 1969 and the subsequent abandonment of this foreign policy cornerstone of the Acción Democrática party that diplomatic relations between the two countries were restored.

The most serious challenge to collaborative relations between Venezuela and Brazil dates from 1966, the year when Brazil's military leaders turned their attention to the development of the Amazon Basin. The government of General Artur da Costa e Silva attached great importance to the development of Brazil's Amazon frontier, which covers 42 percent of the national territory but accounts for only 5 percent of the population. The Costa e Silva government, heavily influenced by a military security doctrine that linked development (defined as rapid industrialization and national integration under technocratic guidance) to national security and to the legitimacy of the military regime, viewed Amazonian development as important for at least three reasons.[11] First, Brazil's rulers wanted to exploit the supposedly vast agricultural and mineral resources contained in the region. Second, the government hoped that Amazonian development might slow the population movement from the impoverished Northeast to the prosperous industrial centers in the South. Third, the Brazilian armed forces believed it essential to develop and maintain a military security presence in this vast, resource-rich, but unpopulated territory at a time when world resources and land were being depleted.

Accordingly, the Brazilian government embarked on a dramatic and ambitious program to transform the Amazon frontier. A major project was the construction of the costly all-weather, 3,350-mile Transamazon highway, which runs from Recife on the Atlantic Coast to the Peruvian border, and the 900-mile Cuiabá-Santarém link that connects the main highway to the Center-West region of Brazil (the main highway was completed in 1975, the link in 1977). The formation of agricultural colonies and small cities adjacent to the transportation system was also encouraged. To attract much-needed capital to the Amazon frontier, a regional development agency, SUDAM (Superintendência da Amazônia), was created, as well as the Credit Bank for the Amazon. SUDAM and the Credit Bank relied heavily on fiscal incentives to attract investors, granting in some cases a 50 percent reduction in income taxes.[12] Over the years, vast tracts of land were acquired for exploitation on very favorable terms by D. K. Ludwig, the King Ranch, the Georgia Pacific Corporation, U.S. Steel and Bethlehem Steel, and the Volkswagen Corporation.

The Brazilian drive to develop the Amazon frontier proved worrisome to neighboring states because it signified the end of the national buffer zone dividing them. In an important sense, Brazil's Amazonian effort was a logical extension of its national economic development strategy, but it nevertheless raised questions about Brazil's geopolitical objectives. The five surrounding countries were disturbed by the overwhelming role of the Brazilian military in the Amazon development program.[13] And in 1967, the headquarters of the Amazon Command of the Brazilian Army was moved westward from Belém, near the mouth of the Amazon River, to Manaus, thereby extending military influence to the upper Amazon.

Even if the possibility of intervention in their affairs by Brazil could be dismissed as far-fetched, the states surrounding the Amazon could not ignore the fact that Brazil was developing an effective presence in the region. Its development of transportation systems and agricultural communities raised the distinct possibility that Brazil could influence the course of the development of the Amazon regions of neighboring states through economic and cultural attractions across the border. And it was not long before reports began filtering back to La Paz, Lima, Quito, Bogotá, and Caracas that peoples in their sparsely populated Amazon territories, especially Indians, were becoming more fluent in Portuguese than Spanish and that they were being increasingly oriented toward colonies on the Brazilian side of the border.

President Rafael Caldera was particularly concerned about Brazil's development activities along Venezuela's southern border. Venezuela's southern region had long been neglected, and the nation did not possess effective control over the territory. The southern region (defined as the state of Apure, the Cedeño district, and the Amazonas Federal Territory) represents 26.5 percent of the national territory, but has a population estimated at only 60,000 inhabitants, or 0.6 percent of the country's population. Moreover, the Amazonas Federal Territory, which borders on Brazil, has a population of only 21,696 inhabitants, most of whom are concentrated in the north, and 40 percent of whom are Indians. President Caldera decided that steps would have to be taken to integrate this southern region into the nation.

In response to the Brazilian Amazon development thrust, Caldera created the Commission for the Development of the South (CODESUR). This agency was placed under the supervision of the Ministry of Public Works, reflecting the priority that would be given to basic works of infrastructure—roads, air strips, communication facilities, and housing. The basic objectives of the program, labeled "The Conquest of the South," were to establish an effective Venezuelan presence in the region through the extension of social and economic services to the area, the construction of transportation systems, and the development of industrial, mining, forest, and agricultural activities. The Venezuelan armed forces were actively involved in the "conquest," and military units participated in the construction of roads, airbases, and other infrastructure development projects. However, no military airbase was created in the region, and most of the security functions for the region were assigned to the Venezuelan National Guard.

In addition to CODESUR, President Caldera directed his diplomatic efforts at strengthening the ties among the Spanish-speaking countries that border Brazil. On a continental tour in early February 1973, Caldera visited six Latin American countries, and it seemed to some the outline of an anti-Brazilian alliance was in the making. A subsequent meeting between Presidents Caldera and Emilio Garrastazu Médici at the border town of Santa Elena de Uairén outwardly smoothed over the disagreements between Venezuela and Brazil, but the meeting was formal and reserved, and Caldera and his foreign minister reportedly returned to Caracas with heightened misgivings about Brazilian intentions.[14]

In December 1973, the Acción Democrática party regained the presidency with the election of Carlos Andrés Pérez. However, the election of Pérez did not signal a major change in Venezuelan-Brazilian relations; foreign policymakers in both countries simply did not attach much priority to improving bilateral relations. President Pérez, for example, was much more interested in carving out a role for himself as a Third World leader, in improving Venezuela's relations with the Andean Pact countries, and in expanding Venezuela's influence in the Caribbean. The Pérez administration did make two gestures toward Brazil—the dismantling of the Copei-inspired CODESUR and a visit by the foreign minister, Ramón Escovar Salóm, to Brazil—but until 1976 Brazil did not figure in Venezuelan foreign policy thinking.[15] It was not until Brazil's overtures regarding the Amazon Pact in late 1976 that relations between the two countries markedly improved.

The Amazon Pact:
A Departure in Brazilian Foreign Policy

Relations between Brazil and Venezuela from 1964 to 1976 were essentially similar to those between Brazil and other neighboring nations. Following the military coup of April 1964, Brazil's foreign policy was increasingly viewed by its neighbors as based on the maintenance of "ideological frontiers," the enhancement of Brazil's geopolitical position in the world, and the attainment of rapid economic development through increased relations with industrialized nations. Brazil's ambitious plans to develop its Amazon territory through reliance on the military and on massive foreign investment only heightened concerns about the ultimate intentions of Brazil's military government.

From the viewpoint of Latin American nations, Brazil was seen as placing little importance on fostering constructive relations with its neighbors. Brazil's closest relations were with other military governments, and the only favorable foreign policy initiatives taken by Brazil were toward the small border states. For example, Brazilian investment in Bolivia increased substantially in the late 1960s, and it is widely believed (though this is unverified) that the Brazilian government acted to support General Banzer in his successful effort to overthrow the liberal administration of President Torres in 1971. In addition, in the early 1970s, Brazilians began moving in large numbers to occupy Paraguayan border lands, and certain parts of Paraguay became effectively integrated with the Brazilian economy.

By the mid-1970s, Brazil's foreign policy began to change direction, responding to changes in the international environment and in domestic political and economic conditions. Brazilian foreign policy has always been highly pragmatic, subject to modification if the nation's economic needs require it. By 1976 it was clear that Brazil's energy requirement, its balance of payments difficulties, and its need to expand and diversify its export markets dictated a reassessment of Brazilian foreign policy.

Brazil's dependence on imported oil and the resultant balance of payments problem constitutes the major challenge to Brazil's development aspirations. Brazil is heavily dependent on oil imports from the Middle East; at present, it receives about 80 percent of its total imports of 800,000 barrels per day from Iran, Iraq, and Saudi Arabia.[16] Moreover, the value of Brazilian oil imports increased from $859 million annually from 1970–1974, to $4.1 billion in 1978, to $7 billion in 1979. In 1980, almost half of Brazil's total export earnings will go toward paying for its oil imports.[17]

Brazil has always utilized its external sector to promote internal economic growth, and by 1976 there were a number of signs that Brazilian foreign policy was changing in response to Brazil's energy vulnerability and its economic difficulties. For example, Brazil changed dramatically its Middle East policy to a pro-Arab stance, and it rushed to recognize the MPLA government in Angola in hopes of gaining more oil and of expanding commercial ties.[18] More slowly, Brazil began to reassess its attitude toward its neighbors.

In November 1976, President Geisel of Brazil proposed to the leaders of Bolivia, Colombia, Ecuador, Guyana, Peru, Surinam, and Venezuela the creation of a mechanism to coordinate the joint development of the Amazon River basin.[19] After a year of diplomatic efforts, the Brazilian Foreign Ministry finally overcame the doubts of its Amazon neighbors and negotiations opened to create the Amazon Pact. In early 1978, the eight countries bordering on the Amazon basin signed a treaty providing for the free navigation of the rivers of the Amazon region; the right of each nation to develop the resources of its Amazon territory, subject only to the restriction that it cause no significant harm to other countries; the promotion of joint research and exchange of information on the flora

and fauna of the Amazon; the rational utilization of the region's water
resources; the adoption of measures to improve health conditions in the
region; the promotion of scientific and technological research; the
development of the transportation and communications infrastructure in
the region; the implementation of joint measures to further regional
economic complementation; and the promotion of tourism to the
Amazon. To implement this agreement, the foreign ministers of each
country are to meet every two years to discuss common courses of action, and each country has created a permanent national commission to
carry out the measures agreed to by the foreign ministers.

Initially, the proposal by Brazil to create the Amazon Pact was not
viewed by most analysts as representing a new departure in Brazilian
foreign policy. Writing in late 1979, Celso Lafer made this assessment of
the pact:

> A successful Brazilian response to the challenges that confront Latin
> America requires more creativity and less reliance on the current tradi-
> tional concept of sovereignty and bilateral relations. In this vein, I do not
> believe that the recently negotiated Amazon Pact represents a significant
> innovation. On the contrary, the agreement falls within the traditional
> style in that it aims at creating a favorable multilateral climate in order to
> facilitate future bilateral relations. It seeks to create an image of construc-
> tive cooperation in the Amazon Basin in order to counterbalance the dif-
> ficulties with Argentina in the Itaipu controversy.[20]

In addition, it was noted that the Amazon Pact was the idea of the
Brazilian Foreign Ministry rather than of the National Security Council
and that the proposal reflected a growing awareness in Brazil of the difficulties and costs involved in exploiting the agricultural, mineral, and
forest resources of the Amazon.

Unquestionably, one of the purposes the Amazon Pact may serve is to
improve Brazil's bilateral ties with its neighbors. But its true significance
must be understood in the broader context of Brazil's changing overall
foreign policy. Brazilian foreign policymakers no longer consider that
the nation's long-term objectives are clearly linked with those of the
developed nations, and they no longer believe that Brazil can attain major power status by the end of the century. And there is an increasing
awareness on the part of the Brazilian government that economic advantages might accrue from closer ties with Latin America. From 1976 to
1979, Brazil increased the percentage of its total exports destined to
LAFTA countries from 12.0 to 15.0 percent and to the Andean Group from
4.2 to 6.2 percent.[21] Brazil also wants to diversify its sources of imported
oil and is looking to its neighbors. In 1980 Venezuela was supplying

Brazil with 50,000 barrels per day (BPD), up from 10,000 in 1977, and Mexico began supplying 20,000 BPD in 1980.

Brazil's initiative in forming the Amazon Pact was the opening salvo in a campaign to transform its relations with Latin America. It was a symbolically important gesture, helping to remove long-standing fears of Brazilian expansionism. Upon assuming office in March 1979, President Figueiredo picked up the initiative of his predecessor, President Geisel, and quickly moved to expand relations with Mexico, Venezuela, Peru, and Argentina. His efforts culminated in the historic signing of ten agreements during his state visit to Argentina, May 14–17, 1980, to hasten the integrated development of the Rio de la Plata area. Brazil's growing responsiveness to increasing ties with Latin America is the result of economic difficulties, a drive to expand export markets, an effort to diversify sources of oil supply, and a growing awareness that Brazil's development problems were aligning it more closely with other Third World nations. By improving relations with its neighbors, Brazil is seeking to enhance its bargaining power vis-à-vis the rest of the world.

Brazil and Latin America: Challenges and Dilemmas

In recent years, it has been fashionable to suggest that Brazil is on the verge of becoming a "major" power and that this "fact" explains Brazil's foreign policy behavior. Policymakers and academics in Brazil and the United States pointed to the outward signs of Brazil's power (gross national product, population, geographic size and location, natural resources) and argued that it was simply a matter of time until Brazil achieved secondary power status in the international hierarchy and a more independent world role.[22] In the interim, Brazil would pursue a pragmatic foreign policy consistent with its position as a "middle power," refusing to align itself automatically with either the Third World or the Western Community.

In the 1970s Brazil was undeniably more active internationally, and growing attention was being paid to its role on the world scene. However, analysts who suggested that Brazil's drive to attain a world role commensurate with its economic potential explained its foreign policy behavior tended to make three unwarranted assumptions about Brazil's international position. First, and perhaps foremost, those who propounded the "Brazil-as-a-major-power" thesis assumed that they were utilizing a well-defined concept. No term in social science is more ill-defined than power, and those who utilized it with regard to Brazil did not even make an effort to give it an empirical referent. Rather, the tendency was to call forth the usual litany of statistics about Brazil's size, population, economic potential, etc., and then to assume that this proved Brazil was an "upwardly mobile power," an "emerging power," a "major power," a "new influential," or a "middle power." What was overlooked was that these terms were being applied to a very diverse set of countries—Saudi Arabia, Iran, India, Nigeria, Venezuela, Mexico, South Korea, etc.—with very diverse economic, military, and political potentialities. In fact, the emperor was naked; the concept of a "new influential" or a "major power" had no empirical meaning, but was instead simply a label employed to differentiate a certain group of more advanced developing countries from their poorer brethren.

The second misconception in the "Brazil-as-a-major-power" school of thought was the confusion of actual and potential power. Analysts simply confused size with power and significantly overestimated Brazil's potential.[23] Economically, Brazil clearly has some clout, but even by the year 2000 Brazil will probably be no more powerful than present-day Italy or Spain. Militarily, Brazil has a very limited capacity, and it could not even sustain a prolonged war with Argentina. Politically, Brazil has been very isolated, not even enjoying significant alliances with its neighbors. In summary, in 1980, Brazil is important internationally in certain economic arenas, but it is by no means a major power (however defined), and it is at least two decades away from achieving this position.

The third difficulty with analyses of Brazilian foreign policy was a tendency to make straight-line projections from the present to the future, assuming implicitly that the favorable political and economic trends of the mid-1970s would continue. This faith in the Brazilian economic miracle, which produced rates of growth in excess of 10 percent per year from 1967 to 1974, seemed justified by Brazil's seemingly easy adjustment to the shock of petroleum price increases after 1973. The Brazilian economy continued to grow at an average rate of more than 6 percent in the 1974–1979 period. However, the decision of the Brazilian government to continue economic growth through reliance on massive foreign borrowing only postponed the tax that had to be paid to the OPEC countries.

The 1973 oil-price increases resulted in a series of problems for Brazil. One is the need for Brazil to maintain its access to the international economy. The magnitude of Brazil's foreign debt, which now exceeds $55 billion, requires it to sustain its access to international foreign markets and to promote rapid export growth. It is estimated that in 1980, service requirements of the debt corresponded to 70 percent of export earnings and that oil imports required another 50 percent. According to Albert Fishlow, "No realistic growth model [for Brazil] can fail to contemplate increasing exports more rapidly than domestic product, and even so, adding significantly to a debt that by the mid-1980s should double."[24] And it should be noted that Brazil must promote rapid export growth and maintain access to external finance at a time of rising international protectionism.

A second problem dominating foreign policy considerations for the 1980s is energy. Originally this problem was confronted as a question of balance of payments constraints. But following the revolution in Iran and additional unpredictable oil price increases, it is now being considered separately as a question of how to reduce Brazil's vulnerability through conservation, the development of hydroelectric resources, the nuclear program, the gasohol experiment, and the search for more diverse and secure suppliers of petroleum. Substituting other sources for oil will be costly, and Brazil will have to bear this burden in the 1980s.

As the 1980s begin, it seems apparent that Brazilian foreign policymakers have come to realize these new economic realities. The historic Brazilian aspiration to assume its rightful place alongside other world powers is being soft-pedaled in official statements, and Brazil is now tending to emphasize its identification with the Third World. Brazil seems reconciled to a status as an advanced developing country that has a long way to go before it is ready to join the Organisation for Economic Co-operation and Development (OECD) countries. Its economic development problems over the next two decades will result in a foreign policy that is more aligned with the "South" than the "North." In addition, Brazilian foreign policymakers now stress friendly relations with Latin America. No longer does Brazil stand aloof from regional organizations, pursuing its interests independently of other Latin American countries.

As Brazil seeks to extend its influence in Latin America, it will confront a number of challenges. Clearly, the Brazilian decisions to forego statements about major power aspirations and to cooperate in regional forums will assuage fears of Brazilian expansionism. Nevertheless, a number of difficulties remain.

One challenge Brazil will face is the modification of its characteristic diplomatic style. In general, Brazilian policymakers have traditionally preferred bilateral to multilateral diplomacy. This aspect of Brazilian diplomacy is well conveyed by Wayne Selcher:

> Multilateral cooperation is regarded as tenuous and undependable at best; the more traditional in the foreign policy establishment go so far as to see presence in Inter-Governmental Organizations (IGOs) almost as a necessary evil, in which Brazil must be ready to assume a defensive or reactive posture against countercurrents. Multilateral foreign policy is therefore

carried out primarily as support for the main modality, bilateral
relations.[25]

This behavior has been particularly marked in Brazil's participation in
regional economic organizations, where it has been very reluctant to
sacrifice national interests on the altar of Latin American solidarity and
regional economic growth. For example, in the formation in 1975 of the
Latin American Economic System, which was vigorously promoted by
Mexico and Venezuela, the Brazilian government expressed its ritual support for the new organization but in practice worked to keep it loosely
structured. Indeed, the basic thrust of Brazilian diplomacy in Latin
American regional organizations has been to utilize multilateral relations
to offset fears of Brazilian hegemony, while reserving "substantive" matters for bilateral dealings.

The Brazilian preference for a bilateral diplomatic style is deeply entrenched in the foreign policy establishment, and old habits will probably die hard. But if Brazil is to forge constructive and mutually
beneficial relations with other Latin American nations, it will have to
break out of this pattern of foreign policy behavior. Historically, the
leaders of Spanish American nations have been strong advocates of Latin
American integration, and they have preferred to deal with the United
States collectively. Moreover, two of the nations Brazil most wants to
cultivate—Mexico and Venezuela—have foreign policy styles that attach
great importance to multilateral negotiations, to collective Latin
American and Third World action, and to Latin American integration. In
order to expand relations with Latin America, Brazilian diplomats will
have to emphasize multilateral diplomacy much more than in the past,
making sure that the Spanish American states do not interpret Brazil's initiatives toward cooperation as a ruse to achieve its own narrower
economic advantages.

A second challenge to Brazil is more substantive: Brazil's commitment
to a good neighbor policy may require it to take stronger positions on
economic issues of importance to Latin American countries than it has in
the past. The economic model Brazil pursued after 1964 had as one of its
central features a heavy reliance upon the international economy, as a
source of capital goods imports, a market for Brazil's exports, and a
source of capital to supplement domestic savings. As a result of its
economic successes and its high degree of integration into the international economy, Brazil tended to take a more moderate position than
most less developed countries on basic international economic questions.
For example, Brazil was less insistent on an internationally negotiated
code of conduct for multinational corporations, it was concerned that

massive debt relief for LDCs would threaten international financial stability, and it was more willing to use the General Agreement on Tariffs and Trade (GATT) to resolve trade disputes (most LDCs prefer UNCTAD, the United Nations Conference on Trade and Development).[26] In general, Brazil recognized that the international economy worked against the interests of developing countries, but its greater stake in world economic stability caused it to play a low-profile role in international discussions of a new economic order.

There are increasing signs that 1981 may witness a fresh round of negotiations over the creation of a "new international economic order." In early 1980, the Brandt Commission released its prestigious report calling for concessions from industrialized nations to spur development in LDCs, and in August 1980 the United Nations held a conference to discuss Third World demands for a restructuring of the world economy. In addition, rumors were plentiful that the Mexican government was making plans to sponsor a summit conference (modeled on the Paris "North-South" talks of 1976) to discuss the findings and recommendations of the Brandt Commission. Clearly, Brazil would be invited as a representative from Latin America, as would Venezuela and perhaps Argentina and Peru. The Brazilian government would come under pressure to support the entire range of LDC demands (commodity agreements, debt relief, a code of conduct for multinational corporations, technology transfer, greater access to the markets of industrialized countries) even though some of them might conflict with Brazil's economic interests. Brazil is certainly as vulnerable today to fluctuations in the international economy as it has been at any time in the past two decades, and its leaders would probably prefer to avoid negotiations that might endanger Brazilian access to markets in industrialized countries, to foreign investment, and to international financial markets. But just as clearly, Mexico and Venezuela would undoubtedly expect Brazil to support Third World demands more firmly, as both these nations have done consistently in the past.

A third major challenge to Brazilian–Spanish American relations concerns the efforts of the Figueiredo government to liberalize Brazil's political system while it tries to cope with a serious economic crisis. Antonio Delfim Netto, Brazil's "super minister" for the economy, is confronting an inflation rate that may exceed 80 percent in 1980 and a current-account deficit that may exceed $12 billion. At the same time, long pent-up popular demands for higher wages and a more equitable distribution of the benefits of economic growth are being expressed. The workers' strike over wages in São Paulo demonstrated the challenges that demands for income distribution can pose to the fragile political consensus to move toward liberalizing the political system. As Albert Fishlow and others have emphasized, "Disappointing economic performance and political liberalization are uneasy partners. Despite the official posture that the economy, if necessary, will be sacrificed to the cause of political participation, one must be skeptical. A reaction and reversal is more likely."[27] In many respects, Brazil's attempt at political liberalization is the test case of redemocratization in Latin America, and its experiment is being closely watched by other countries in the hemisphere.

The abandonment of political liberalization by the Figueiredo administration would have important consequences for its new policy toward Latin America. It is unclear whether a return to authoritarian government would significantly alter Brazil's foreign policy consensus, but it seems at least plausible to speculate on a resurgence of geopolitical thinking and of a renewed drive to achieve *grandeza*. But more importantly, a turn by Brazil to more authoritarian political measures would seriously undermine its efforts to build constructive relations with the nations of the Andean Group and of the Amazon Pact. In particular, the Andean countries have taken strong positions in support of democratic governments, as evidenced by their actions with respect to the Bolivian military coups of 1979 and 1980. During the Figueiredo state visit to Venezuela, President Herrera Campins went out of his way to stress Venezuela's pleasure with Brazil's strides toward democracy, and relations would surely cool if governmental repression increased. On the other hand, the reactions of the Southern Cone countries would be distinctly favorable to an authoritarian political solution to Brazil's economic crisis. A retreat from political liberalization by Brazil in the face of economic deterioration would tend to support the advocates of harsh political and economic medicine in Argentina and Chile. What impact this would have on relations among the authoritarian regimes in the Southern Cone is difficult to foresee, but the possibility of closer relations among them and a corresponding deterioration of relations with the northern tier countries of South America is a plausible prospect.

Conclusion

The prospects for mutually constructive relations between Brazil and Spanish America have been considerably enhanced by Brazil's new policy initiatives. In particular, the creation of the Amazon Pact in 1978 and the agreements between Brazil and Argentina of May 1980 have reduced historic fears of Brazilian expansionism on the continent. Whether Brazil will be able to follow up these initiatives with expanded commercial and political relations with Latin America will depend on its ability to alter its traditional diplomatic style, to make concessions on international economic issues, and to continue its progress toward a more open political system. The United States, Latin America, and the Third World are all anxious spectators in this drama.

Notes

1. Embassy of Brazil, Washington, D.C., March 9, 1979.

2. *Latin American Regional Reports: Southern Cone*, May 23, 1980. Newsletter published in London by Latin American Newsletters, LTD.

3. William Perry, *Contemporary Brazilian Foreign Policy: The International Strategy of an Emerging Power*, Foreign Policy Paper, Vol. 2, No. 6. (Beverly Hills, Calif.: Sage Publications, 1976), p. 36.

4. Brady Tyson, "Brazil," in Harold Davis and Larman Wilson (eds.), *Latin American Foreign Policies* (Baltimore, Md.: Johns Hopkins University Press, 1975), p. 226.

5. Riordan Roett, "Brazil Ascendant: International Relations and Geopolitics in the Late 20th Century," *Journal of International Affairs*, Vol. 29, No. 2, 1975, p. 150.

6. Ronald M. Schneider, *Brazil: Foreign Policy of a Future World Power* (Boulder, Colo.: Westview Press, 1976), pp. 32–43.

7. Wayne A. Selcher, *Brazil's Multilateral Relations: Between First and Third Worlds* (Boulder, Colo.: Westview Press, 1978), p. 245.

8. Roett, "Brazil Ascendant," p. 139.

9. The Venezuelan-Brazilian border is the best defined of all of Venezuela's borders. Venezuela has active boundary disputes with Colombia, Trinidad and Tobago, and Guyana.

10. See Richard E. Dibble, "Population and the Protection of the Frontiers: The Case of Venezuela," unpublished paper, February 1977.

11. See David J. Meyers, "Frontier Settlement in the Amazon: International Provocation or National Development," unpublished paper, Pennsylvania State University, February 1978; and Wayne Selcher, "The National Security Doctrine and the Policies of the Brazilian Government," *Parameters*, Vol. 7, No. 1, 1977.

12. See John C. Jahoda and Donna L. O'Hearn, "The Reluctant Amazon Basin," *Environment*, Vol. 17, No. 7, October 1975, pp. 16–30.

13. Selcher, "National Security Doctrine," pp. 18–19.

14. See John Martz, "Venezuelan Foreign Policy Toward Latin America," in Robert Bond, *Contemporary Venezuela and Its Role in International Affairs*, A Council on Foreign Relations Book (New York: New York University Press, 1977), pp. 162–163.

15. See the interview with Ramón Escovar Salóm, "Venezuela ofrece amistad al gigantesco vecino, Brasil," *Resumen*, January 23, 1977, pp. 46–49.

16. The following breakdown of Brazil's oil imports in 1976 illustrates its vulnerability:

Brazil: Sources of Crude Petroleum Imports, 1976
(millions of dollars, C.I.F.; percentages in parentheses)

Source	Value in Dollars	Percentage
Persian Gulf:		(54.7)
Saudi Arabia	1,134	(29.9)
Kuwait	470	(12.4)
United Arab Emirates	100	(2.6)
Iran	370	(9.8)
Africa:		(10.4)
Algeria	63	(1.7)
Gabon	100	(2.6)
Libya	152	(4.0)
Nigeria	81	(2.1)
South America:		(2.4)
Peru	35	(.9)
Venezuela	57	(1.5)
Other:		(32.2)
Egypt	11	(.3)
USSR	13	(.3)
Iraq	1,197	(31.6)

Source: Brazil, Ministério da Fazenda, 1976.

17. *Latin America Weekly Report*, November 30, 1979, estimates that Brazil's 1980 oil import bill will be $10–12.5 billion.
18. Thomas Skidmore, "Brazil's Changing Role in the International System: Implications for U.S. Policy," in Riordan Roett (ed.), *Brazil in the Seventies* (Washington D.C.: American Enterprise Institute, 1976), pp. 22–23.
19. See Robert D. Bond, "Venezuela, Brazil, and the Amazon Basin," *Orbis*, Vol. 2, No. 3, Fall 1978, pp. 635–650.
20. Celso Lafer, "Brazilian Foreign Policy, Retrospect and Prospects," unpublished paper, October 1979.
21. *Latin America Regional Report*, January 14, 1980. Published in London by Latin American Newsletters, LTD.
22. This theme is reflected in the titles of the books and articles by Roett, Perry, and Schneider previously cited. Even as careful an analyst of Brazil as Ronald Schneider began his 1976 book, *Brazil: Foreign Policy of a Future World Power*, with this statement:

Brazil, one of the most upwardly mobile actors in the current international political system, is moving from a policy of engagement toward one of expansion in international affairs. In terms of foreign policy capacity, it is an upper-middle power with the potential to move into the ranks of the five great powers that presently occupy a place in the international stratification system below that of the two superpowers, the United States and the USSR. Brazil's continental expanse (it is fifth in the world in area), its population of 113 million (it has overtaken Japan for sixth place among the nations of this globe), its rapidly growing economy (its GNP recently surpassed India's for tenth place), and its expanding foreign trade all underscore its potential for achieving major power status within a relatively short period.

23. See commentary on this theme in Chapter 2.

24. Dionísio Diaz Carneiro, Albert Fishlow, and Pedro Malan, "Issues in Brazil's Economic Development," background paper prepared for the May 20–21, 1980, Conference on Brazil's Future International Role, cosponsored by the Council on Foreign Relations and the Center of Brazilian Studies, p. 12.

25. Selcher, *Brazil's Multilateral Relations*, p. 280.

26. Ibid., Chapters 2 and 9.

27. Diaz Carneiro, Fishlow, and Malan, "Issues in Brazil's Economic Development," p. 17.

6

Brazil and the Southern Cone

Carlos J. Moneta and Rolf Wichmann

The aim of this chapter is to present the main perception the Southern Cone countries of South America have of the present and future role of Brazil in the subregion. Indeed, the image that the decision makers in Argentina, Bolivia, Chile, Paraguay, Peru, and Uruguay have of Brazilian designs will affect the tone, mood, and postures of their foreign policies. In all cases, the ideological setting and the type of regime in power will exert influence on the general strategy and particular policies to be shaped. Nevertheless, there always exists the risk of overemphasizing the ideological aspects, reducing the importance of concrete economic and geopolitical factors that are likely to endure in spite of political changes. Therefore an attempt will be made to take both into account in the analysis of the relations between this group of countries and Brazil.

Brazil and the Southern Cone Countries in the 1970s

The development of Brazil's relations with the Southern Cone countries must be analyzed within the context of the opening of the Latin American economies and the emergence of new models of insertion into the world economy. During the last decades important changes have taken place in Latin America. The modernization process, with its emphasis on a style of development copied from the economic patterns and life styles of the Western industrialized countries, brought benefits and problems that were unevenly distributed among countries and within them. The new strategies of development that acquired importance by the middle of the 1960s were based on a model that opens the economy to external forces, leading to the transnationalization of the internal market. The internationalization of capital has been followed by the internationalization of the processes of production.[1] This has resulted in a redefinition of the world division of labor, allowing for the transfer of sectors of industrial production to the developing countries. Those that offer convenient conditions (e.g., labor force, raw materials), such as Brazil, were able to profit from this, obtaining significant growth and becoming exporters of certain manufactured products.

However, these new models of insertion into the world economy, with their emphasis on the external sector (exports and imports, finance, technology, heavy participation of transnational corporations) and with a miniaturized internal market focused on sophisticated goods for the high-income sectors of the population, have deeply affected the socioeconomic and political structure of these countries as well as those economic needs that relate to foreign policy. The economic strategies designed to attract foreign capital and facilitate penetration of a domestic economy reoriented toward external markets required—among other things—lower costs and a passive labor force. The state imposed these policies under authoritarian regimes most often dominated by the military. This is the trend prevailing—with important structural economic differences in the minor countries—throughout the Southern Cone, with military-technocratic regimes in Argentina, Brazil, Chile, Peru, and Uruguay and a type of traditional autocracy in Paraguay. In 1979–1980 a shaky democratic regime emerged briefly in Bolivia, and Peru returned to an uncertain democratic future in the middle of 1980.

This process has had two important consequences: (1) A modified structure of relations emerged between the countries of the region, resulting in new political-economic schemes that involve both cooperation and conflict (Rio de la Plata Basin Treaty, Amazon Pact), diversification of markets reaching beyond the region, and new needs and capabilities for the major countries, which in practice meant a different stratification in the international relations of the Southern Cone; and (2) given the political-economic features of the regimes in power and the dynamic nature of the internal, intraregional, and international processes involved, it will be necessary to examine certain scenarios that will also take into account the possibility of regime changes in these countries.

The states of the Southern Cone display different levels of national viability as relatively autonomous entities, as well as great heterogeneity in the degree of power and influence that they are able to exert. This situation arises from their historical patterns of development, inequalities of resources, and differing degrees of efficiency in converting disparate demands into a coherent program of action. If we examine the Southern Cone from the mid-1960s to the present day, it is possible to identify some of the major changes that have taken place in the distribution of power and influence. Asymmetrical growth has meant, among other things, a realignment of economic interests and the emergence of new needs, coupled with increasing inequalities in the total capability of the major countries—Argentina and Brazil—to project themselves into the subregion in order to satisfy their political, economic, and security goals. One of the consequences of this has been that all the countries of the subregion have become more important for Brazil as markets for its manufactures and technology and as suppliers of raw materials.

As a result of its important economic interests in Bolivia, Paraguay, and Uruguay, such as trade, direct investment, joint projects, aid, and transport and communications, Brazil has succeeded in altering the balance of power with Argentina, attracting these countries to its area of influence. Political instability in Argentina, together with irregular growth, frequent changes in government policy, and the Beagle Canal dispute with Chile greatly facilitated Brazilian ascendancy during this period. Furthermore, Brazilian economic and political relations with Chile were consolidated after the overthrow of Allende in 1973. The advances made by Brazil in the exploitation of its Amazonian territories and the construction of a geopolitically planned system of highways to connect its eastern and western borders began to remove geographical barriers to Peru. Brazil's interest in the development of Peruvian oil fields and other resources and the political changes that occurred in Peru after the fall of Velasco and the rise to power of Morales Bermúdez in 1975 began to dismantle some of the existing political obstacles to closer relations between Brazil and Peru, bringing the two a step closer after a period of formally correct but otherwise distant relations.

Simultaneously, the asymmetrical relations of Brazil and Argentina with Bolivia, Paraguay, and Uruguay raised the specter of an increased dependency of the latter countries on the former, but also the possibility of a better bargaining position and an inch more of maneuvering space vis-à-vis the major regional powers, especially in regard to the exploitation of critical resources. Examples of this Argentinian-Brazilian competition and how it has increased the bargaining power of smaller regional states are Paraguay's negotiations with both Argentina and Brazil over water projects in the Rio de la Plata basin, and Bolivia's manipulation of both Argentina and Brazil in their desire to gain access to Bolivian energy and iron resources in order to seek more benefits for itself.

Besides the economic links that have developed to reinforce the previous influence of Brazil in the Southern Cone, restraining that of Argentina, the political-economic models of these two nations have affected the types of government that have emerged in Chile, Uruguay and, to an extent, in Bolivia. The military regimes that took power in the early 1970s were influenced by the Brazilian model established in 1964.

These governments also paid close attention to the military regime that overthrew President Isabel Perón in Argentina in 1976, and not only for security reasons (they looked to the Argentinian government as a model for the elaboration of a national security doctrine) or because of overall anti-Marxist ideology. These models claimed that they could—and the Brazilian one did—achieve the kind of economic growth that from the point of view of the internal power groups could be considered successful. In spite of significant differences in the degree and orientation of state participation, all these models share the basic features of opening up their economies to the process of transnationalization.

All the states of the Southern Cone must therefore ponder the future of the Brazilian model in all its likely trajectories, the limits and possibilities presented by a model of "pragmatic nationalism"—a nationalism of ends and not of means—and the future role of Brazil in subregional and regional affairs. But most important, the impact of Brazil's evolution on each one of these countries and the policies that must be followed to contain, appease, or cooperate with Brazil are among the main concerns of the military leaders, politicians, and dominant economic groups in Asunción, Buenos Aires, La Paz, Lima, Montevideo, and Santiago.

Brazil in the 1980s and Beyond: Potential Scenarios

Without needlessly speculating on the more probable outcomes of the present political process in Brazil, it is nevertheless necessary at least to consider them. This is because these outcomes will determine the predominance or hegemony of one or the other of the major political factions in the country, which will then establish the goals on which future foreign policy will be formulated.

The first scenario is a form of classical liberal democracy. It presupposes that the present political liberalization will continue and will be brought rapidly to fruition with the election of a democratic multiparty civilian regime. This would result in a loss of strength and relevance of the aggressive aspects of Brazilian geopolitical strategy and the mystique of anticommunism. Brazilian economic policy, however, would retain most of its previous drive and continental expansion would continue. Multinationalization of Brazilian state enterprises, like Petrobrás, would continue and would be likely to lead to an expansion of their operations throughout Latin America, especially in the export of financial and technological services.

A second scenario is a populist-democratic outcome. This scenario implies changes in economic policy that would reinforce Brazilian capital against transnational corporations and supply a wider internal market.

Exports would be likely to lose part of their present importance as import-substitution strategy acquired new momentum. However, as in the previous case, the need to maintain an input of capital goods and the pressure of the external debt and the continued need to pay for high oil imports would require a certain level of exports. Therefore, the Latin American market would retain its importance, especially in light of possible restraints on Brazilian exports in extraregional markets, such as the protectionist trend in developed countries. Attempts at Latin American integration might receive a better reception in Brazil, but the present trends of bilateralism and sectoral approaches are likely to continue, as they correspond better to Brazilian interests.

A military-technocratic scenario would mean a retreat from the present gradual opening towards democratization. The military regime would remain in control, formally or informally, retaining both its old geopolitical vision and an aggressive policy of economic expansion. The economic model would continue as before, reinforcing the effects of the geopolitical model with which it interacts. The result would be a reaffirmation of the "subimperialist" role (although a diversified one, since "special relationships" are evolving also with Japan and Western Europe), leading toward a major Brazilian economic penetration, either partial or total, of the economies of the neighboring states, especially Bolivia, Paraguay, and Uruguay.

The last scenario, that of progressive groups forming the government, need not be discussed. It is most unlikely in the foreseeable future for a variety of factors, such as the present structure of the political and economic system in Brazil, the alignment of political forces, and the strength of the state and the external forces that would oppose such a development.

In all these scenarios, it is possible to perceive that economic factors impose limits on political options. Brazil's interests will require the maintenance of significant economic relations with neighboring countries. The difficulty of changing the trend of the 1970s—as well as the political opportunity offered by such a change—rests on the political nature of these relations. Brazil requires the contribution of Latin America, given the present international stratification, either to become a great power (as a gradual upward climb will require Brazil to first obtain—and get support from—the status of predominant regional actor) or to become a leader of the developing nations' drive for a change in the present international economic order. Brazil's "middle class" status in the society of nations has pushed the military regime to adopt an ambiguous policy, showing its "Third World" or "emerging power" features when this was most suitable for the audience and the goals pursued.[2]

Future regimes may be able to inject a new meaning into these economic restraints in accordance with their sets of values. If "autonomy" prevails, then a more extended and cooperative policy could be expected in Brazil's relations with Argentina and/or the middle and minor states of the Southern Cone. If the political outcome in Brazil results in the continuation of a rational, self-conscious dependent path, relations with Argentina would require at best a sort of selective sectoral alliance that would contain inequalities and the continuation of the previous trend of competition, although in a more sophisticated manner, to achieve "special relationships" with the United States and other industrialized powers. This would mean the loss of a perhaps unique opportunity to achieve more individual as well as collective Latin American autonomy and bargaining power vis-à-vis the United States and other developed countries. With regard to the other states of the Southern Cone, however, this would not offer too much help in changing the present patterns.

The problems outlined here and their possible consequences are the basic factors that have to be taken into consideration by the governments and the dominant groups in the Southern Cone countries. Their perceptions of the future Brazilian role will be tied to a subjective evaluation of the concrete benefits or losses that will be incurred under specific conditions by the political and economic actors involved. Therefore, the social legitimization or rejection of the Brazilian actions toward these countries by their domestic elites and public opinion will depend to a great extent on the economic and political results that are achieved.

Argentinian Perceptions of Brazil

Perceptions of Brazilian behavior in Argentina are multifaceted and complex, blending both positive and negative aspects. They reflect more than a hundred and fifty years of conflict, competition, and mutual distrust between the two countries and have created in Argentina a national consciousness regarding the "Brazilian problem." But they are also shaped by the ideological visions of the dominant groups, alliances, and competing factions; more often than not there are important differences among these visions. These views represent divergent "nationalist" perceptions of Argentina, the outside world, and the strategies that must be followed to reach certain goals (whose value content changes from faction to faction). To this must be added a national situation (geographical location, population, resources, etc.) that becomes simultaneously the environment to be changed and a restraining element.

There are several interpretations of the foreign policy perspectives and the decision-making process of Argentina.[3] One approach—the geopolitical—focuses on historical patterns of behavior and goal-setting, taking into account the country's position in the world system during each period under consideration, the particular situation, and the political and economic forces in power. In another major approach, emphasis is placed on the existence of different schools of thought and on the ideological characteristics of the political, economic, and military actors.[4]

Of these schools, the geopolitical approach takes on particular relevance as it represents the world vision of the military and that of a small, but sometimes influential, number of civilians who have had direct control of the government for relatively long periods since the Second World War. Strongly influenced by traditional European political thinking, by post–World War II U.S. geopolitical approaches designed to secure U.S. influence in the developing areas, and by indigenous Latin American geopolitical elaborations, these groups have developed a "doctrine of development and security" in Argentina, as well as in Brazil, Bolivia, Chile, and Uruguay. Generally, Brazil is taken into account within the framework of bilateral relations, the distribution of power in the Southern Cone and in the South American continent, and in relation to the hegemonic power, the United States. Lately, certain extraregional, although unequal, projections of both Brazil and Argentina have also to be considered.

Although some schools of Argentinian geopolitical thought do not fear Brazil's growth as long as Argentina maintains parity and in fact favor cooperation with Brazil, attitudes toward Brazil have changed as governments have changed in Argentina. Ongania in the middle and late 1960s believed that Argentina could become a first-rank power in Latin America through collaboration with Brazil based on a common ideological and security position. Perón in his second period (1973–1974) looked toward building a working relationship with the rest of Hispanic America in order to increase Argentina's bargaining position and regional influence vis-à-vis Brazil. With the ouster of Peronism in 1976, the Videla regime again sought a modus vivendi with Brazil, fully aware of the disparities of economic and military power that by now had evolved between the two countries. This meant accepting solutions to outstanding issues that would not be acceptable to certain elements in the military alliance but that were preferable to suffering further losses to Brazil should these issues remain unresolved. An example of this current Argentinian policy is the Itaipu-Corpus Hydroelectric Agreements for the Rio de la Plata basin recently concluded with Brazil.[5]

What this serves to illustrate is that there exists no single line of thought among geopoliticians in Argentina, nor for that matter in Brazil or throughout the Southern Cone. In describing the major shades of opinion among the governing factions in the region, it may be more accurate to distinguish between a liberal-internationalist approach, which favors the opening of the economy to transnational capital and is essentially pro-Western, and a statist-nationalist approach. Each one of these is shared by different segments of the military, intelligentsia, technocracy, labor, and capital, not just in Argentina, but also in Brazil and throughout the region. In the case of Argentina, what unites these two approaches is a common desire to enhance Argentinian capabilities, influence, and prestige. What divides them is their perception of foreign actors and of the economic model that is appropriate for Argentina. Their differences reflect the different political and economic interests of the dominant economic groups and classes.[6]

Common to all Argentinian schools of geopolitical thought is the centrality assigned to Brazil, either as the fundamental ally in opposing the United States and in obtaining greater influence for Latin America in world affairs, or as the opponent and a menace to Argentinian national integrity. (Until a few years ago, a quite parallel process could be observed on the Brazilian side.) In all likelihood, this ambivalence toward Brazil will continue into the future.

On the other hand, the conflicts in the Argentinian-Brazilian relationship should not be emphasized at the expense of the cooperative aspects of that same relationship. Bilateral trade between the two states is quite significant, and as middle powers seeking to increase their influence among developing nations, Brazil and Argentina share many positions on economic and political issues in the North-South negotiations and in other regional and international forums. It is at the regional Latin American and the Southern Cone levels, as well as in perceptions of the United States, that their differences appear.

Finally, any analysis of Brazilian interactions with the Southern Cone on the basis of national interest must take into account internal-external linkages. This means that any future trend toward conflict or cooperation will reflect the dominant interests in Brazil and Argentina and shifts in the alliances of socioeconomic factions in each of these countries. The dominant socioeconomic groups will act for or against cooperation depending on their own evaluation of the cost-benefit equation. For this reason, any study on the feasibility of future cooperation between Argentina and Brazil must begin by focusing on the concrete issues that could unite or separate them.

Argentina and Brazil:
Possibilities of Conflict and Cooperation

During the last decades several issue areas have occupied the attention of Argentinian decision makers in their relations with Brazil. These are: (1) the Rio de la Plata basin; (2) influence over Bolivia, Paraguay, and Uruguay; (3) South Atlantic, African, and Antarctic policies; and (4) general bilateral relations.

The Rio de la Plata Basin

A joint development program of the water and other rich resources of the Rio de la Plata watershed was agreed upon by Argentina, Brazil, Bolivia, Paraguay, and Uruguay in 1967. This giant basin occupies the total territory of Paraguay, more than two-thirds of Uruguay, and significant parts of Argentina, Bolivia, and Brazil. Of the five signatory states, Argentina and Brazil possess more than 80 percent of the industrial power and the more developed urban centers and regions within the basin.

With more than 50 million kilowatts of electric power ready to be exploited from the basin's water system, conflict arose over the way in which these resources were to be exploited in bilateral or multilateral projects already in place or being planned in the upper section of the Paraná River. Involved were joint projects between Brazil and Paraguay (Itaipu Dam) and between Argentina and Paraguay (Corpus Dam). Certainly some of these projects would have been more efficient with trilateral design and management. What was at stake was not only the benefits or losses that Brazil and Argentina might incur depending on the way the resources would be handled technically, but also, given the gigantic developmental impact of the projects on the region, the future distribution of power between the two countries and their respective future influence over the minor partners in the Rio de la Plata agreement.[7]

Argentina had been the initiator of the agreement and had originally sought to enlist the cooperation of Bolivia, Paraguay, and Uruguay in presenting a joint negotiating position vis-à-vis Brazil in order to prevent any unilateral use of the water resources by Brazil that could seriously damage the ecological and economic systems of Argentina and, to a lesser extent, of Paraguay. Brazil perceived this as a deliberate Argentinian attempt to prevent it from developing the hydroelectric resources that it desperately needed and in fifteen years of struggle largely succeeded in preventing the formation of an Argentinian-led group in the Rio de la Plata region that would oppose Brazilian planning and development of water resources. This effort was especially successful in the case of Paraguay, which is a partner of both Argentina and Brazil in major hydroelectric projects.

As a consequence, a national consciousness emerged in Argentina, shared to a degree by elements within neighboring countries, concerning the "Brazilian menace." The Plata basin issue soon became the most important source of conflict between Argentina and Brazil, creating a mutual animosity that reached far beyond the limits of the Southern Cone. The "Brazilian menace" also became an issue of domestic politics and governments were rated on their ability to confront it. Finally, in October 1979, a tripartite agreement was signed by Argentina, Brazil, and Paraguay concerning the Itaipu and Corpus hydroelectric dams.[8] Officially, the agreement was heralded as extremely important and as one that would change the tone of the relations between Argentina and Brazil. Nevertheless, critical voices were raised from within the military, economic circles, and the media in Argentina. These critics felt that even with this agreement Argentina would still suffer irreparable damage from the Itaipu project. According to this perspective, "if the agreement is called 'excellent' in the future, it will be because it was better than no solution at all to the *fait accompli* of the Brazilian giant dam at Itaipu, constructed in partnership with Paraguay."[9]

Nevertheless, the agreement has paved the way for future Argentinian-Brazilian cooperation, and the Plata basin is the terrain where the new political climate will be put to the test. If the Itaipu-Corpus settlement is really carried through, it would be a significant step in the direction of bilateral cooperation, although it would not necessarily mean an end to conflict. For example, establishment of the rules of the game regarding competing Argentinian and Brazilian influence in Bolivia, Paraguay, and Uruguay lies in the future.

Influence Over Bolivia, Paraguay, and Uruguay

The participation of Bolivia, Paraguay, and Uruguay in the Rio de la Plata agreement has given these states a new opportunity to test themselves in bilateral and multilateral diplomacy with their two powerful neighbors. The existence of military or semimilitary authoritarian regimes in all of these countries since the birth of the agreement (with some minor exceptions), all sharing a common anticommunist ideology, was not a deciding factor in their orientation toward either Buenos Aires or Brasília. In fact, even the close personal ties that existed between President Banzer of Bolivia and top military men in Argentina did not secure a pro-Argentinian orientation in Bolivian policy. As in each of these three states different military and economic factions favor close relations with Brazil, while others favor Argentina, policy will probably follow the time-honored principle of avoiding a close association with either in order to extract maximum advantage while incurring a minimum of dependence.

However, in order to maintain such a delicate balance, both sides have to be able to offer approximately equivalent benefits. With the decline of Argentina in capabilities relative to Brazil in recent years, combined with serious Argentinian policy mistakes, there has been a discernible shift in favor of Brazil. A very dynamic flow of investment, aid, and military assistance has helped to strengthen the political, economic, and cultural ties of these countries to Brazil. But this emerging close relationship, together with the important land purchases by Brazilian agribusiness interests in the frontier zones of Bolivia, Paraguay, and Uruguay, has also raised concerns in economic and political circles in these countries over the loss of national sovereignty, political and economic penetration, and increasing dependence on Brazil.[10]

The present Argentinian ruling circles are frustrated and feel threatened by what they perceive to be a dangerous imbalance in the region and they have publicly criticized the growing Brazilian presence in Bolivia, Paraguay, and Uruguay. As a result, a renewed effort is being made to redress this imbalance and to reclaim lost terrain. It has been only partially successful so far, although some advances have been made by Argentina in that direction, such as the Apipe Dam agreement with Paraguay and new commercial and investment agreements with Bolivia and Uruguay.

What can be expected is continued competition between the two regional powers, but even if Argentina is successful in gaining more political and economic influence in its three smaller neighbors, it would be very difficult to restore a situation of comfortable equilibrium with Brazil. Although political and economic systems may change in either Argentina or Brazil, the determining factor in the competition for influence will be the respective economic capabilities of the two rivals to satisfy the needs of Bolivia, Uruguay, and Paraguay. Moreover, any renewed effort on the part of Argentina to catch up must take into account new factors, such as changes in the international system and the emergence of new power centers at the regional level, such as Venezuela and the Andean Pact.

South Atlantic, Antarctic, and African Policies

Brazilian geopoliticians, supported by Brazilian admirals, have suggested a "manifest destiny" for Brazil in the South Atlantic Ocean, claiming it as a sort of *mare nostrum*. Brazilian naval and merchant marine capability is growing, and in 1975 Brazil received adherent status to the Antarctic Treaty after stressing its security requirements and its desire to participate in Antarctic exploration and exploitation of Antarctic natural resources. In the meantime, various private groups, with apparent government encouragement, have publicly demanded that the Brazilian authorities issue an official claim over parts of Antarctica.[11] Brazil has also successfully expanded its ties with Black Africa, while maintaining discreet political ties and profitable trade with South Africa. However, Brazil has repeatedly and publicly rejected formal suggestions from Pretoria that it participate in a military alliance with Argentina, Uruguay, and possibly Chile for the defense of the South Atlantic.[12]

Whatever the viability of these policies, they have affected the Argentinian armed forces, especially the navy, which is responsible for the defense of Argentina's territorial waters and the important sea lanes that pass through them. The Argentinians were quite embarrassed by Brazil's rejection of the South African treaty offer, which they supported and from which the Argentinian government hoped to obtain internal and external political rewards.[13] Thoughts of Brazilian encroachment on the Antarctic involve the armed forces deeply, because over the last few decades it has become a national objective to defend Argentinian territorial claims in the Antarctic.

The Brazilian claim, although not yet formally announced, overlaps with the Argentinian one, and it is feared that it would set a precedent for other Latin American states to claim territory in a part of the Antarctic already in dispute, with rival claims by Argentina, Chile, and Great Britain. Although the Antarctic Treaty clearly inhibits signatory states from changing the terms of national sovereignty claims and the trend now is to work toward some kind of common access to Antarctic natural resources by signatory states, Argentina is deeply troubled by a possible Brazilian presence there. This preoccupation must be seen in light of Argentina's dispute with Chile over the Beagle Canal in Tierra del Fuego and with Great Britain over the Malvinas (Falkland) Islands.

For this reason, the Videla government has at least momentarily adopted a policy of "low profile" in regard to overt military cooperation with South Africa, while encouraging the growth of economic and political ties with Pretoria. At the same time Argentina is attempting to maintain good relations with Black Africa in order to be assured of African support in international forums. Argentina would like to match Brazil's economic and political success in Black Africa, but is hamstrung by its relations with South Africa, relations that in the first instance were brought about by ideological considerations. Its ties with South Africa could be damaging to Argentina in the future, especially if at some still unforeseen date the racist regime in Pretoria is replaced with an autonomous black regime, as South Africa is a signatory member of the Antarctic Treaty and controls the sea lanes between the Atlantic and Indian oceans.[14]

With regard to their respective spheres of influence in the South Atlantic, tensions exist between Brazil and Argentina, despite formally correct and even friendly relations between their navies. Political changes in both countries may help to establish a modus vivendi or even lead to cooperation, but they might also worsen the situation, especially if the trend toward eventual Brazilian naval superiority continues. Even more ominous would be a serious Brazilian alliance with Chile, for either military or economic purposes.

All these factors together create a very fluid situation. In regard to Antarctica, Argentina seems to be more worried about possible Brazilian exploitation of natural resources, such as natural gas and oil, than about actual territorial claims. Argentina over the long run will most probably attempt to cooperate with, rather than oppose, Brazil in Antarctica, but this will depend on the satisfactory settlement of other outstanding bilateral issues. A joint venture, especially if Chile could be included, could be mutually rewarding by pooling technical, financial, and human resources, but as a precondition Argentina would probably demand a formal renunciation of any Brazilian territorial rights in the Antarctic. This will not be easily negotiated.

General Bilateral Relations

Trade. Trade between Argentina and Brazil will total $1.5 billion by 1980 and may reach $3 billion during the 1980s. The pressure to export is imposed by the present economic situation, the role assigned to export in both countries' economic models, and by the fact that important sectors of the Argentinian and Brazilian economies are complementary. Trade has often become a hostage to politics, as during the Plata basin conflict, but both sides have tried to insulate commerce from politics as much as possible, to avoid any adverse effects on the interests of economic groups in both countries. The common need to export industrial products with a relatively high technological level to both Latin American and world markets could in fact form the basis for mutual cooperation. The transfer of indigenous and adapted technology to less developed countries could be another field in which collaboration is feasible and could be mutually rewarding.

On the other hand, Argentinian industrialists fear Brazilian competition in their domestic market and elsewhere, and this fear is growing, especially in light of Brazilian advances in the Argentinian market and the higher efficiency level of Brazilian industry. Argentinian economic interests view with apprehension the tendency of foreign investors to favor Brazil and are afraid that eventually key sectors of the multinationals operating in Argentina, such as the automobile industry, will relocate to Brazil.[15]

A variety of circumstances or policy shifts could change this situation, such as a shift in Brazilian economic policy toward the domestic market, controls over transnational corporations, and changes (including higher efficiency) in the Argentinian economic model. In the medium term, what is likely to be more successful is internal cooperation and integration among transnational companies which would not be favorable to Argentina, given present trends. Nevertheless, there exists the possibility of collaboration between state-owned and private enterprises in both countries in such areas as food and energy, with Argentina selling grain and natural gas to Brazil in return for industrial goods and raw materials. Argentina would, however, still have to improve economically; otherwise disadvantageous asymmetries would arise. A common policy regulating the activities of transnationals could also offer new challenges and opportunities, but it would have to recognize that no matter what understandings are reached, important areas of economic competition would still exist between the two states, especially in regard to the export of industrial goods, technology, and services to external markets.

Nuclear and military policies. The nuclear competition between Argentina and Brazil is a dangerous source of rivalry and, according to some experts, could and should be reversed, creating the possibility for a crucial cooperative undertaking that could give a major impetus to regional autonomy vis-à-vis the great powers.[16] At present, Argentina has the capability to build nuclear weapons and Brazil will soon have it. The "atomic threat" (either Argentinian or Brazilian) is ever-present in national planning and in the mass media of both countries. By following separate paths in nuclear development, Brazil and Argentina have spent precious resources and lost the opportunity to pool human and financial inputs, but after experiencing difficulties in obtaining external technological assistance, as well as minor setbacks in their respective programs and economic constraints, a policy of collaboration seems to be shaping up. Three agreements on nuclear collaboration were signed in May 1980 when President Figueiredo visited Argentina.[17]

A substantial reduction of mutual suspicions in the military could also be achieved by cooperation in development and production of weapons for export and internal deployment. Up to now, both Argentina and Brazil have concentrated on expanding their armaments industries, and, as has happened in other areas, economic growth has given the edge to

Brazil. For the time being the policy of separate military development and self-reliance is not likely to change in either country and is reinforced by the geopolitical thinking of their military establishments. Especially in Brazil, advances obtained through the "separate path" may tend to confirm it as it is considered an essential prerequisite to obtaining greater capabilities. But economic constraints, technological difficulties, and political changes may encourage closer collaboration in the future, perhaps foreshadowed in the May 1980 agreement between Brazil's Siderbrás steel firm and Argentina's Fabricaciones Militares.

Argentinian-Brazilian Relations: Conclusions

Future relations between the two nations will probably be marked by either a continuation of the historical trend of conflictive-cooperative interaction based on competition or by an attempt to collaborate closely in order to achieve a more autonomous position in the world system for both states. At present, the latter possibility seems the more likely. After the impediment of the Itaipu-Corpus dispute was removed by constructive diplomacy during 1979, moves toward rapprochement occurred with unexpected swiftness in 1980, culminating in an exchange of presidential visits. The advantages of economic complementarity and mutual awareness of sufficient similarities in global international relations to encourage cooperation resulted in the signing of a broad range of agreements that have the potential of turning the rivalry into a partnership, spurring Latin American integration, and changing the whole calculus of South American international relations, especially around the Rio de la Plata basin. Various forms of technological exchange (including nuclear and military), private sector collaboration through a joint commission, joint ventures, and regular intergovernmental consultation on matters of common interest are foreseen.[18] Any such ambitious programs, in order to be feasible, will have to be precisely defined and organized, however. Existing internal constraints, together with real sources of competition and structural contradictions, are very capable of stifling any collaborative attempt that does not avoid the ideological determinants of sociopolitical and economic styles. The concrete long-term interests of both Argentina and Brazil must be separated from stereotypes and parochial perceptions and demands. A step towards collaboration in the long term would be to work in the medium term through ad hoc sectoral policies, without reaching an overall agreement. This would create a good environment for enhancing cooperation and trust. Meanwhile, it is hoped that the two states will achieve the necessary harmony between the democratic participatory demands sought at the world level and the internal changes needed to reach a comprehensive coherence between internal and international behavior.

Bolivian-Brazilian Relations

Bolivia's relations with Brazil have become the subject of increasing domestic political controversy, and, whether directly or indirectly, have been among the factors that have led to political upheaval and change in Bolivia in recent years. This has made Bolivia unique among Brazil's periphery states in the sense that Brazilian economic penetration and perceived interference in Bolivian politics contributed to the ouster of what was widely considered a pro-Brazilian faction in 1978 and its replacement with military and civilian factions more determined to resist Brazilian hegemony over all or part of the country. It is still too early to tell whether the current holders of power in La Paz will enjoy a long incumbency, or whether the Bolivian example will mark the beginning of a pattern that will be repeated in other periphery states like Paraguay or Uruguay, but it should cause Brazil's policymakers to reflect on the impact of Brazilian expansion and on the possibility that increased political and economic influence in smaller states along its borders has the potential for producing a nationalist backlash.

Bolivian Perceptions of Brazil

Although Bolivia has historically suffered in conflict with Brazil, perceptions of Brazil in contemporary Bolivia are sharply divided along regional and political lines. Economic self-interest also colors the vision of Brazil. Differing perceptions of Brazil mirror domestic political polarization, which has meant in practice that the country's relations with Brazil have become a key issue in domestic political debate. Bolivia is most often described as divided between the traditional center of political and economic power, the Altiplano, where the capital, La Paz, is located, and the new dynamic economic region in eastern Bolivia around Santa Cruz. The interests that dominate eastern Bolivia, apart from their conservative inclination, look towards Brazil as the logical market for their products and take a benign view of Brazilian economic penetration of the area, as they hope to benefit from it and thus strengthen their own position in the struggle for hegemony in domestic Bolivian politics. It therefore comes as no surprise that Bolivia's traditional Altiplano elite views Brazilian activities in eastern Bolivia with more misgivings, since it could ultimately influence its hold on political power in the country. In addition to these partisan considerations, the increasing Brazilian presence in the Bolivian economy following the Banzer coup d'état in 1971 has provoked a widespread fear in some quarters of eventual Brazilian domination of Bolivia's economy and control over its natural resources on terms very disadvantageous to Bolivia. This nationalist reaction has been simmering ever since the Cochabamba Agreement signed by Banzer and President Geisel of Brazil in 1974, and it finally helped to oust General Banzer and his followers from power in 1978.

Given the fact that the Bolivian armed forces are divided into political factions, with ever-shifting alliances among them, it is no surprise that the issue of Bolivia's relations with Brazil divides them as well. Opposition to Brazilian penetration has been expressed by the Bolivian Confederation of Labor (COB) and the parties of the left, now principally grouped in the Democratic Popular Union (UDP), which is headed by Hernán Siles Zuazo. Significant anti-Brazilian sentiment is also present in the center-right National Revolutionary Movement (MNR) of former President Paz Estenssoro. The pro-Brazilian factions are primarily linked with the Falange Socialista Boliviana (FSB), a party closely identified with the Banzer period in Bolivia. This split between right and left on perceptions of Brazil should not be surprising in view of Brazil's right-wing authoritarian military regime. Bolivian conservatives look to Brazil as an ally against domestic upheaval and revolution, whereas the Bolivian left views Brazilian influence as an impediment to the realization of its political objectives.

Close association with Brazil would be more palatable if it had led to a successful resolution of Bolivia's quest to regain the access to the Pacific Ocean that it lost to Chile during the last century. After the right-wing coup in Chile in 1973, the way seemed to be open to Brazilian mediation between two like-minded regimes. Brazil used the occasion of the inauguration of President Geisel in 1974 to engineer a meeting between Banzer and President Pinochet of Chile. Negotiations began in earnest but, after a flurry of hope, broke down in 1977. A successful outcome would not only have improved Banzer's political standing, but would also have helped to promote Brazilian aims in the region by helping to establish harmonious relations between two regimes friendly to Brazil. As it was, the breakdown sped Banzer's removal from power and dealt a serious blow to Brazil's political influence in Bolivia.

Prospects for Bolivian-Brazilian
Political Collaboration

In the 1970s Bolivia collaborated closely with Brazil, to the point that the opposition accused Banzer's government of being an instrument of Brazilian policy in the Southern Cone. In fact, the opposition generally interpreted the coup d'état of 1971 as the work of the Santa Cruz oligarchy assisted by Brazil. No doubt Brazil found Banzer more to its liking than the left-leaning Torres. Banzer's regime opened Bolivia to Brazilian economic penetration and attempted to install a Bolivian version, albeit a corrupt one, of the Brazilian model of development. Political and labor opposition was muzzled, Brazil was given access to Bolivian natural gas and iron ore, and the transportation network between the two countries was improved to link their economies more closely.

The removal of Banzer and the new and fragile democratic phase in Bolivia lead to serious speculation on future political relations between the two states. Even though the pro-Brazilian factions have been at least temporarily removed from political power, the political stalemate that has emerged in Bolivia in the aftermath of the August 1979 elections may give them increasing leverage in the political bargaining process. This possibility was demonstrated during the political negotiations that put an end to the Natusch episode in November 1979, after that rightist colonel had brought down the interim administration of Walter Guevara Arze. The negotiations ended with the formation of another interim government headed by Lidia Gueiler, but not until the bargaining process had included the Falange Socialista Boliviana and Banzer's new Alianza Democrática Nacional (ADN) party.[19] If this stalemate is not broken by the spring 1980 elections, pro-Brazilian factions may continue as political brokers, extracting concessions from the major political factions.

Should this democratic period continue into the near future, it is likely that Bolivia will distance itself from Brazil and move closer to the states of the Andean Pact. This realignment must be seen in the light of a democratizing trend in the Andean region encouraged by the United States. In fact, U.S. pressure was a key factor in bringing the Gueiler administration to power. It is very unlikely that Brazil would move in Bolivia contrary to U.S. policy. Bolivia also hopes that its new democratic image will be helpful in winning regional and international support in its quest for a land corridor to the Pacific Ocean through Chilean territory. Support for this goal by the Organization of American States at its October 1979 meeting in La Paz will help to strengthen the Bolivian position. If democratic government and collaboration with the other Andean Pact states, as well as with Argentina, can give Bolivia its access to the sea, Bolivian democracy may become more viable.

However, whatever government emerges in Bolivia, it cannot ignore the economic ties that have been forged with Brazil over the last decade. Also, even though anti-Brazilian sentiment can now be voiced freely, future Bolivian governments will most probably be dominated by the moderate MNR, which is likely to maintain correct, if not overly friendly, relations with Brazil, while trying to improve Bolivia's bargaining position on bilateral economic issues. At present, Bolivian nationalism is obsessed with the Pacific corridor, and unless there is a clumsy Brazilian intervention in domestic politics, fear of Brazilian domination will be relegated to second place. There are also domestic considerations. No Bolivian administration can completely alienate the powerful pro-Brazilian interests in Santa Cruz and hope to stay in power long. Concessions will have to be made to them, which in fact means making concessions to Brazil. Given Bolivia's weak economic situation, exports to Brazil of natural gas and other resources are vital and will continue to be a top priority for any regime. This fact makes a complete turnabout in Bolivian-Brazilian economic relations quite unlikely, although Brazil may find its political clout reduced in the future. Bolivia's attempt to strengthen ties with Peru and Argentina will also diminish Brazilian political leverage, although this Bolivian move is aimed more at Chile than at Brazil. Nevertheless, Peru and especially Argentina are also rivals of Brazil.

All this means that Brazil will not be able to use Bolivia as a political chess-piece in its geopolitical and economic strategy. However, the instability of Bolivian politics makes any conclusion of this kind tentative. Regime change in Brazil may also affect bilateral relations during the next decade.

Economic Relations: Past and Future

Any future Bolivian administration must confront the greatly expanded role of Brazil in its economy, which will circumscribe Bolivian policy toward its eastern neighbor. As a member of the Rio de la Plata Basin Treaty, its economic future is tied to Brazil and the other treaty members. This could become a source of tension with Bolivia's partners in the Andean Pact. In a sense, Bolivia's membership in the two subregional blocs indicates indecision in Bolivian policy as well as internal divisions.

Brazilian economic penetration of Bolivia began in earnest with the Agreement on Industrial Trade Complementation signed by Presidents Banzer and Geisel in May 1974. The negotiations that led to that agreement had already caused a rupture between the more pro-Argentinian MNR and the FSB, the two pillars of the Banzer regime in the early years. The agreement provided for the sale of 240 million cubic feet per day of natural gas to Brazil at a price of $0.65 per 1000 cubic feet. It also contained provisions that could lead to Brazilian exploitation of Bolivia's rich iron and manganese deposits at Mutún. For its part, Brazil committed itself to build up Bolivia's industrial infrastructure, including a steel plant and a petrochemical complex, providing capital outlays totaling more than $1 billion. With this agreement, Bolivia decisively shifted away from Argentina and towards Brazil.[20]

With this economic and trade pact, commonly referred to as the Cochabamba Agreement, Brazil realized its major objectives in Bolivia. Control over Bolivian iron ore meant that Brazil would increase its role as an ore supplier for the Argentinian metallurgical industries by denying Argentina access to the Bolivian ore by virtue of the Cochabamba Agreement. The Santa Cruz region would also benefit, since most of the Brazilian-financed projects would be located there. In the wake of the 1974 pact, Bolivia moved closer to the Brazilian economy, whether one looks at trade, direct investment, or arms sales to the Bolivian armed forces. In the banking sector, for example, the Banco do Brasil gathers more local capital than all other commercial banks in Bolivia put together. Between 1969 and 1978 this enabled Brazil to expand its exports to Bolivia from $4 million to $133.8 million. After the United States, the Banco do Brasil is the largest supplier of credit in Bolivia. It finances railways and highways constructed by Brazilian firms, as well as natural gas and mineral exploitation, hydroelectric dams, steel mills, and petrochemical plants. The bank does not funnel Bolivian funds to Brazil, but provides additional credits from Brazil to finance further Brazilian exports to Bolivia.[21]

It would be very difficult for Bolivia to withdraw from this web of economic relations. It is more likely that Bolivia will seek better terms, especially for its natural gas exports. The proximity of the Brazilian market as well as Bolivia's lamentable economic situation will provide the incentives for increasing Bolivian exports to Brazil during the next decade. The first major step in this direction was the agreement in principle between the countries in October 1978 that would increase Bolivian natural gas exports from 240 to 500 million cubic feet per day.[22] Bolivia may try to increase its leverage in negotiations with Brazil by moving closer to its Andean Pact partners and Argentina, but Bolivia's membership in the Rio de la Plata group binds Bolivia to Brazil, although Bolivia may use the Argentinian-Brazilian rivalry in the Rio de la Plata agreement to its advantage.

Bolivian Military Factions and Relations with Brazil

It has become fashionable to say that Bolivia has had more coups than years of independence. Not only is this a comment on Bolivian political stability, it also reveals the nature of the Bolivian armed forces. To say that the armed forces are politicized is an understatement, and as a result Bolivian politics has increasingly been determined by factional alliances within the armed forces. Each of the major military factions in turn has allies among the major political factions. Roughly speaking, divisions in-side the military reflect the political divisions within the country. At present, the major factions in the armed forces are referred to as *golpistas, institucionalistas,* and the *Grupo Generacional.* The first is rightist and generally sympathetic towards Brazil. The second has been the principal force behind the return to democratic rule and includes many moderate and conservative senior officers who support the MNR; this group has been strengthened by the latest promotions within the Bolivian military. This faction is committed to military professionalization and modernization with an eye toward Chile. The last faction, the *Grupo Generacional,* is made up of those younger officers who graduated from the military academy after the 1952 MNR-led revolution.[23] It includes many progressive officers who may even be willing to collaborate with the Siles Zuazo forces in the future.

What has kept Bolivian democracy afloat so far has been the alliance between the *institucionalistas* and the *Grupo Generacional,* as demonstrated during the finally unsuccessful Natusch coup in late 1979. An end to this alliance could profoundly affect Bolivian politics, and, directly or indirectly, Bolivian relations with Brazil. As long as the alliance holds, Bolivia may see a string of weak democratic regimes. Unfortunately, the Byzantine world of Bolivian armed forces politics is not very predictable, tied as it is to yearly promotion lists and control by one faction or the other over key military units. Rumblings from the right continue and a deteriorating economic and political situation could produce a coup, especially in order to prevent a leftist electoral victory. Should this happen, the *golpistas* could count on the direct or tacit support of the conservative and even the moderate *institucionalista* officers. Such a coup would be welcomed by the Santa Cruz interests and could lead again to a closer Bolivian alignment with Brazil. But once the senior *institucionalista* officers pass from the scene, a confrontation between *golpistas* and the *Grupo Generacional* could occur, which would raise the possibility of Brazilian, not to speak of U.S., intervention, especially if the left-wing forces gained the upper hand. The continuation of democracy in Bolivia, therefore, is dependent on a delicate and constant balancing of mutually antagonistic forces, as well as on a healthy economy.

Brazil's Future Relations with Bolivia

Internal developments in Brazil may have a more profound impact on Bolivian politics than even the outcome of the Pacific corridor dispute with Chile. Bolivia is already benefiting from the increased subtlety of Brazilian diplomacy that has accompanied the Brazilian liberalization process in recent years. No doubt Brazil is today more open to diversity in the Southern Cone than it was nine years ago. In practical terms, this means that Brazil might be willing to accept a number of political outcomes in Bolivia, with the probable exception of a radical leftist government. A reversal of the democratization process in Brazil, however, and the emergence of an entrenched bureaucratic-authoritarian regime that would include extreme right-wing elements of the Brazilian armed forces would spell trouble for Bolivia. Not only would strident anticommunism and the idea of ideological frontiers again assume their former importance (if not primacy) in Brazilian foreign policy, but right-wing elements in Bolivia would also be encouraged to emulate their Brazilian counterparts. Moderates in Bolivia would have to be seriously concerned about the future of Bolivian democracy and the Bolivian left would have to accept the possibility of Brazilian intervention if it ever reached power, even if this should occur through the electoral process. Bolivia would find itself under more overt Brazilian political pressure, and Brazil might use arms purchases to politically influence the Bolivian armed forces.

Should the liberalization process in Brazil finally bring about a civilian democratic regime, the *golpistas* and their civilian allies in Bolivia would be increasingly isolated. A Brazilian democratic regime would most likely favor the MNR moderates, but even the Bolivian left would have more options than before. Whatever the political outcome in Brazil, some degree of political influence will be exercised by Brasília in Bolivia by virtue of the economic links that have been forged between the two states.

There is also the possibility that as the Argentinian economy revives, Argentina may become an attractive alternative economic partner for Bolivia. Also, even if the rivalry between Argentina and Brazil seems to be subsiding after the latest Paraná agreements, that rivalry could revive, and some level of competition will always be present, as both states compete for the same regional and subregional markets. Bolivia could use this rivalry to its benefit. In fact, smaller and poorer states such as Bolivia must use competition between regional powers to the fullest extent if they do not want to risk being dominated by either.

Chilean-Brazilian Relations

Chile is one of two South American states that does not have a common frontier with Brazil (the other is Ecuador). The absence of geographic contact has meant that Chilean relations with Brazil have not been marked by fears of creeping Brazilian annexation, as in the cases of Bolivia and Paraguay. Thus Chile may adopt a more benign view of a growing Brazilian role in the Southern Cone and in South America as a whole. Chile can also afford a more serene attitude because it has historically relied on Brazil as a geopolitical counterweight to Bolivia and Peru, as well as to Argentina at certain times.

The overthrow of the left-wing Allende government in September 1973 and its replacement by a right-wing authoritarian military government opened the way for Chilean-Brazilian cooperation. Brazil had viewed the Allende regime as a regional focal point of opposition to Brazil and Brazilian regional objectives. In the early 1970s Brazil was concerned about a radicalization of the Southern Cone that would lead to its isolation and eventually threaten domestic stability in Brazil. The left-wing military government in Bolivia, the socialist regime in Chile, guerrilla warfare in Uruguay, the left-wing military regime in Peru, and the announced return to civilian rule in Argentina, which would assure a return of Peronism, certainly provided a basis for these Brazilian fears. No doubt Brazil was pleased with the shift to the right in the Southern Cone, which began with the Banzer coup d'état in Bolivia in 1971 and ended with the fall of Isabel Perón in 1976. There is also substantial circumstantial evidence that Brazil helped this shift along, as it would remove many of the political obstacles to Brazil's goals in the Southern Cone.[24] It is therefore within the context of Brazil's subregional policy that Chilean-Brazilian relations must be evaluated.

Chilean Perceptions of Brazil since 1973

The authoritarian Pinochet regime has looked to Brazil as a natural ally and model ever since it came to power in Chile. However, the Pinochet regime has tried to emulate the results of the Brazilian model while employing very different practices to achieve them. This is true in the case of both political control and stability as well as economic growth, which are the two aspects of post-1964 Brazil that Chile has hoped to copy. Different structural economic conditions, higher levels of political and social development, as well as a less favorable international economic environment have dictated the application of different methods in Chile, although broad similarities exist with Brazil. But in the severity of some policies Chile has surpassed Brazil. Concretely, what all this has meant is that the political, economic, and social costs of creating a Chilean version of the Brazilian success story have been higher and the economic success (as measured by rapid and continuous economic growth) of the Chilean policies in the medium and long term is much more problematic than in Brazil.

In the subregional and regional context, Chile has looked to Brazil as a geopolitical ally in its disputes with Bolivia, Peru, and Argentina, a strategy that has historically been used by Chilean governments. As long as tensions with its neighbors persist, Santiago will count on Brasília for support. A number of factors stand in the way of an open Santiago-Brasília axis, however. Not only is such an alignment dependent on the continued existence of the present regimes in both countries, but it also assumes the permanence and deepening of the Brazilian-Argentinian rivalry without taking into account the possibility of reconciliation and even of cooperation between them. Brazil may also want to distance itself from isolated Chile in order not to imperil relations with Bolivia and Peru. This last point illustrates a fundamental difference between Chile and Brazil; whereas a close relationship with Brazil is a top priority for Chile, the reverse does not hold true. Brazil must balance its interests in Chile with its objectives in other parts of the Southern Cone and Latin America. Chile is simply not a top priority for Brazil in its subregional and regional policies.

Sooner or later, the current Chilean regime will realize this and adjust its policies accordingly. Brazil's failure to support full Chilean membership in the Rio de la Plata Basin Treaty after Chile left the Andean Pact in 1976 was the cause of some disenchantment in Chile, and although Chile was granted observer status, second-class status in a subregional economic association does not meet Chilean aspirations. A lowering of Chilean expectations of the political and economic benefits it could obtain from Brazil may eventually alter Chilean perceptions of Brazil and lead to more pragmatic policies with more limited objectives.

Bilateral Economic Relations: Up, Up and Away?

The real success story in Chilean-Brazilian relations since 1973 has been economic and it will continue to be so in the future. Chile looks to Brazil as a market for its raw materials, especially copper and fruits and other agricultural products, for which there is increasing Brazilian demand. For Brazil, Chile provides an outlet for its manufactured goods as well as opportunities for banking activities and direct investment. The expansion of Chilean trade with Brazil has been part of an overall expansion of Chilean trade. In 1973 Chilean exports to South and Central America totaled $147.9 million; by 1978 that figure had climbed to $641 million.[25] Principal exports have been minerals, wood products, and fruits and vegetables, as well as finished and semifinished goods. Brazil has occupied a key place in the Chilean export drive and the Export Promotion Bureau of the Chilean Foreign Ministry has opened one of its six offices abroad in São Paulo.[26]

Brazil has rapidly expanded its trade with Chile. In the first four months of 1979, Brazilian exports to Chile totaled $107.6 million, putting Chile in second place behind Argentina, with $162.7 million in Brazilian exports, not only within the Southern Cone, but within all of LAFTA, surpassing such countries as Mexico, Venezuela, Colombia, and

Paraguay.[27] Chilean exports to Brazil rose from $286 million in 1977 to $345 million in 1978 and a similar expansion was expected to take place during 1979.[28] The dramatic increase in Brazilian exports to Chile in the first months of 1979 can be attributed to the Argentinian decision not to export "strategic goods" to Chile during the Beagle Channel crisis in late 1978. Brazil quickly filled the gap in Chilean import needs, and unless the trend is reversed, Brazil will most probably replace Argentina as Chile's leading regional trading partner, which would be quite a blow to Argentinian industry. However, a rapid increase in Brazilian exports to Chile could turn the Chilean surplus in bilateral trade into a deficit, creating pressures on Chile to expand her exports to Brazil. In 1979, Chile's current-account deficit amounted to approximately $450 milllion, primarily the result of increased imports brought about by lower tariffs.[29] Given this global situation, Chile cannot afford to have the lucrative trade with Brazil slip into permanent deficit.

It is not probable that Brazil will assume in Chile the kind of predominant role it enjoys in all or part of the Bolivian and Paraguayan economies. The absence of common frontiers and massive joint projects prevents the creeping economic annexation that is taking place in eastern Bolivia and parts of Paraguay. Chile has a policy of buying from the most competitive supplier, which means that Brazil has to compete for the Chilean market with suppliers from the advanced industrial countries and from the rest of Latin America. Chile is just not as dependent on Brazil as are some of the smaller states of the Southern Cone, and although Brazil has made some investments in Chile and Brazilian banks have expanded their activities there, Brazilian capital must compete with other major foreign investors as well as with very dynamic local financial and economic groups. Also, Brazil cannot provide the kind of technology and the amount of capital needed to exploit Chile's mineral resources, such as copper, and in other sectors, such as timber, agribusiness, and ocean fishing, Brazil again is faced with North American, European, and Japanese competition. But we may indeed see some Brazilian agribusiness investments in Chile in the future, together with ventures in construction and urban development. Recently, Petrobrás signed an agreement with the Chilean national oil company Empresa Nacional de Petróleo (ENAP), for joint exploration of Chile's petroleum resources.[30]

Political Factions and Future
Brazilian-Chilean Relations

It would be incorrect to describe the current holders of political and economic power in Chile as pro-Brazilian. Chilean politics never has been and in all likelihood never will be divided into pro- and anti-

Brazilian factions, as is the case in Bolivia, Paraguay, and Uruguay. It is true, however, that Chile and Brazil have drawn closer together since 1973.

No doubt Pinochet would like to see closer overt collaboration between Chile and Brazil, but Chile's current isolation within the Southern Cone stemming from territorial disputes and human rights violations, in contrast to Brazil's slow but steady move towards domestic liberalization and more subtle and less strident regional policies, makes that kind of collaboration difficult. No doubt the two countries appear to be on opposite paths in both domestic and regional policies. Chile's internal policy of confrontation and suppression of opposition is matched by a confrontational stance towards its neighbors; Brazil is moving in the direction of domestic reconciliation and regional collaboration and compromise. Brazilian geopolitical planners lost some of their early enthusiasm for Chile after the failure of the Chilean-Bolivian negotiations on Bolivian access to the Pacific. Brazil had promoted these negotiations, hoping to gain economically and politically from Chilean-Bolivian collaboration. Breakdown of negotiations and political change in Bolivia have dashed these hopes for the time being. Brazil has also begun to stop giving unconditional support to Chile in international forums that regularly condemn the human rights violations of the Pinochet regime. Brazil has consistently rejected proposals by Chile to form an alliance of Southern Cone military regimes, and high-level contacts between the two countries have been surprisingly sparse. After Pinochet's 1974 visit to Brazil, the next visit by a high dignitary did not take place until the summer of 1979, with the visit of air force commander Fernando Matthei, the most moderate member of the Chilean junta.[31] This indicated a Brazilian desire to minimize *public* association with the Santiago government.

If the Pinochet regime begins to lose its pariah image, Brazil may not mind a more open association. The October 1980 state visit by President Figueiredo revealed some mutual uneasiness between the two governments as Chile continued under indefinite military rule and Brazil progressed in political liberalization. But public distance may hide a degree of behind-the-scenes cooperation.[32] The crisis between Chile and Argentina in late 1978 over the Beagle Channel demonstrated to Chile that in the crunch it can count on some Brazilian economic support. Although Brazil was officially neutral and offered to mediate, hostile Brazilian reactions to Argentinian blockades of Brazilian goods passing over Argentinian territory en route to Chile, as well as the visit to Brazil by the Chilean chief of staff, General Washington Carrasco, at the height of the crisis, demonstrated that Brazil was tilting towards Chile. Future cooperation between Argentina and Brazil and a lessening of their rivalry would, however, make continued Brazilian support less certain in the absence of a resolution of the Beagle Channel dispute.

Politically, there has been a degree of emulation of Brazil in Chile. Santiago has developed its own national security doctrine to justify the institutionalization of the authoritarian regime, complete with a national security school, the Academia Superior de Seguridad Nacional, to indoctrinate civilian and military bureaucrats.[33] After 1973, close links were established between the Chilean and Brazilian security services, with Chileans receiving training in Brazil. Links between the Brazilian National Information Service (SNI) and the Chilean secret political police, now called National Information Center (CNI), in all probability still exist.[34]

Since 1973, fraternal ties between the Chilean and Brazilian armed forces have increased. Chile, however, continues to purchase arms and equipment primarily from the United States, France, and Israel because it is faced with the Soviet- and French-equipped Peruvian and Argentinian armed forces. Brazil has sold some military aircraft to Chile's naval air wing, as well as other conventional arms to the army. But technological considerations will limit Chilean arms purchases from Brazil in the future and will be limited to less sophisticated weapons, although Brazil has publicly declared its willingness to sell arms to Santiago.[35] Technological developments in the Brazilian arms industry could end this Chilean hesitation. Relations between the armed forces of both countries are likely to remain good in the future, but Brazil will probably try to avoid a quasi-alliance with Chile in order to maintain sufficient room for maneuver in the region. There exists the distant possibility of Brazilian assistance to Chile's problem-plagued nuclear program if Brazil ever decides to become a regional exporter of nuclear technology.

This all presupposes, to a great extent, the continued existence of the present Chilean regime. Although the Pinochet government is stable at present, its future may not be that rosy. Pinochet has become a caudillo-like figure, with the armed forces increasingly being converted into an appendage to his person. Chile is not governed by a collective decision-making process among the armed forces, but by one man and his close circle of civilian and military advisors, which includes the president's wife and daughter. Beyond the armed forces, the government finds support in sectors of the middle classes, other conservative and traditionalist circles, and those economic interests that benefit from the current Chilean economic model. Broad sectors of the population are excluded or have been silenced, which means that although Pinochet has the support of the powerful, a mass base of support escapes him. A return to civilian democratic government would probably result in a shift in the political outlook of the Chilean government, from the right to the center or center-left, which would affect Brazilian-Chilean relations, especially in the area of military and intelligence cooperation, rather negatively. Political relations could cool, Chile could try to reenter the Andean Pact, and Brazil might find its economic activities in Chile restricted by new regulations. Bilateral trade would in all likelihood not be affected as it is too important to both countries.

Should the return to democratic rule in Chile be complemented by a civilian government in Brasília, relations between the countries would remain close and even military ties would not be adversely affected. In fact, given the intransigence of the Pinochet regime, it is more fruitful to speculate on how changes in Brazil will influence bilateral relations. A democratic Brazil would profoundly change the political climate in the Southern Cone and throughout South America, as Brazil has served as both a model and a sponsor for right-wing forces throughout the region since 1964. Chile would find itself isolated and domestic pressure to return to civilian rule would increase. In fact, Brazil may even push Chile in that direction; given Brazil's projected regional power in the 1980s, such pressure would be difficult to resist.

This is the optimistic scenario. The problem with the Brazilian liberalization process is that democracy always seems to be over the next mountain. Economic troubles and domestic unrest could force an entrenchment of the military-authoritarian apparatus in Brazil. This could lead to circumstances favoring closer Brazilian relations with Chile, much to the comfort of President Pinochet, who might be facing significant domestic opposition by that time. This would, of course, have a negative impact on the eventual return to civilian democratic rule in Chile.

In any event, Chile and Brazil will continue to have important economic links. But in the Chilean market Brazil will have to compete with the major industrial powers and will not have either a privileged position or hegemonic influence. Whatever the outcome of their respective political processes, what is certain is that Chile and Brazil have drawn closer together in the course of the last decade, and it is unlikely that they will totally draw apart in the foreseeable future.

Peruvian-Brazilian Relations

Peruvian-Brazilian relations are distinguished by their lower salience for both countries, at least when compared with Brazil's ties with other neighbors in the Southern Cone. Although Brazil and Peru share a long Amazon border, the absence of surface communication links has reduced contact. In recent years, the desire of both countries to develop the Amazon region has led Peru and Brazil to draw closer. Significant bilateral agreements have been formalized at important meetings between the presidents of the two countries. As Brazil seeks further markets for its exports and establishes more ties with the Andean Pact, further Peruvian-Brazilian cooperation may emerge, with Amazonian development providing the solid basis for such collaboration.

Changing Peruvian Perceptions of Brazil

At the beginning of the 1970s, the progressive military government of General Velasco Alvarado was seen as a populist alternative to the kind of military-led development taking place in Brazil. There was even speculation on how the Peruvian model could influence the thinking of younger Brazilian officers. Certainly Brazil did not look favorably upon its left-leaning military colleagues in Lima, and the more paranoid among Brazil's geopoliticians saw the Peruvian regime as part of a leftist encirclement of Brazil that seemed to be emerging in the Southern Cone. During the same period, Peru was a driving force behind the creation of the Andean Pact, a subregional economic association with mechanisms for regional integration and foreign investment control quite different from those of Brazil. It would be incorrect to say that this was part of a deliberate Peruvian anti-Brazilian policy. The two countries had been separated for so long that no clear perception of Brazil had developed in Peru.

All this changed with the rapid Brazilian development of the Amazon basin, which awakened Peru to the need to develop its own Amazonian territory before the region developed extensive ties with the Brazilian economy. The next shock came with the fall of the progressive governments around Peru and their replacement by right-wing regimes with close ties to Brazil. Peru's increasing isolation led to fears of becoming the next target of Brazil's geopolitical drive towards regional hegemony. At this juncture, General Morales Bermúdez removed Velasco from power and shifted the Peruvian revolution to the right.

Since the removal of Velasco in 1975, Peru has tried to establish good, neighborly relations with Brazil and has become a partner of Brazil in joint Amazon projects. But Peru is not likely to look to Brazil as a model or to subordinate itself to Brazilian interests. Peru has a leadership position in the Andean Pact and some of the best-equipped armed forces in Latin America, thanks to Soviet and French military credits and assistance. By accepting Soviet arms, the Peruvian armed forces asserted their independence in Latin America, which they are unlikely to surrender. All shifts to the right notwithstanding, the Peruvian and

Brazilian armed forces just do not share the same ideological outlook, and many of their regional and international perspectives do not coincide. Besides, the assumption of power by Morales Bermúdez was linked with a return to civilian rule, completed in 1980. Over the next decade, the Amazon issue in particular offers opportunities for cooperation as well as for conflict. Increased contact with Brazil in the 1980s and beyond will offer ample opportunity for Peruvians to form an opinion on Brazil, if they have not formed one already.

Political and Economic Relations

Amazonian development will most probably provide the springboard for closer Peruvian-Brazilian collaboration in the future. Peru has responded positively to the proposed Amazon Pact, calculating that it is better to benefit from joint Amazonian development using Brazilian capital and resources than to see Brazil develop the Amazon basin on its own. The first movement in this direction began after the 1976 meeting between Morales Bermúdez and Geisel, and further agreements were signed in 1977. Brazil has relied on Peru to sell the Amazon Pact to more reluctant neighbors such as Colombia and Venezuela.[36] Peru's status in the Andean Pact can be put to use here. Brazil's recent overtures towards the Andean Pact must be understood within the context of the Brazilian Amazon schemes, since all the Andean Pact members possess Amazon territory and all, with the exception of Ecuador, share borders with Brazil. Peruvian-Brazilian collaboration will not be without political pitfalls, especially if Peru begins to feel that Brazil is receiving greater benefit from their cooperation or if Brazil tries to gain direct control of or privileged access to Peru's Amazon resources. This is especially true of Peru's Amazon petroleum resources, should they turn out to be more plentiful than is now thought.

Always looking for markets for its exports, Brazil had already begun by the early 1970s to grant Peru credits in order to finance imports of Brazilian goods. Brazil, in fact, looks upon Peru as a market with great potential. But the volume of Brazilian exports to Peru is still modest when compared to those to other countries in the region. Exports from Brazil to Peru actually fell from $80.2 million in 1976 to $34.2 million in 1978, reaching $12.2 million for the first four months of 1979.[37] This reduction can be attributed to the Peruvian economic crisis and fiscal measures that have reduced imports. But the outlook for future economic relations is good. In October 1979, while on an official visit to Brazil, President Morales Bermúdez signed agreements that provide $20 million in credits for Brazil to purchase nontraditional Peruvian exports and that commit Brazil to organize a $89 million finance package for the

Charchani Hydroelectric Project.[38] The latter agreement provides an opportunity for Brazilian banks and may lead to large-scale Brazilian financing of development projects in Peru that benefit both countries. A more active role for Brazilian banks in Peru's capital markets will depend on further relaxation of Peruvian banking regulations, but this will be subject to the vagaries of partisan politics after the 1980 elections.

Bilateral trade will most probably increase, as will joint ventures. Direct Brazilian investment in the Peruvian economy will have to take into account Andean Pact restrictions on the activities of foreign companies, including phase-out and limitations on remittances of profits. The conservative fiscal policies of Morales Bermúdez aside, there are strong autarkic tendencies in Peru, and the economic nationalism that accompanied the military revolution of 1968 is just not going to dissipate after the military returns to the barracks. Depending on the direction of domestic politics, economic nationalism could even intensify, which may have an adverse effect on bilateral economic relations. Such a development could, however, be offset by the creation of a network of economic ties between the Andean Pact as a whole and Brazil, a prospect that appeared more likely as 1980 progressed.

Prospects for the Future

As relations between Peru and Brazil are really only in the infant stage, they are unlikely to be severely affected by political changes in Brazil. Neither an entrenchment of the present Brazilian regime nor the emergence of a civilian democratic regime of one form or another will have much of an impact. A civilian regime in Brazil could increase sympathy for Brazil among moderate and leftist political forces in Peru, but even a right-wing reassertion would cause little alarm, unless it led to an aggressive Brazilian policy in the Amazon basin. Brazil is not as yet central to Peruvian concerns. For example, even if Peruvian exports to Brazil doubled over the next decade, they would still only account for 2 to 3 percent of total Peruvian exports.[39]

Political changes in Peru are not likely to cause much concern in Brazil either, unless a revolutionary leftist regime comes to power. This is not likely, given the present attitude of the Peruvian armed forces. Furthermore, the development of the Amazon basin calls for courteous relations between Peru and Brazil, something which no Peruvian government is likely to forget in the near future.

Tensions could arise if Brazil tries to take unfair advantage of the Amazon Treaty, or if Brazil tries to turn economic cooperation into political clout. From a subregional perspective, tensions could occur if Bolivia tried to move closer to Peru in order to gain leverage vis-à-vis

Brazil, or if Argentina and Peru established better relations (as they seem to be doing) while relations between Buenos Aires and Brasília worsened. In fact, Argentina may initiate such close collaboration in order to avoid isolation in the Southern Cone as Brazil begins to cooperate with the Andean Pact. Argentina's offer in 1979 to assist the Peruvian nuclear program must be seen in this light. Given greater Peruvian-Brazilian cooperation, speculation will begin to focus on the possibility of Brazilian penetration leading to hegemony. This is not likely, but Peru will have to weigh its actions carefully if it is to retain its leverage and independence in its relations with its powerful eastern neighbor.

Brazilian Relations with Paraguay

Among the minor states of the subregion, Paraguay has demonstrated the possibilities open to a small nation to increase its bargaining power in negotiations with powerful neighbors, in this case Argentina and Brazil. Both these countries need access to Paraguay's water resources, and the Brazilian Itaipu and the Argentinian Corpus dams are both located partially on Paraguayan territory. Playing its role as an arbiter with superb skill and preventing a direct bilateral understanding between Argentina and Brazil, Paraguay has managed to receive substantial rewards in trade, investment, construction of transportation infrastructure, and financing of its share of the dams' construction expenses from Argentina and Brazil. Ties with Brazil developed through the construction of Itaipu and the complex set of bilateral relations that have evolved in other areas have increased Paraguay's overall dependence on Brazil. This has reduced Paraguay's flexibility and has affected its ability to maintain its independence by playing Brazil against Argentina. In trade alone, Brazilian exports to Paraguay rose from $132 million in 1976 to $224 million in 1978 and reached $92 million in the first quarter of 1979.[40] In the social arena, Itaipu has led to a reduction of unemployment, as 65 percent of the dam's labor force is Paraguayan and approximately $100 million entered the country annually during the period 1973–1975 alone as a direct or indirect consequence of the dam.[41] However, an opponent of President Stroessner has claimed that banks and companies controlled by foreign capital—most of them North American and Brazilian—control 30 percent of Paraguay's land and 80 percent of its external trade.[42] It is also a fact that the land around Itaipu was bought up by members of the Stroessner government and by Brazilians.

When Itaipu becomes fully operational in 1988, Paraguay will earn more than $130 million annually by exporting electricity to Brazil. To this figure must be added the sale of electricity to Argentina from the

Paraguayan share of the Yaciretá-Apipe Dam, which will be operational by 1986. Finally, another $52 million will come in annually from the Corpus Dam when that hydroelectric project is completed around 1990.

Consequently, Paraguay will practically double its export earnings. In the next decade, Stroessner or his successor will be faced with the economic, social, and political consequences of sudden modernization in a very backward socioeconomic and political environment. Besides the obvious problems of inflation and social dislocation, what is at stake is the survival of the present governing combination, which consists of a repressive military clique and the Colorado Party, which controls the parliamentary majority. The opposition Radical-Liberal and Liberal parties have platforms similar to the Colorados, and the Communists and Christian Democrats are excluded from politics. The development program adopted in these circumstances, which has been basically conservative so far, is likely to be influenced by Paraguay's neighbors. Changes in leadership caused by either the death or the overthrow of Stroessner are likely to reinforce the potential instability that rapid change may bring. Furthermore, changes or consolidation of the present political-economic models in Argentina and Brazil could help either to precipitate or to block the process of internal transformation that Paraguay will be facing in the coming years.

Brazilian Relations with Uruguay

Uruguay is the only former Argentinian stronghold that has not completely shifted into the Brazilian sphere of influence. At the economic level intense competition has been taking place between Argentina and Brazil for predominance. During the last five years Uruguay has received significant economic concessions from both countries in the form of advantageous trade quotas and tariffs, joint industrial ventures, credits, aid, joint development of border zones, offers of custom unions and preferential commercial zones, and technology transfer agreements. More important may be the fact that during the second Perón government (1973–1974) an old conflict over Rio de la Plata limits and Atlantic maritime zones was satisfactorily resolved with Argentina, as was the issue of the 200-mile economic zone in the Atlantic with Brazil. Finally, the long awaited Argentinian-Uruguayan Salto Grande Dam was built, becoming operational in 1979.

As a result of economic support, Argentina has retained substantial leverage in Uruguay, but Brazil has also been able to make advances. Brazil's exports to Uruguay increased in the early 1970s, reaching $162.6 million in 1976, and by the end of the decade leveled off at about $140 million annually.[43] At the political level, the military regime in Uruguay contains both pro-Argentinian and pro-Brazilian factions. From the sociocultural standpoint, Uruguay has been traditionally and still is attached to Argentina. The more visible aspects of the new Brazilian presence, such as the purchase of *estancias* as well as the commercial and financial participation in the economy, have not only been resisted by the powerful cattle interests, but have also been denounced by pro-government newspapers, which speak of "a real invasion" from Brazil.[44] Nevertheless, economically, Uruguay has been partially drawn away from Argentina as a commercial partner. For example, Brazil received most of Uruguay's beef exports after the great decline in the European meat market.

With regard to other issues, the Uruguayan military—like the Argentinians—is very interested in reaching a defensive agreement with South Africa. Even if Brazil does not participate, the Uruguayan navy is pressing for full official support from the military government in Montevideo. An official Antarctic Institute has been established and Uruguayan Antarctic strategy is under study.[45] Brazil's informal claims in Antarctica have been taken into consideration, as well as the logistical possibilities that the port of Montevideo would offer to Brazilian naval task forces en route to Antarctica. On the other hand, there is the eventual possibility of an arrangement in Antarctica with Argentina. This depends more on decisions that will be made in Buenos Aires and Brasília, but it could nevertheless become a source of bilateral irritations.

With regard to future Uruguayan-Brazilian relations, much depends on the existence or absence of new political formulas in the Southern Cone. The liberal democracy that previously flourished in Uruguay has been demolished by the military, and it will not be easy to reestablish even a rudimentary form of democracy, given the total harassment of political institutions and parties, the changes introduced in the economic model, and the forced emigration of the most skilled segments of the population. The military will attempt to keep rigid control over the pace of the gradual return to civilian rule that they have promised for the 1980s. The extent to which they can be flexible will depend to a significant degree on the attitudes of Argentina and Brazil. In a dangerous precedent, when the revolutionary Tupamaros were gaining political strength in Uruguay in the early 1970s, Brazil was prepared, if necessary, to invade Uruguay.[46] At that time, the Argentinian decision makers were confronted with a dilemma. They wanted to stop subversion in Uruguay as much as the Brazilians did, but they could not accept Brazilian troops there, fearing that a permanent form of Brazilian tutelage would emerge in Uruguay. Strategic thinking at the time contemplated both a rejection of any foreign intervention in Uruguay and a military move by Argentina to stop a Brazilian advance into Uruguayan territory. But even without such extreme measures as military intervention, Brazil and Argentina are in a position to press for what they may consider to be a desirable direction for the Uruguayan political process.

Conclusion

A Brazil is emerging that is cementing extensive economic ties throughout the Southern Cone, drawing the subregion closer together and creating a web of economic interdependence that in the future may restrict the maneuvering space of decision makers in the area if they seek to redefine or restructure their relations with Brazil. Although Brazil's political clout in any particular state may depend on political factors, such as regime changes both in Brazil and throughout the Southern Cone, Brazil's ever-increasing economic weight throughout the region and its importance as a market and source of goods will propel her into an influential, if not hegemonic, position in such issue areas as regional economic development and trade.

On the political front, regime changes in Brazil will probably affect other Southern Cone states, with the exception of Argentina, more than political changes in the Southern Cone, with the exception of a complete regional revolutionary upheaval, will affect Brazil. Unless paralleled by similar developments in all of the Southern Cone countries, a successful conclusion of the liberalization process in Brazil, culminating in the election of a democratic government, would lead to a possible stabilization of the uncertain democracy in Bolivia, easier cooperation with the new civilian regime in Peru, and public distance from the governments of Chile, Paraguay, and Uruguay. In the case of the last two countries, Brazil could even exert pressures in the direction of political liberalization. A democratic Brazil would probably result in a deepening of competition and rivalry with the military government in Argentina, but should Brazil gain regional and international prestige as a result of its democratic institutions, Argentina would feel a powerful motivation to move toward civilian government again. An authoritarian entrenchment in Brazil would most probably result in the retention of the political status quo in Uruguay and Paraguay; it could also undo the delicate political balance in Bolivia, encourage authoritarian forces in Chile, and lead to closer cooperation between Argentina and Brazil and a lessening of their rivalry. But the latter scenario seems less and less likely; it is hoped that it will not be too long before the political constellation of the Southern Cone includes a democratic Brazil to which the other states in the subregion will have to accommodate themselves.

Although there is no doubt that Brazil's economic strength will increase over the next decade and that economic relations with Brazil will increasingly become central concerns of Southern Cone countries, there is no guarantee that the reaction to such overwhelming economic clout concentrated in one country will be totally benign or positive. The reaction will depend on the way in which Brazil uses that economic power. Brazilian policy will have to be subtle and must adopt a low political profile, looking for regional consensus rather than trying to impose its views on the rest of the states. Any crude Brazilian power play would only provoke an anti-Brazilian reaction, not just in the Southern Cone, but throughout Spanish America. In this regard, Brazilian relations with Argentina, Peru, and Venezuela, as well as with Mexico in the future, must be handled with great diplomatic finesse if new rivalries are not to develop or old ones to intensify. If Brazil begins a drive for hegemony, however, or is perceived to be contemplating such a move, states like Argentina will rise to the challenge, and the Southern Cone may move toward conflict rather than cooperation.

Notes

1. Economic Commission for Latin America (ECLA), *Latin America and the New International Development Strategy*, Doc. E/CEPAL/L.210 (Santiago, Chile, 1979), Chapter 1.

2. C. Orrego Vicuna, "Las alternativas de América Latina como clase media de las naciones," *Estudios Internacionales* (Santiago, Chile), No. 40 (1977).

3. See, for example, Edward Milenky, *Argentina's Foreign Policies* (Boulder, Colo.: Westview Press, 1978).

4. See J. Tulchin, "The Argentinian-Brazilian Relationship: An Argentinian View," Occasional Papers Series, Center of Brazilian Studies, Johns Hopkins University, Washington, D.C., 1979.

5. See *Review of the River Plate* (Buenos Aires), October 31,1979.

6. Milenky, *Argentina's Foreign Policies*, Chapter 3.

7. *La Opinión* (Buenos Aires), August 4, 1977, and March 19, 1977.

8. Argentina, Foreign Ministry, Permanent Mission at the United Nations, New York, October 22, 1979 (notes interchanged between Argentina, Brazil, and Paraguay on the construction of hydroelectric projects on the Paraná River).

9. *The Review of the River Plate*, October 31, 1979, pp. 684–687.

10. See *New York Times*, January 21, 1975; *El Cronista Comercial* (Buenos Aires), April 28, 1975; and articles in *El Pueblo* (Asunción), April 24–27, 1975.

11. T. de Castro, *Rumo à Antarctica* (Rio de Janeiro: Livraria Freita Bastos, 1976), p. 113.

12. C. Moneta, "Las vinculaciones políticas, económicas, y militares de la

República Sudafricana con los paises latinoamericanos del Atlántico Sur," in C. Moneta (ed.), *Geopolítica y Geostrategia del Atlántico Sur* (Buenos Aires: Editorial Pleamar), forthcoming.

13. Ibid.

14. Ibid.

15. *Clarín* (Buenos Aires), January 20, 1980.

16. See Jorge Sabato and Raul Frydman, "Energia Nuclear en América Latina," *Estrategia*, No. 42 (1976), pp. 54–62.

17. *La Opinión*, November 13, 1979; *Washington Post*, November 14, 1979; "Figueiredo and Videla Sign Historical Agreements," *Latin America Weekly Report*, May 23, 1980, p. 3.

18. "Brazil and Argentina Make It Together," *Latin America Weekly Report*, May 9, 1980; and "A Giant Step for the Southern Cone," *Latin America Weekly Report*, May 23, 1980.

19. *Latin America Weekly Report* (London), November 23, 1979, p. 43.

20. See Mariano Malaver, "La Bolivie dans les griffes du Brésil," *Afrique-Asie*, No. 58 (1974), pp. 43–44.

21. *Relatório do Banco do Brasil, 1974*; for 1978 export figures see *Latin America Regional Report* (London), January 4, 1980, p. 4.

22. *Quarterly Economic Review, Bolivia and Peru, First Quarter 1979*, London: Economist Intelligence Unit (EIU), 1979, p. 18.

23. Ibid.

24. See Hugo Abreu, *O outro lado do poder* (Rio de Janeiro: Editora Nova Fronteira, 1979); *Washington Post*, January 6, 1974.

25. *Economist*, February 2–8, 1980, "Survey on Chile," p. 4.

26. Ibid.

27. *Latin America Regional Report*, January 4, 1980, p. 4.

28. *Quarterly Economic Review, Chile, Second Quarter 1979*, London: EIU, 1979. See appendix for statistics.

29. Chile, Banco Central. Cited in *Latin America Regional Report*, March 7, 1980, p. 8.

30. *Latin America Weekly Report*, March 21, 1980, p. 4.

31. *Hoy* (Santiago), No. 120, November 1979.

32. *Latin America Weekly Report*, March 21, 1980, p. 4.

33. For the training of both civilians and military personnel, see "Los Chicago Boys," *El Mercurio* (Santiago), August 19, 1979; *Que Pasa* (Santiago), No. 464, March 1980, p. 8.

34. For evidence of Brazilian-Chilean intelligence cooperation see, for example, the widely circulated document, Dirección de Inteligencia Nacional (DINA), Ref. No. 1495/107, *Re: Clarification Regarding Requested Increase in Budget*, September 16, 1975.

35. *The Military Balance, 1978* (London: International Institute for Strategic Studies, 1978). For Brazilian willingness to sell arms, see *Uno Mas Uno* (Mexico City), December 7, 1979.

36. Wayne Selcher, *Brazil's Multilateral Relations* (Boulder, Colo.: Westview Press, 1978), p. 267.

37. *Latin America Regional Report*, January 4, 1980, p. 4.

38. *Latin America Economic Report*, October 26, 1979, p. 329.

39. *Statistical Abstract of Latin America*, Vol. 18, 1977 (Los Angeles: University of California Press), p. 364.

40. *Latin America Regional Report*, January 4, 1980, p. 4.

41. *New York Times*, January 21, 1975.

42. *Manchester Guardian*, February 27, 1977.

43. *Latin America Regional Report*, January 4, 1980, p. 4.

44. *La Opinión*, June 24, 1978 and August 23, 1978.

45. See H. Arbuet Vignati et al., *Antárctica: Continente de los más para los menos* (Montevideo: Fundación de Cultura Universitaria, 1979).

46. See the recollections of a former top military insider, now deceased, General Hugo Abreu, titled *O outro lado do poder*, published in Brazil in 1979 against government wishes.

7
Brazil and West Germany: A Model for First World–Third World Relations?

Wolf Grabendorff

Brazil is the Third World country with which the Federal Republic of Germany maintains the closest relations. It is also one of the most important "take-off" countries (*"Schwellenland"*)[1] on the verge of industrialization and is one of the leading Third World regional powers. Brazil considers itself to be a "superpower-in-waiting" and acts as a link between the interests of the First and Third Worlds. In the discussion within the Federal Republic about improving relations within the North-South configuration, German-Brazilian relations can be considered a model for the problems and perspectives of the bilateral relationship between a rich industrialized country and a poor Third World country on the threshold of industrialization.

Three different political events in recent years have caused the relationship with Brazil to become particularly relevant to the Federal Republic. The first event was the German-Brazilian nuclear treaty of 1975, which aroused worldwide discussion because of the anticipated increased risk of nuclear proliferation. Second, toward the end of the 1970s the Federal Republic of Germany classified Brazil as a "take-off" country. And, finally, Chancellor Schmidt's visit in 1979 to Brazil and other Latin American countries gave rise to a reevaluation of the complete spectrum of Germany's relations with Latin America.

Against this background it would seem meaningful to examine Brazil's position in the international system with respect to its long-term implica-

An earlier version of this paper was presented at the Center of Brazilian Studies, School of Advanced International Studies, Johns Hopkins University, Washington D.C., April 11, 1979. This version has benefited greatly from the comments of Manfred Nitsch, Wayne A. Selcher, and Helga Strasser.

tions for bilateral relations with the Federal Republic. It will not be possible to take into consideration all aspects of the German-Brazilian model of a First World–Third World relationship. Rather, those factors in particular will be examined that have become evident in the difficulties encountered in the current sphere of cooperation. Therefore, neither an examination of the historical dimensions of cooperation between the two countries nor a study of the role of German immigrants in Brazil will be included.[2]

Of greater significance here is an examination of the extent and importance to both sides of bilateral relations in the fields of economics, science, culture, politics, and development policies. At the conclusion of this survey the convergences and divergences in these relations will become apparent. It will thereby become clear that these convergences between Brazil and the Federal Republic will in the future no longer play the decisive role that they did in the 1960s or 1970s. Here one must point out the divergences and their origins in order to avoid making any potentially faulty estimates about the stability or sensitivity to crises of those bilateral relations. The divergences that necessarily exist between two countries so dissimilar as the Federal Republic and Brazil must be considered in conjunction with specific external and internal determinants in both countries. In view of the relatively high level of homogeneity and stability in the Federal Republic, the emphasis of this study must lie on the determinants in Brazil. The apparent Brazilian structural heterogeneity and the resulting political instability must be seen as one of the main causes of future divergences.

It is not yet possible to evaluate comprehensively the conflicts of interest that are becoming apparent within either the internal or external determinants. In both cases the potential for change in Brazil at the start of the 1980s is clearly discernible. A few general conclusions about the possibility of using German-Brazilian relations as a model for First World–Third World relations will be drawn from this review of the differing conceptions and interests of both sides. Because the Federal Republic's foreign policy profile is typical of a certain type of behavior of industrialized countries and because Brazil displays a type of behavior relatively characteristic of developing countries, consideration of the specific content of these close relations between two such countries takes on a certain relevance for the development of the North-South relationship. It is therefore important to determine the different goals and expectations of both sides and simultaneously to describe to what extent changes in the international constellation have already led or could lead to corrections in their respective concepts.

The central question arising from the comparison between the Federal

Republic and Brazil is this: To what extent are agreements primarily in the economic sphere capable of producing a lasting relationship, positively perceived on both sides, in spite of existing structural differences? Beyond the German-Brazilian relationship, any such statement should also be of decisive importance to North-South relationships between industrialized nations and "take-off" countries.

Scope and Importance of German-Brazilian Relations

Brazil and the Federal Republic have often indicated that their bilateral relations are "exemplary and permanent."[3] At least from the viewpoint of the Federal Republic, it is in fact impossible to compare the scope of these bilateral relations to that of relations with any other developing country. Brazil is the Federal Republic's most important Third World economic partner, even with the continuous oil-price hikes that have increased the value of Germany's trade with oil-rich Third World countries. And in Brazil the Federal Republic, in turn, takes second place only to the United States in the fields of trade, investment, and development aid.

Since the 1950s the level of trade between the two countries has steadily risen; in fact, it tripled in the 1970s. Presently Brazil accounts for almost 1 percent of all German exports and imports, while exports to the Federal Republic make up 10 percent of Brazil's total exports. In 1973 the share of imports from Germany was more than 13 percent of Brazil's total imports. Because of the increasing cost of oil imports, this share has dropped to approximately 9 percent since 1976. (See Table 7.1.) However, present figures indicate that the German share of Brazil's foreign trade is again increasing,[4] as Brazil would like to see the Federal Republic become a major market for the growing exports of its manufactured products. Of particular interest when considering these trade figures is a comparison of the Federal Republic's imports over the last several years. In the early 1970s the share of agricultural products in FRG imports from Brazil was over 50 percent, but it fell in 1978 to somewhat more than 40 percent. Similarly, the share of raw materials imports in FRG imports from Brazil decreased from approximately 30 percent in 1973 to about 25 percent in 1978, whereas its share of imports of manufactured products rose from only 5 percent in 1973 to more than 17 percent in 1978. (See Table 7.2.) In Brazil the greatest rate of increase in imports from the Federal Republic occurred mainly in chemical raw materials, rising from only 1 percent in 1973 to almost 9 percent in 1977. On the other hand, the share of machinery and equipment as well as metal processing machinery imports fluctuated only insignificantly. (See Table 7.3.)

TABLE 7.1

Brazil's Foreign Trade with the Federal Republic of Germany
(Percentage of Brazilian Totals)

	1973	1974	1975	1976	1977	1978 (1)
Imports	13.1	12.5	11.0	8.8	8.6	8.2
Exports	9.0	7.2	8.1	9.1	8.8	8.4

1) Calculations based on data from the Deutsch-Südamerikani-
    sche Bank

Source: Brasiliens Wirtschaftliche Entwicklung (Cologne:
Bundesstelle für Aussenhandelsinformationen, January 1979).

TABLE 7.2

Distribution by Product Sector of the Total Imports of the
Federal Republic of Germany from Brazil, in Percentages

	1973	1974	1975	1976	1977	1978
Agricultural products	50.6	46.3	50.4	43.3	48.8	41.4
Raw materials	29.9	31.9	26.7	29.4	22.8	25.9
Semi-manufactured products	13.9	13.3	11.1	13.5	15.2	15.3
Manufactured products	5.6	8.5	11.8	13.8	13.2	17.4
TOTAL	100.0	100.0	100.0	100.0	100.0	100.0

Source: Data from the Deutsch-Südamerikanische Bank
(January 1980)

TABLE 7.3

Share of Selected Goods in the Total Exports of the Federal

Republic of Germany to Brazil, in Percentages

Export goods (purchased by Brazil)	1973	1974	1975	1976	1977
Machinery/Equipment	15.0	12.6	17.3	16.3	18.7
Chemical raw materials	1.0	6.8	6.0	9.0	8.9
Metal-processing machinery	7.4	7.7	8.9	8.3	8.4

Source: <u>Länderkurzbericht Brasilien 1979</u> (Stuttgart:

Statistisches Bundesamt Wiesbaden, 1979).

Perhaps of even more importance to the bilateral relationship is Brazil's position as host country for investments of German capital. Here it ranks fifth in the world and first among the developing countries. Fifty-five percent of all private German investments in Latin America are concentrated in Brazil, a total of over 4.5 billion deutsche marks. This is approximately 8 percent of total German foreign investments, but the figure would be almost twice as large if reinvestments and investments via third countries were included. In 1961, however, almost 17 percent of all German foreign investments were made in Brazil; clearly Brazil's share of the Federal Republic's overseas investment capital has decreased.[5] In spite of this relative decrease in Brazil's importance for German capital investment, the value of accumulated German investment property increased approximately 458 percent between 1963 and 1978. Thus it is by no means astonishing that the Federal Republic was able to achieve considerably higher growth rates in new investments as compared to the United States, the major foreign investor in Brazil. (See Table 7.4.) Presently, approximately 500 German industrial and 200 German service firms have branches in Brazil, 75 percent of which are concentrated around São Paulo. These businesses have been responsible for creating between 200,000 to 250,000 jobs in Brazil.[6]

In contrast, the Federal Republic's expenditures for development aid to Brazil are relatively small,[7] even though Brazil, because of its size, stands at the head of the list of Latin American recipients of development aid from the Federal Republic. Credits and subsidies through 1978 totaled

1.4 billion deutsche marks. Here again the Federal Republic ranks second
after the United States, as is the case with trade and investments. Its
development aid is concentrated primarily in four areas:

1. Technology development and transfer;
2. Security of raw materials supplies, including the encouragement
   of alternative energy sources;
3. Social development in particularly underdeveloped areas;
4. Regional development, including checking the exodus from rural
   areas.

It is precisely this technical-scientific cooperation with Brazil, institu-
tionalized at various levels in the last ten years, that has turned this country into a major partner of the Federal Republic. Governmental cooperation with Brazil has contributed particularly to an increase in private
economic dealings.[8] The importance of technical-scientific cooperation is
shown by the fact that as early as November 30, 1963, the Federal
Republic of Germany and Brazil signed an agreement establishing a

TABLE 7.4

Foreign Investments of Major Countries in Brazil (as
percentage of total foreign investment in Brazil)

	1973*	1974	1975	1976	1977	1978
USA	37.5	33.5	32.8	32.2	30.4	27.8
Federal Republic	11.4	11.8	11.9	12.4	13.6	15.3
Japan	6.9	9.9	11.5	11.2	10.7	10.2
Switzerland	7.8	9.3	10.1	10.9	10.7	11.8
United Kingdom	7.1	6.6	5.9	4.7	4.9	5.4
Canada	7.9	6.6	5.6	5.3	4.6	5.1

Source: Data from the Deutsch-Südamerikanische Bank

*All dates as of December 31.

framework for technological cooperation, the first of six treaties between the two countries. This agreement was replaced on June 9, 1969, by a treaty on cooperation in scientific research and technological development, which was in turn supplemented by an additional treaty on nuclear research signed on April 23, 1971. These bilateral agreements formed the basis for the treaty on cooperation in the field of peaceful uses of nuclear energy of June 27, 1975.[9]

The importance of economic and scientific-technological relations has also become evident in the political contacts between the two countries. Three German foreign ministers (Willy Brandt in 1969, Walter Scheel in 1971, and Hans-Dietrich Genscher in 1975) have visited Brazil, and in 1978, for the first time, a Brazilian president, General Ernesto Geisel, made a state visit to Bonn. This visit was returned in 1979 by Helmut Schmidt, who thus became the first German chancellor to visit Latin America. The fact that the policy planning staffs of both foreign ministries are now meeting regularly is a good indication of the extent to which political consultation between the two countries has flourished. Similar German agreements exist only with France, Great Britain, the United States, and Japan.[10] These regular consultations demonstrate the political importance attached to Brazil by the Federal Republic.

What importance does the scope and form of this bilateral relationship hold for both partners? Brazil's expectations are apparent: Brazil's political leadership is attempting to reduce those development problems arising from capital, technological, and energy needs through cooperation with the Federal Republic. Naturally this broadening of foreign relations—reducing the dominating role of the United States through increased cooperation with Western Europe and Japan—has led to a diversification of Brazil's dependencies and interests. Brazil today, at least in certain areas (e.g., technology and capital transfer), is also dependent on the Federal Republic. The German-Brazilian nuclear treaty in particular will certainly contribute to expanded trade and to German industries' increased willingness to invest in Brazil.[11] Of particular importance to Brazil is the fact that German investments are concentrated far less in the primary sectors than in growth-oriented industries such as the automobile, chemical, and capital goods industries.[12] Brazil is counting on the Federal Republic to encourage its integration into the world market by increasing its ability to compete in the field of manufactured products exports.

In the meantime, the nuclear treaty of 1975 marked the high point of the partnership. This treaty between the Federal Republic and Brazil paved the way for the most extensive and advanced technology transfer between an industrialized nation and a Third World country to date. It is not yet clear to what extent the developments of recent years, the domestic Brazilian debate, and economic development have in the meantime contributed to a decrease in the scope of this transfer and an extension of the original time-line of the treaty.[13]

In any case, the Federal Republic remains a significant partner for capital and technology imports as well as for raw material and manufactured product exports. In spite of the increased value of Brazil's trade with oil-exporting countries resulting from the rising price of oil, the country's close relationship with the Federal Republic should in the medium term remain indispensable.

From the point of view of the Federal Republic, Brazil's significance takes on a different dimension. Among the major imports from Brazil, only iron ore plays a really significant role. Brazil is regarded primarily as a future market; it already enjoys the greatest import capacity of any Third World country.[14] The expectation that Brazil could become a leading industrialized nation[15] explains the above-average interest that German business has shown in this market. Already 1.4 percent of world industrial production and 18.4 percent of the industrial production of the developing countries is concentrated in Brazil.[16] Above all, the Federal Republic considers its expansion of bilateral relations with Brazil as an investment in the future. From the German viewpoint, any disadvantages arising from Brazil's economic development and social and political instability are outweighed by the chance that Brazil will become not only a leading regional power but also an important industrialized nation.[17]

The German-Brazilian nuclear treaty reveals a certain dependence or interdependence between Brazil and the Federal Republic. The Federal Republic's willingness to compromise during the treaty negotiations certainly stemmed from its need to reduce surplus capacity in its reactor industry through increased exports, for which only a small circle of customers exists. The present cooperation with Brazil has certainly stabilized tens of thousands of jobs. At the same time, however, given the German interest in carrying out its nuclear program, Brazil's bargaining power with the Federal Republic has increased sharply. In general, the Federal Republic must also be interested in further Brazilian economic growth; only then could the long-term involvement of German business prove lucrative. In spite of this, however, Brazil is not nearly as important to the German economy as was, for example, Iran (until the upheavals of 1979–1980).

In contrast to the Federal Republic's relations with other important partner nations, its relations with Brazil are of a predominantly economic nature. And even when the economic benefits to the two countries are not immediately discernible, as for example within the framework of technical-scientific cooperation, Brazilian-German relations are still primarily concerned with improving and extending the conditions of economic cooperation between the two countries. It is becoming increasingly apparent in the widespread discussion about the nuclear treaty and the role of German firms in Brazil that this emphasis on the economic aspects of cooperation has produced a certain lack of flexibility where political change is concerned. Thus one could assume that the political aspects of cooperation with Brazil will become more important. The conditions for such an intensification have certainly improved through the emerging democratization in Brazil. On the one hand, the political opening has increased the probability of economic differences. On the other hand, it offers the chance to redefine Brazil's importance to Germany more in terms of political goals.

The Federal Republic's position in relation to Brazil has changed significantly since the signing of the nuclear treaty in 1975. The statement by the former Brazilian foreign minister, Azeredo da Silveira, "The Federal Republic occupies for us a privileged position and no other country can offer us this measure of cooperation,"[18] applies only partially because of the difficulties encountered in implementing the nuclear treaty and in the political opening of the country. Nevertheless, Brazil's importance to the Federal Republic is still great enough to warrant the latter's making an effort to adapt to the altered political and economic conditions in Brazil.

Convergences and Divergences Between the Federal Republic and Brazil

The ability of any bilateral relation within the international system to survive under stress is dependent upon the convergences and divergences that exist or develop between the two partners. In each case, these must be examined in terms of their determinants, as both domestic political changes as well as changes in relations with third countries can have both direct and indirect consequences for the bilateral relationship. In the case of German-Brazilian relations it is particularly difficult to determine the convergences and divergences, because Brazil at present finds itself in a state of domestic political fluidity, the consequences of which for its foreign policy and thus also for its bilateral priorities are not yet foreseeable. The following discussion of the convergences and divergences must therefore be based on Brazil's past behavior, although certain signs are already visible of a new orientation that tends to indicate an increasing divergence of interests in the bilateral relationship.

When considering the convergences, the mutual acceptance of a market economy and the rejection of a Marxist-collectivist system[19] are in the forefront. Here it is relatively insignificant that Brazil's market economy is more state-controlled and the German market economy is more market-oriented. Both countries also accept the principle of noninterference in the domestic affairs of other countries. In the Federal Republic, however, a distinction is made between violation of property rights and of human rights in Brazil. In the latter case, Brazil has repeatedly insisted on maintaining the principle of noninterference.

Externally, a complete array of common interests has resulted not only from Brazil's historical ties to the world economy and the resulting growth of relations with the Western industrialized nations, but also from its close cultural involvement with Europe. In addition, the fact that both countries are extremely dependent on oil imports and thus reject any form of raw materials cartel forms another convergence.[20] (Of course Brazil, because of its own raw materials exports, does not support this standpoint quite as rigorously as the Federal Republic.) Furthermore, both countries, because of their own dependence on exports, tend to support liberalization of trade and to reject protectionism.

On the political level as well there are certain commonalities: Both powers consider themselves—even though at different levels—to be climbers in the international system and both claim the right to a larger role than they now have in the international system that has existed since 1945. The need of Brazil to catch up is, of course, considerably greater than that of the Germans. In addition, the preferred position of both nations as informally accepted leaders of their respective regions carries with it certain commonalities, such as a "junior" relationship with the United States. These convergences result in at least temporary complements: on the one hand, the capacity to produce raw materials and finished products; on the other, the export of technology and capital. However, these convergences, concentrated mainly in the economic area, stand in direct contrast to a large number of divergences in several other areas.

Both sides consider the convergences between them as mostly advantageous, but when studying the divergences one must pay particular attention to the differences specific to each side. Because the Brazilian government lacks legitimation it is difficult to identify the actual interests or conflicts of interest which may exist. In particular the political opening from 1975 to 1980 has made it obvious that Brazil as a partner is far more stratified than Germany and therefore its position vis-à-vis the Federal Republic is considerably more complicated than one could assume from the relations up to the present.

Until now, one of the major problems in relations with Third World countries has been how to establish a confidential working relationship with and include the ideas of the counterelites—that is, these countries' governments of the future—in the bilateral relations.[21] Authoritarian states, such as Brazil since 1964, are not interested in expanding bilateral relations beyond the strictly economic sphere into a pluralistic relationship. Brazilian sensitivity about any possible external interference by an otherwise highly valued partner during the current process of democratization is particularly obvious, as seen in the reaction to the work of the German political foundations.[22]

In the case of Brazil the internal determinants of the divergences between the two countries are of particular importance. Brazil's political self-concept is basically different from that of the Federal Republic. Each Brazilian government must take into consideration certain political determinants whose size and importance the Federal Republic would find difficult to comprehend. The fact that the majority of Brazil's population has remained on the margin of Brazil's quite successful industrialization process during the last fifteen years has also cast doubt on the economic legitimacy of the current political system. As long as all alternative ideas about development and participation were repressed, stability was guaranteed for the military government, but no popular majority support for foreign and foreign economic policy decisions could be expected. Thus Brazilian-German relations have been concentrated for the most part on that sector of Brazilian society that identifies itself with the interests of Western industrialized nations. Therefore, the close relationship exists primarily between the Federal Republic and a privileged sector of Brazil and does not reflect the very heterogeneous profile of the whole country.

A number of internal dualisms are to be found in Brazil's self-concept, only the most important of which can be mentioned here. First, there is an ever-growing discrepancy between those sectors of the society oriented toward Western standards of living and the majority of the population, which finds itself living on the margins of this society. Moreover, there is a regional dualism in the country, which has to struggle with enormous structural problems and hunger in some areas (the Northeast) and in others has reached a certain level of industrialization (in particular Rio de Janeiro, São Paulo, and Belo Horizonte). This double image has also placed a strain on bilateral relations, as the various Brazilian governments had until now been interested in maintaining this image in order to achieve the greatest possible resource allocations for their country. At the international level this contradiction manifests itself in the fact that it is advantageous for the country, when seeking aid, to define itself as a particularly underdeveloped land but, when doing business with industrialized countries, to define itself as being on the verge of industrialization.

In view of this dualism, upon which, in the current process of political opening, is superimposed the conflict between government and opposition, there exists the danger that the good relations that existed until now between the two countries based on bilateral cooperation with an internationally oriented elite can no longer be maintained. The emphasis on economic relations in conjunction with an "underdeveloped" system of political communication results in a high level of sensitivity in the relations model to shifts in economic emphasis that could arise from any correction of the development model due to the political opening.

The present widespread criticism in Brazil of the Federal Republic, which emanates not only from the opposition, is fed from three sources: First, the Federal Republic is being forced to share the responsibility for the stabilization of a political and economic system that was in no way desired by all Brazilians; second, the shape and scope of the nuclear treaty and the associated involvement of private German firms in Brazil's state-owned firms are considered to offer a one-sided advantage to the Federal Republic; and third, the strong presence of German industry—above all the major firms like Volkswagen, Bayer, Mannesmann, and Siemens—is seen as a threat to the Brazilian national economy. The danger that German firms will get an "exploiter" or "multinationals" image because of a generally increasing nationalist tendency in Brazil cannot be underrated. The threatening discrepancy between the apprehensions of the host country and the economic interests of the Federal Republic could probably be reduced if the big German concerns could build up a kind of exemplary presence in Brazil. This should not be limited to a technological and economic contribution, but should also be expressed in questions of codetermination and ecology as well as in the fields of local community and cultural affairs.

The widespread sensitivity among Brazilians to uncontrollable external economic influences in their country is well known. But investors from the Federal Republic may face new tensions or adjustment problems in connection with the impending changes in Brazil's economic and development model, whose cause is certainly to be found not only in democratization but also in changes in the world economic situation. Experience has shown that "development achievements of foreign firms are not usually the result of their own initiatives,"[23] so that the possibilities for German firms in Brazil under new "rules of the game" should not yet be exhausted. A general appraisal of the bilateral relations will certainly not be quite so positive in the future as in the years from 1964 to 1978, when stability was enforced by the military and any public sensitivity about economic relations with and the privileges of German firms could be largely prevented.

In the area of foreign policy the differing assessments of the maneuverability and intentions of both partners in the bilateral relationship become even clearer. Brazil never left any doubt that it wanted to use the Federal Republic and Japan to reduce its dependence on the United States. In the fields of trade, finance, and technology, both countries can offer advantages similar to those of the United States, although they do not enjoy the U.S. ability to exert political pressure. Brazil's desire for diversification of its foreign relations has in the last several years not been limited to the Western industrialized countries but has also increasingly included the "new rich" (e.g., the Arab states and Nigeria).

A decisive difference in the international classification of bilateral relationships is that Brazil is attempting to rise in the international system much as the Federal Republic did in the 1950s. Now, however, the Federal Republic has largely consolidated its international position and consciously chooses to remain in the shadow of the United States, while Brazil is standing at the foot of its global role. It is highly unlikely that Brazil's goal is a tight bond with the West similar to that of the Federal Republic. To this extent the decisive external determinant of the German-Brazilian relationship lies in the dissimilar postures of the two countries in the international system. Brazil is primarily concerned with the North-South conflict and has only a very minor interest in the East-West conflict. By contrast, the Federal Republic's political identity has developed in the midst of the East-West conflict, and it has considered the North-South conflict until now to be a dimension of only secondary, albeit rapidly increasing, importance.

This fundamental difference and the resulting divergences could not be eliminated even if Brazil were to try to solicit understanding in the Third World for its partner, the Federal Republic. On the contrary, Brazil's credibility has already suffered in the eyes of certain radical leaders of the Third World to the extent that it has become a privileged partner of industrialized nations. Because it has served as a link between the First and Third Worlds it is no longer considered to be a trustworthy ally in the North-South conflict. But in spite of its present ideological alignment and Western development strategy, Brazil still largely supports the demands of the Third World on the industrialized countries. Its foreign policy of "responsible pragmatism" is more an expression of the dilemma of having to reconcile the country's economic possibilities and structural necessities, rather than proof of any long-term interest in certain forms of bilateral cooperation.

Precisely because of its far-reaching and direct dependence on the industrialized nations, Brazil attempts to put indirect pressure on its partners, including the Federal Republic, by way of the North-South
dialogue. It is unlikely that it will permit itself to become an instrument
of the interests of the industrialized nations, since it would thereby lose
its bargaining power with those nations and thus reduce its
maneuverability within the international system.[24]

Therefore, Brazil, in contrast to the Federal Republic, is not of the
opinion that it is currently the most important obligation of the international community to ensure the economic strength of the industrialized
nations by safeguarding an appropriate supply of raw materials. Rather,
it is arguing for a new international economic order as the logical consequence of world economic developments since 1973. In this attempt to
bolster its own position, Brazil is running into ever-greater conflicts with
the industrialized nations. On the one hand, Brazil knows very well that
it would lose its preferential treatment, in particular in the field of
technology transfer, should it speak out more strongly in favor of the
Third World's ideas about restructuring the patterns of world trade. It
therefore tends to exploit for its own advantage the divergences between
itself and both the industrialized nations and Third World countries in
the multilateral framework as well as in the conferences on raw
materials. Brazil is not bent upon assuming a leadership role in the Third
World, but rather is attempting to demonstrate solidarity with the
demands of the Third World in many spheres. This is also true for the
political demands of, for example, the Arab states, as Brazil's
dependence on Arab oil supplies has become of greater consequence than
its dependence on the import of capital and technology from the industrialized nations.

Brazil's moderate attitude toward foreign investments, nationalization, and multinational concerns can be considered a result of its current
development situation and should in no case be judged to be indicative of
permanent Brazilian policy. Brazil knows very well how to make use of
its dependence, as the levels of foreign investments and foreign debt have
risen so high that even with increased pressure on foreign concerns and
an alteration of the rules of the economic game it can count on foreign
support for its economic development. The Brazilian government is well
aware that here it can gain leverage for the improvement of its position in
foreign trade and as a debtor in the world market.[25]

The fact that Brazil, under its foreign policy motto of responsible
pragmatism and with its wish to keep all options open, is unwilling to
enter automatically into alliances is another external divergence between
the Federal Republic and Brazil. It means that Brazil's political reliability,

in particular on the wider international level, remains questionable.[26] Thus Brazil has also been able to use the rivalry between the Federal Republic and the United States in the field of nuclear energy to its own advantage. Although Brazil appreciated the steadfastness of the Federal Republic in the face of the pressure that the United States attempted to exert between 1975 and 1977, it showed little understanding for the Federal Republic's unwillingness to enter into a conflict with the United States. Since Brazil, because of its historical experience, defines its dependence almost exclusively in economic terms, it is politically almost impossible for Brazil to understand security dependencies such as exist between the Federal Republic and the United States. Thus Brazil will continue to smile at the Federal Republic's continued deference in all questions concerning Latin America to the "predominant and natural role of the United States in the Western Hemisphere"[27] and will classify it as a burden on any bilateral relations. It necessarily follows that Brazil expects far too much from the Federal Republic. In addition, the importance of the two countries' commonalities as regional leaders is often less than could be expected, since these commonalities are unable to outweigh the grave differences existing between Europe and Latin America and between the two countries themselves.

Whereas for Brazil the Federal Republic's foreign policy rationality is relatively calculable, their differing interests in the North-South conflict and in relation to the supremacy of the United States make any assessment of Brazil's rationality more difficult. Here previous experience with the nuclear treaty is a good example. Brazil was primarily interested in improving its political status within the international system. This goal will be achieved even if the implementation of the treaty is delayed or its planned scope reduced. What was for the Federal Republic a strategy for gaining acceptance of a promising technology on the world market was for Brazil primarily the key to becoming a superpower. Thus the treaty was subject to entirely different interpretations from both sides because of the structural differences of both societies and their different positions in the international system. The political costs that this treaty has brought to the Federal Republic will be entered as a debit in the books of the bilateral relationship.

Bilaterally, a close relationship between a nation on the rise in the international system, which by definition represents anti–status quo interests, and a defender of the status quo in the international system must in the long run be most questionable. The Federal Republic, with Brazil's help, would like among other things to maintain the status quo, that is, its position in the world economy. Brazil would like to establish its own position at the expense of the industrialized nations. In questions about the international division of power, influence, and property, Brazil's goals must differ from those of the Federal Republic, regardless of any internal constellation of elites. Precisely because Brazil considers its ascent in the international system to be predestined, it must cease to identify itself with the Federal Republic's economic interests.

A Model for First World–Third World Relations?

If one speaks about the exemplary nature of the perfect cooperation within or even paradigm of the North-South relationship in the case of Brazil and the Federal Republic of Germany, one must not ignore the fact that this obtained only during a certain phase when the two countries economically complemented one another.[28] A change in the demand structure—and this is true for the domestic market as well as for certain areas of the world economy—could place considerable political strains on such a close relationship. The emphasis on the perfect congruence of interests has for too long concealed the fact that until now this congruence has lacked a firm basis and tight moorings.

The goals and expectations of both sides are just too different. Brazil hopes to gain far more from its cooperation with the Federal Republic than the latter is able to offer.[29] The expectations on both sides become all the more unrealistic the more their relationship is held up as a model. In such circumstances, any "normal" crisis in the bilateral relationship, which is now and then unavoidable between two states with such different structures and interests, is seen as an exceptional strain. In this connection, the negative experiences that the United States has had with its concept of a "special relationship" are an important indication that particularly far-reaching and economically stable relations are actually possible only between states that can come to share a large number of conceptions and expectations, not only in the economic sphere but also at all levels of interaction. This kind of model relationship exists, for example, between the United States and Canada and between the Federal Republic and France. It is no accident that the United States has been unable to establish such model relationships with the Latin American countries. There are also few indications that the Federal Republic will succeed in establishing such a relationship with Brazil.

The interactions on the government level and between multinational concerns and their daughter firms are certainly not sufficient for the establishment of a permanent model relationship. The feeling of belonging to different regional groups and of representing different worldwide interests must necessarily cause each country to seek allies whose international political goals differ from those of the other's allies. At the same time, an overly close alliance with and too great expectations from the partner country could prevent each country from adapting to changes occurring elsewhere in the international system. When assessing the ability of the bilateral relationship to act as a model, the political costs—e.g., from the Federal Republic's viewpoint, of neglecting other countries in the region—that could result from concentrating on such "take-off" countries, as well as those costs that could result from the favoring of a particular developing country at the expense of the relationship with the United States or other partners, must be taken into consideration.

Experience has shown that privileged relationships with states that, because of their wealth of natural resources and regional influence, are in a position to contribute to one's own situation in the international system are especially fragile. Here Iran can be seen as an extreme case. A close relationship with an industrialized nation has never produced either domestic or regional stability for a "take-off" country. The consideration that these states or their ruling elites show for the interests of the industrialized nations has proved profitable to both partners for only a limited time. The "nation-building process" takes far longer and is considerably more difficult as long as a certain sector of the indigenous elite attempts to prevail, with the continued ideological and financial support of the industrialized nations, against the majority of the population. In the case of Brazil, as a result of the increasing political opening, a course correction is becoming evident that brings with it a certain turning away from Europe in general and the Federal Republic in particular in favor of stronger South-South relationships (with Latin America, Africa, and the Arab states). Developing countries in Brazil's category can adapt to such altered international circumstances much more quickly than their partners among the industialized nations.

For the Federal Republic, Brazil is in many respects an archetypal "take-off" country and the relations that have been established between the two countries should serve as a model for its relationship with other "take-off" countries. However, as soon as the internal inequalities are reinforced and national participation encouraged by the modernization thrusts, as is the case in other "take-off" countries—that is, as soon as the excessively strong ties to the interests of Western industrialized nations cause political instability—the areas of agreement between the partners will diminish. What remains of the model for First World–Third World relations is a sharing of economic interests independent of the level of development, but upon which are superimposed structural differences in foreign policy goals and domestic political needs. A sober examination of the divergences of interests between Brazil and the Federal Republic, which will continue to crystallize, probably will eliminate the concept of a model for First World–Third World relations but will in no way foreclose a good bilateral partnership without excessive expectations on either side.

Notes

1. The term "take-off" countries (*"Schwellenländer"*), which was introduced into the development politics terminology of the Federal Republic in 1977, has several meanings. It should separate the "relatively developed" from the "less developed" countries of the Third World. It is, however, often used as a synonym for the term "threshold power" (*"Schwellenmacht"*), which applies to candidates for "nuclear weapons status." For a critical analysis of this group of Third World countries, see Ralf Dahrendorf, "International Power: A European Perspective," *Foreign Affairs* 56, no. 1 (October 1977), pp. 72–86, especially p. 83.

2. Contrary to the many explanations given for the close relations between the two countries as due to the German element in Brazil, this is hardly an important factor. Of all the European immigrants to Brazil from 1884 to 1963, less than 4 percent were German. And only slightly more than 3 percent of all Germans who emigrated between 1871 and 1957 went to Brazil. See Albrecht von Gleich, *Germany and Latin America* (Santa Monica, Calif.: Rand Corporation, RM-5523 RC, 1968), pp. 6–7.

3. Quoted from the joint communiqué issued on the occasion of Chancellor Helmut Schmidt's visit to Brazil on April 4, 1979. See *Bulletin* 52, p. 464.

4. Carlos von Doellinger, *Der historische Zusammenhang zwischen Auslandsinvestitionen und Aussenhandel in den deutsch-brasilianischen Wirtschaftsbeziehungen* (Universität Göttingen, Ibero-Amerika-Institut für Wirtschaftsforschung), p. 16.

5. Ibid, p. 11.

6. "Der Beitrag deutscher Auslandsinvestoren für die Entwicklung Brasiliens," in Bundesstelle für Aussenhandelsinformation, *Mitteilungen* 29/BM159 (May 1979), p. 1.

7. India, the country with top priority in German development politics, received more aid than all Latin American countries taken together—5.8 billion deutsche marks. Pakistan, Israel, Indonesia, and Egypt also received far more than Brazil. See Wolfgang Hoffman, "Bonner Geld für die Dritte Welt," in *Die Zeit*, June 15, 1979, p. 29.

8. The fourteen bilateral agreements that have already been signed demonstrate where the emphasis in German-Brazilian cooperation lies—in nuclear research, space research, astronomy, aviation research, computer technology, mathematics, scientific documentation, geology, oceanic research, material control, biochemistry, medicine, agriculture, and veterinary studies. For detailed information on the technical-scientific cooperation between the Federal Republic and Latin America, see Germán Kratochwil, *Wissenschaftlich-*

Technologische Entwicklung und Internationale Zusammenarbeit in Lateinamerika (Tübingen, 1976). For the results of German-Brazilian cooperation in the scientific fields, see Deutscher Akademischer Austauschdienst, *Beiträge zu den brasilianisch-deutschen Beziehungen* (Bonn, 1978).

9. The remaining three treaties are an agreement on double taxation, which went into effect on January 1, 1976; an agreement on cooperative film production of June 3, 1976; and an agreement on shipping, which was signed on April 4, 1979.

10. This is dated June 16, 1978; it envisages regular consultations on current questions of foreign policy of mutual interest. The joint talks of the policy planning staffs take place separately from the annual consultations between the foreign ministers, alternating between Bonn and Brasília. See *Bulletin* 71, p. 626.

11. Even if the prediction that German investments in Brazil would surpass those of the United States in the 1980s seems exaggerated, it does accurately reflect the trend. See Ronald M. Schneider, *Brazil, Foreign Policy of a Future World Power* (Boulder, Colo., 1976), p. 192.

12. Manfred Nitsch, *Rich Country Interests and Third World Development: The Federal Republic of Germany* (Berlin: Institute of Latin American Studies, Free University of Berlin, 1979), p. 41.

13. On the effects of the German-Brazilian nuclear treaty on Brazil's nuclear policy see Wolf Grabendorff, "Bestimmungsfaktoren und Strukturen der Nuklearpolitik Brasiliens," in Lothar Wilker (ed.), *Nuklearpolitik im Zielkonflikt* (Cologne, 1980), pp. 41–71.

14. Except for the oil-exporting countries, which occupy a special position, Brazil can also be classified as the greatest exporting country of the Third World. See Celso Lafer, "El estudio de las relaciones internacionales: necesidades y perspectivas," in *Estudios Internacionales* 11, no. 43 (July-September 1978), pp. 47–56, especially p. 47.

15. Compare the optimistic assessment of a member of the board of Siemens AG, Paul Dax, "Können die deutschen Grossfirmen zur ausgewogenen Entwicklungs Brasiliens beitragen?" *Deutsch-Brasilianische Hefte* 17, no. 6 (November-December 1978), pp. 398–411.

16. This is true only if one excludes China. See the data in Organisation of Economic Co-operation and Development, *Interfutures, Final Report* (Paris, 1975), p. 214.

17. Schneider, *Brazil*, p. 166.

18. German Federal Press Office (Bundespresseamt) reprint of Second German Television (ZDF) interview with Azeredo da Silveira, June 27, 1975.

19. See the article by the then State Secretary in the Foreign Ministry, Peter Hermes, "Aspekte und Perspektiven der deutschen Lateinamerika-Politik," in *Europa-Archiv* 14 (1979), pp. 421–430, especially p. 425. See also the interesting critique by William Waack, "Os velhos dilemas da nova política alemã para a América Latina," in *Jornal do Brasil*, August 19, 1979.

20. See the remarks by Chancellor Helmut Schmidt at the reception in Brasília on April 3, 1979: "Neither the suppliers of industrial goods nor the suppliers of raw materials nor the suppliers of oil have the right to dictate to or even to

dominate economically the other countries. Brazil today senses, just as does the Federal Republic of Germany, how dependent we are upon the large energy producers and energy suppliers of the earth." *Bulletin* 52, p. 462.

21. This kind of behavior, which is typical of the bilateral relations between the democratic states of the West, has not permeated their relations with the politically unstable countries of the Third World. The realization that it has become necessary is evident in Hermes, "Aspekte," p. 430, where it is assumed that the role of nongovernmental institutions in relations with Latin America will expand.

22. The Friedrich Ebert Foundation, the Konrad Adenauer Foundation, and the Friedrich Naumann Foundation are all active in the fields of trade union organization, the cooperative movement, and adult education, although with varying emphases. The Friedrich Ebert Foundation has been accused in the Brazilian press of interfering in the new formation of the Brazilian political party system. See, for example, Assis Mendonça, "Alemães confirmam: financiam partidos," in *O Estado de São Paulo*, June 19, 1979.

23. "Der Beitrag deutscher Auslandsinvestoren," p. 3, and Rudi Maslowski, *Deutsches Geld und Dritte Welt, dargestellt am Beispiel Brasilien* (Wuppertal, 1973).

24. See in particular Wayne A. Selcher, *Brazil's Multilateral Relations: Between First and Third Worlds* (Boulder, Colo., 1978), and Wolf Grabendorff, "La Política Exterior del Brasil entre el Primer y Tercer Mundo," *Nueva Sociedad* 41 (March-April 1979), pp. 108–119.

25. On these tactics, see Werner Baer and Carlos von Doellinger, "Determinants of Brazil's Foreign Economic Policy," in Joseph Grundwald (ed.), *Latin America and the World Economy: A Changing International Order* (Beverly Hills, Calif., 1978), pp. 147–161, especially p. 159.

26. This fact has become obvious in light of Brazil's intention to undermine the United States' embargo of grain shipments to the Soviet Union.

27. Hermes, "Aspekte," p. 426.

28. Thus Chancellor Helmut Schmidt, for example, speaks of "an exemplary case of cooperation between a great industrialized country and a country in the last stages of development," *Die Welt*, April 6, 1979. And again in a speech to business leaders in São Paulo, "If you wish, our economic structures are almost perfectly complementary. We can ideally mutually supplement one another and thus fulfill the prerequisites for tackling together those tasks which stand before us in the future," *Bulletin* 52, p. 466.

29. Furthermore, this is generally true for the relations between Latin America and the Federal Republic. "Certainly, the expectations of the Latin Americans are exaggerated and the possibilities open to the Federal Republic are often overestimated. Nevertheless, the German side will have to decide if it doesn't have to do more to fulfill the wishes of the Latin Americans if it wants to maintain its position." Karl-Alexander Hampe, "Lateinamerikas Eintritt in die Weltpolitik," *Zeitschrift für Kulturaustausch* 24, no. 4 (1974) pp. 16–23; quote on p. 21.

8
African-Brazilian Relations: A Reconsideration

Anani Dzidzienyo and J. Michael Turner

As frustrations continue to mount in the North-South dialogue between the nations of the developed and underdeveloped worlds, nascent relations among the less developed countries of the South become increasingly important. A particularly noteworthy example of intra-South cooperation—and one that has generated much discussion—is the current relationship linking Brazil with various countries in Africa.

Brazil's interest in Africa is in no way accidental. Over the last seven years—the period immediately following what has come to be known as the miracle years, 1969–1974, during which hopes were high that Brazil would achieve its wished-for great power status—this nation of 123 million, occupying a landmass of equally impressive size, has pursued an activist foreign policy aimed at securing a foothold in the little-tapped consumer markets of Africa. The timing of that move was critical: The oil crisis of 1973 forced Brazil to consider the benefits to be derived from closer association with the larger oil-producing countries of Africa, namely, Angola, Nigeria, and Gabon. But, lest the "conquest"—or "scramble" or "invasion," as it has been variously described in Brazil (words with decidedly pejorative connotations in Africa)—raise hackles and suspicions in certain quarters, Brazil made its moves armed with a reassuring rationale: Its ties with Africa were rooted in history and culture. In the case of Lusophone Africa, the commonalities transmitted by way of Portugal made for a special relationship. And, too, Portugal's eclipse as a colonial power and subsequent inability to function in any meaningful neocolonial capacity willy-nilly paved the way for Brazil to emerge as a dominant force in the Portuguese-speaking world. No longer identified with Portugal, Brazil was now free to adopt a reborn Third Worldism.

What, then, is the observer to make of African-Brazilian relations at the beginning of the 1980s? In practice, Brazil's activities in Africa have been largely confined to a few key countries: those with large populations, hence providing significant consumer markets for its goods and services; the oil producers; and the countries of Lusophone Africa. Our discussion will necessarily focus on these target countries. (For the purposes of this chapter we shall restrict our treatment of Africa to the countries of the sub-Saharan region; thus Algeria, Libya, Morocco, and Tunisia, all countries with a substantial Brazilian trade, do not form any significant part of the discussion.)

Brazil's Africa Policy Since Quadros

A brief comment on the history of Brazil's contact with Africa is appropriate here, if only because Brazil itself has given so much emphasis to it in its current outreach to Africa. From the discovery of Brazil in 1500 to the abolition of slavery in 1888, an estimated 3.5 million African slaves arrived in Brazil. From 1835 on, some Afro-Brazilians were to migrate back to West Africa—to Nigeria, Benin, Togo, and Ghana—either as deportees following the 1835 slave revolt in Bahia or as voluntary returnees.[1]

The period under review, 1961–1980, opens with the ground-breaking policy of *aproximação* introduced during the administration of President Jânio Quadros. This major shift in Brazil's foreign policy—away from its traditional alignment with the United States and the Western world—gave primacy to its place in, and relations with, the non-Western world, especially the countries of Africa and Asia. The dramatic flurry of activity during the seven-month Quadros regime was perhaps best symbolized—that is, from the African perspective—by the appointment of the black journalist Raymundo Sousa Dantas as ambassador to Ghana. For the first time in the history of Brazil a black ambassador was sent overseas. The epoch-making event was accompanied by the establishment of embassies throughout West Africa.[2] African students were awarded scholarships for study in Brazilian universities. Symbolically, and appropriately, the orientation program for the first group of students was held in Salvador, Bahia, the most visibly African community in Brazil.[3]

But this *aproximação* to Africa, which was not backed by concrete political and economic initiatives or actual policy changes, was short-lived, eventually foundering and dying with the overthrow of the João Goulart regime in 1964. The new power-holders were quick to return Brazil to its traditional foreign policy orientation, with a concomitant dissociation from the anticolonial liberation movements in Africa.[4]

Ironically, not even during the *aproximação* phase did Brazil ever make a clean break with her identification with Portugal's role in its African colonies. And in the period immediately following, 1964–1972, one finds a veritable nadir in Brazil's relations with Africa brought about by the dictates of internal Brazilian politics, preoccupation with "national security" and the threat of subversion, and solidarity with Salazarist Portugal; Brazil could no longer count itself even theoretically among the group of nations that identified with the aspirations of Africans in their struggle to overthrow colonialism and imperialism.[5] In accepting the validity of Portugal's claim to its dual mandate of "civilizing" Africans and protecting the South Atlantic from communism and subversion of Western ideals, Brazil became identified with another purported defender of Western civilization on the African continent: the apartheid regime of the Republic of South Africa.

By the last quarter of 1972, the bogging-down of Portugal in the African wars (especially that in Guinea-Bissau), the increasing international recognition accorded to liberation movements in Lusophone Africa and consequent isolation of Portugal and its supporters, and Brazil's need for overseas markets all contributed to a change in Brazil's African policy. In 1972 Foreign Minister Mário Gibson Barbosa made an official visit to seven African countries.[6] The two-pronged emphasis of that tour (as suggested by official pronouncements at the time) was (1) the strength of historical and cultural ties between Brazil and Africa, bolstered by the exemplary nature of race relations in Brazil, and (2) Brazil's ability to export tropicalized technology, goods, and expertise to Africa. Not only were these Brazilian products more suitable than U.S. or European models, they could also be procured under better financial conditions.[7]

Barbosa met with a lukewarm reception from those informed African observers who identified, and indeed raised, the critical question: Could Brazil's bona fides be correctly judged unshakable, given its equivocations on the question of Portuguese colonialism and its fraternization with the apartheid regime? Independent Black Africa, the foreign minister learned, would resolutely reject any form of expansionism.[8] The immediate result of the Barbosa visit was the so-called aggressive policy aimed at the African market. Although obviously inspired by economic factors, this push was supported by some overtly political moves, notably (1) recognition (in July 1974) of the PAIGC (Partido Africano de Independência da Guiné e Cabo Verde) as the legitimate ruler in Guinea-Bissau and Cape Verde (in this instance Brazil formally advised Portugal of its intent a mere three hours in advance of its realization, thus contravening the terms of the treaty of friendship duly signed by Brazil and

Portugal in 1961); and (2) formal recognition (in December 1975) of the MPLA (Movimento Popular de Libertação de Angola) as the sole and legitimate government of Angola—before any other Western country and even before the majority of independent African countries saw fit to do so.[9]

But not even these gestures, dramatic though they were, could obliterate the notion of a Janus-headed Brazil, one face looking expectantly to a newly rediscovered Black Africa and the other—as it were, much the more mature—nodding to the apartheid regime. Brazil, after all, still traded with Pretoria; Varig, the national airline, still flew to South Africa. And rumors persisted about Brazil's interest in the proposed South Atlantic pact, an interest in part predicated on its own strategic considerations—specifically, protection of the 4,500-mile sea route separating the African west coast and the eastern bulge of Brazil.[10] But looking beyond matters of security, we find Brazil in an apparently schizophrenic predicament in which it considered entering an alliance with forces known—or at least assumed—to oppose the very liberation movements in Africa that on two other occasions it had quite pointedly sanctioned.

By the end of the 1970s Brazil had attempted to resolve some of these contradictions. Varig no longer flew to South Africa, for reasons that remain unclear. Did Brazil act in response to ideological considerations or, more pragmatically, to economic losses? And a spokesman for the Brazilian defense establishment, Navy Minister Admiral Maximiano Fonseca, publicly declared that Brazil did not need a South Atlantic pact to ensure the security of her coastline.[11]

But what can be said about the African perspective in the matter of Brazilian-African relations? The literature to date has largely ignored the question, preferring to concentrate instead on Brazil's role as a future great power, the geopolitics of its domestic and foreign policy and its search for markets. One learns how Africa can benefit from Brazil's technological expertise and how Brazil can most effectively conduct its business dealings in Africa.[12] Some, paying tribute, wittingly or unwittingly, to Brazil's "racial democracy," count this among the pluses in its unique list of qualifications.[13] Perhaps the most disappointing treatment of the subject is d'Adesky's generally well-written and informative analysis of the increasing trade and commercial relations between Brazil and Africa and the prospects and problems therein. It is careful to point out certain infrastructural problems peculiar to Africa that would act to hamper progress and calls for a greater flow of information about Brazil to Africans, as well as support for organizations in Brazil that are concerned with developments in Africa. But the discussion sheds no light on the crucial African viewpoints. We are left to wonder about the political considerations, no less significant because unstated, that must surely affect Africa's acceptance of and at times seeming acquiescence to Brazilian overtures. How, Selcher atypically has noted, do Africans perceive the image and reality of Brazil's race relations? And how is that perception relevant to Brazil's foreign policy initiatives in Africa and to Africa's dealings with Brazil?[14]

Current Initiatives

To answer those questions, or more realistically (as will become clear as this discussion unfolds), to show why to date they remain unanswerable, we must cite some of the specifics of Brazil's carefully orchestrated strategy, whose implementation has involved a wide range of participants, among them diplomats, politicians, businessmen, and even religious leaders.[15] A cornerstone of that strategy is trade, and the success of its pursuit, measured in monetary terms, is in fact quite remarkable. Africans are buying and consuming a wide range of Brazilian products—automobiles, ceramics, shoes, meat, grains, sugar, coffee—valued at $571 million in 1977, a sixfold increase over the 1972 figure. African exports to Brazil rose from $153 million in 1972 to $550 million in 1977. So the total value of the bilateral trade swelled to $1.1 billion in 1977.

The Brazilian presence in Africa is not confined to goods alone, but extends to experts and technicians at work on a variety of projects, including road building in Mauritania, soya cultivation in the Ivory Coast, construction of tile and brickwork factories in Ghana, and improvement of telephone communication networks in Nigeria. In Angola management specialists from a major Brazilian supermarket chain have been called in to apply their expertise to the operation of the state-owned people's stores.[16]

Brazil has played host to African heads of state and ministerial delegations over the past five years—in 1979 Nigeria alone sent eighteen delegations, with the most influential visitor being General Shehu Yar'adua, chief of staff, Supreme Military Headquarters, in the government of General Obasanjo. Africans are studying a variety of subjects in Brazil's institutions—medicine, international relations, fine arts.[17]

All in all, it is the relationship with Nigeria that has produced the most far-reaching results. Total bilateral trade between Nigeria and Brazil is projected to rise to $5 billion in 1983.[18] Under the terms of an agreement signed in early 1980, Brazil will quadruple its oil imports from Nigeria, and Nigeria will in turn increase its food imports from Brazil, particularly of sugar and soya. These assurances, bolstered by a number of joint ventures in cattle raising and agricultural processing, are expected to contribute mightily to the growth of bilateral trade.[19] Optimistic projections aside, the trade picture to date shows that Brazil's exports to Nigeria have increased over 200-fold in the eight-year period of "conquest." Specifically, in 1972 Brazil exported goods valued at $1 million to Nigeria; in 1978 the value soared to $233 million, representing 85 percent of Brazil's total sales to Africa.[20] Nigeria has consistently received the lion's share of Brazil's expenditures in West Africa: $20.8 million of a total of $21.3 million spent in 1972 and $90.4 million of a total of $94.6 million in 1977.[21]

Brazilian firms have made effective use of public relations in their efforts to reach the Nigerian market. One of the more ambitious campaigns was launched in 1978 by Interbrás, whose goal was to sell a line of electrical products designed for use in the home. The "sales force" consisted of a Brazilian soccer team and Pelé himself. It was indeed Pelé's collaboration and sympathetic personality to which Interbrás vice president Carlos Sant'Anna paid tribute in his assessment of the campaign's success.[22] Lloyd Brasileiro has entered into a joint venture to found the Nigerbrás shipping line, a joint Nigeria-Brazil venture, and under a 1977 agreement Brazilian vessels are granted priority treatment at the port of Lagos. Once again looking to the future, we note that an accord of friendship, signed in 1979, provides for periodic consultations at the ministerial level on subjects of mutual interest to Nigeria and Brazil in the areas of internal affairs, scientific cooperation, and transfer of technology.[23]

Not unexpectedly, oil-exporting countries—Algeria, Libya, Gabon, and of course Nigeria—have been Brazil's largest trading partners, together accounting for 14 percent of its exports to Africa in 1972, 63 percent in 1975, and 55 percent in 1977.[24] But in the case of Gabon the balance of trade is heavily weighted in Gabon's favor: Gabon's exports to Brazil totaled $3.9 million in 1972, $645,000 in 1974, and $97.8 million in 1975. Gabon in turn bought from Brazil goods valued at $15,800 in 1973, $166,000 in 1976, and $1.2 million in 1977—figures that pale in comparison to the Nigerian equivalents. Brazil's trade relationship with Gabon exemplifies the heavy burden it has borne as a result of the various crises in the world petroleum situation.[25]

Alone among the Lusophone countries, Angola ships crude oil to Brazil. Bilateral trade between the two countries totaled $4 million in 1975, and by 1979 that figure had risen to $400 million. The international division of Petrobrás, Braspetro, has secured the right to prospect for oil in Angola; under the agreement, Brazil and Angola will enter into a joint venture in the event that any oil discoveries are made.[26]

Elsewhere in Lusophone Africa, Brazil is establishing her natural prominence predicated on those commonalities, noted early in this discussion, representing the Portuguese connection, primary among them language. Following the dictates of pragmatism—that is to say, ignoring the obvious differences in political outlook—the Lusophone countries have turned to Brazil for teachers, researchers, administrators, technicians, and experts, as well as educational materials, books, records, and films.[27] Brazilian agronomists, architects, urbanologists, and dam engineers are at work in Mozambique, which will use a $100 million line of credit to purchase Brazilian goods. Between 1976 and 1979 Mozambican trade with Brazil increased tenfold, from $8 million to a total of $80 million; in the first month of 1980 alone that trade was valued at $4.6 million.[28]

To end this recitation of Brazilian initiatives in Africa, we turn to Brazil's relations with South Africa—a conundrum defying pat resolution. As we noted earlier, Brazil has effectively maintained a Janus-headed stance on the question of her diplomatic and economic relations with the apartheid regime, on the one hand publicly condemning apartheid, ordering cessation of the Varig flights to Johannesburg, accrediting to its embassy in Pretoria not an ambassador but a chargé d'affaires; and on the other maintaining an active trading relationship with the regime. For the fact is that the bilateral trade figures have steadily grown: $7.0 million in 1972, $33.8 million in 1976, $109.6 million in 1977. The 1980 figure is expected to reach $150 million.[29] Yet Brazil has successfully assuaged the fears of conservatives at home—and it would seem among her Black African trading partners as well; ideological considerations, be they rhetorical or actual, need not stand in the way of fruitful commerce.[30] The extent to which Brazil's "pragmatism" continues to be effective will largely depend on whether independent Africa concretizes condemnation of apartheid with commensurate action against those countries—African and non-African—that maintain profitable commercial relations with the regime.

Culture, Race, Politics, and Trade—
African and Afro-Brazilian Perspectives

Throughout this discussion we have made repeated reference to Brazil's articulation of historical and cultural ties with Africa. What, one may ask, properly constitutes those ties, and what inferences can Africans draw from Brazil's manipulation of the ties in pursuit of its African policy? On the nature of the ties, it can be said that Brazil acknowledges—indeed, appears to celebrate—the identifiably African contribution to its culture. The African influence, so deeply ingrained in Brazilian society, can be seen in customs, life styles, belief systems, and the physical aspect of its people. Thus, extraordinary as it might seem to the observer, an official spokesman has declared Brazil the second largest *African* country after Nigeria in terms of population.[31] These retentions constitute an indestructible bridge of centuries-long duration that (the imagery here is President João Figueiredo's) both Africans and Brazilians must build on for their mutual material and social progress.[32]

All heady stuff for the African observer. But what, one might well ask, lies beyond the fervently iterated litany of retentions? Brazil, it would appear, has so effectively used the shared heritage to establish credibility in Africa, making it at once a cornerstone of its African policy and an instrument for its implementation, that Africans for the most part willingly accept Brazilian pronouncements. This despite the conspicuous and nearly complete absence of Afro-Brazilians—the most visible symbols of Africa in Brazil—from participation in their country's African initiatives.

Central to this issue is the role of race in national and international politics. While it may very well be the case that race is rarely the crucial factor in the decisions of sovereign states, it is not so unusual for racial and ethnic groups in plural societies to have some impact on their society's actions in the international sphere.[33] That Afro-Brazilians appear to have no such impact is consistent with their marginalization within Brazilian life and society. Afro-Brazilians, generally speaking, are excluded from the middle and higher levels of government, academia, business, diplomacy, the military—a fact that has been amply documented. The subject, sad to say, has elicited little discussion among Africans.[34]

Brazil and Brazilian affairs are rarely, if ever, given space in the African press. The reporting that does appear is at best a perfunctory recording of official communiqués and details of official visits.[35] For a brief period during the Second World Black and African Festival of Arts and Culture (FESTAC), which was held in Lagos and Kaduna, Nigeria, in January 1977, the Nigerian press devoted considerable coverage to the controversial rejection of a position paper that the Afro-Brazilian activist Abdias do Nascimento had hoped to deliver at a colloquium on black education and civilization. His subject: the deprivations and discrimination suffered by Afro-Brazilians. The *Daily Sketch* (Ibadan) serialized Nascimento's paper in its entirety.[36] At no point did press observers confront a basic issue: Participation in the colloquium had been restricted to official delegations, which of course meant in practice that distinguished individuals from the New World who themselves belonged to the group under discussion could make no contribution.

Those seeking critical appraisal must turn to overseas publications that treat African affairs, but here, too, coverage is sporadic. In 1972 and 1973 *West Africa*, a weekly published in London and widely circulated among Africans, carried a two-part essay on Brazil's view of Africa and another on the role of Afro-Brazilians in contemporary Brazilian society.[37] In 1978 an article entitled "Brazil Goes Africa" touched on some of the political problems involved in Brazil's relations with Africa, with particular attention to its dealings with South Africa.[38] But such treatments are exceptional. Another London-based publication, *Africa* magazine, in individual pieces appearing between 1972 and 1980, has dealt with survivals of African culture in Brazil, South Africa's relations with Latin American countries, including Brazil, and the controversy surrounding the inclusion of a racial category in Brazil's 1980 census.[39] An article in *Jeune Afrique*, a weekly published in Paris, examined the theory and practice of race relations in Brazil. The writer concluded that in the land of "King Pelé" the descendants of Africans were victims of an insidious form of racism.[40]

Given the persistence of the original colonial lines of communication, Africans look primarily to the former metropoles for news. Not surprisingly, therefore, African perceptions of Brazil are influenced by images filtered through Britain and France, as well as the United States, that powerful disseminator of news throughout the world. A different situation obtains in Lusophone Africa. There, awareness of Brazil has been closely linked to the Portuguese connection. In justifying its presence in Africa, Portugal held up the example of Brazil as testimony to a unique ability to create successful multiracial societies in the tropics. Not unexpectedly, the liberation movements in Lusophone Africa rejected that rationale out of hand.[41]

A certain skepticism is to be noted in the attitudes as reflected in public statements of Lusophone Africans toward Brazil. Speaking at the University of Dar es Salaam in 1974, Agostinho Neto declared that Afro-Brazilians did not in his view enjoy the full freedom or national equality of which Angolans had heard so much talk.[42] Indeed, the Angolan government later refused to broadcast a Brazilian television film on the grounds that it projected a pejorative image of blacks. Samora Machel has taken Brazil to task for its alignment with Portugal during the liberation struggle.[43] Brazil was excluded from the official roster of guests invited to the ceremonies celebrating Mozambique's independence, for only those who had identified with and supported the struggle of

FRELIMO (Frente de Libertação de Moçambique) were welcome; rather it was a Brazilian in exile in Moscow, the legendary Luis Carlos Prestes, then secretary-general of the Bra ilian Communist Party, who was asked to be present.[44] While on a visit to Brazil in 1979, Aquino de Bragança, an adviser to the president of Mozambique, voiced objections to the notion that a common language per se could guarantee fruitful cooperation; after all, he pointed out, the people who fought in the liberation struggle and the Portuguese troops who fought to quash them both spoke Portuguese.[45]

As increasing numbers of Africans go to Brazil, their direct experience of Brazilian society could broaden the dialogue in interesting ways. And here the issue of race—one that Africans are least likely to ignore, and one that Brazil has arguably forced them to look at by oft-repeated pronouncements of racial democracy—will surface. An incident involving four Nigerian students in Brazil merits comment. While in the company of university colleagues, the Nigerians were arrested on campus and hustled off to a police station for questioning in connection with a local robbery allegedly committed by a group of blacks. Itamaraty identity cards notwithstanding, the students, as they themselves acknowledged, were victims of a form of harassment that blacks are all too often subjected to.[46] On two occasions the ambassador of Ghana has been the target of discriminatory acts on the part of Brazilian policemen in Rio de Janeiro and Brasília. Despite his diplomatic status, he, too, suffered the harassment meted out to blacks in a society that effectively excludes them from positions of power and authority.[47]

The reemergence in recent years of Brazil's black press can have important consequences for African-Brazilian relations. For one thing, that press is actively making known the opinions—little heard in official circles—of a sector of the Afro-Brazilian population that regards those relations with keen interest.[48] One notes in the black press a particular sensitivity to the perceived manipulation of historic and cultural ties, with both the manipulators and those Afro-Brazilians they push forward as living symbols of those ties, in other words the manipulated, coming in for criticism. Prominent among the "manipulated" are the well-known *mãe do santo* (priestess) Olga de Alaketo and Pelé, whose latter-day incarnation as supersalesman was mentioned earlier.[49] Crucial to the criticism of Pelé is what is perceived to be Uncle Tomism, for he has never identified himself satisfactorily with his fellow Afro-Brazilians and their special predicament.

What is hoped, it appears, is that the current predicament of Afro-Brazilians—defined as economic, political, *and* racial, in contradistinction to the official notion of a social disadvantaging that is essentially color-blind[50]—together with the shared heritage, will link Afro-

Brazilians and Africans in an authentic and mutually beneficial relationship. Thus Africa's awareness of and solidarity with Afro-Brazilians become important. When Angola rejects a Brazilian-made film that in its view projects a negative image of Afro-Brazilians, official Brazil, it is felt, might very well reconsider its thinking about black protest: To wit, when Afro-Brazilians make similar condemnations they are usually accused of racism. No such accusation, it is argued, could be made against the government of Angola.[51]

Toward a Broadened African-Brazilian Relationship

What we can glean from Afro-Brazilian press statements would point to a specific Afro-Brazilian dimension to African-Brazilian relations that official Brazil has shown little inclination to valorize. And those few members of the Afro-Brazilian community whose services are enlisted in the promotion of official initiatives in no way pose a challenge to the status quo, for in the final analysis it is matters of trade that govern their involvement.[52]

In decrying existing relations between Africa and Brazil for their failure to take into meaningful account the Afro-Brazilian dimension, the renowned Afro-Brazilian educator and activist Abdias do Nascimento exemplifies the alternative view. A truly genuine relationship between Africa and Brazil, he has said, would include Afro-Brazilians in an honored position, the real benefits of which would accrue to Africa, Brazil, and Afro-Brazilians themselves.[53]

Following Rosenau's thesis, to the extent that the coming together of Brazil and Africa acts to rearrange or remodel the existing system of international relations, which is the larger framework within which their growing relationship exists, a certain confusion and excitement will result as the two areas shift away from the traditional relations that history, colonialism, and neocolonialism have imposed on both.[54]

In the sphere of East-West relations several observations can be made. Given the severe strains on détente that we have seen in recent times, especially in the wake of the Soviet invasion of Afghanistan, renewed calls have come for a reassessment of Western strategies to deal with such activities on the part of the Soviets. Africa's importance here becomes obvious because of the existence on the continent of the apartheid regime, which aggressively asserts its commitment to defending both Africa and the South Atlantic from communist threats to their freedom. Were the changing global situation to result in the resurfacing of the idea of a South Atlantic pact, what can be said about the African and Brazilian responses?

Brazilian resolution of that issue and the priority that it will give to its pursuit of relations with Africa will, in short, very much depend on the durability of the *abertura democrática*, the balancing of forces and influence within the elite military-civilian decision-making complex, and Brazil's ability to manage and/or resolve the socioeconomic and political crisis—specifically, a crippling foreign debt and great disparities between haves and have-nots—that has accompanied the demise of the "miracle."[55] And here Africans would do well to temper their enthusiasm over the merits of the "miracle" and its possible emulation by Africa with some careful analysis of its real costs in human, social, and political terms.

In the case of Africa (excluding South Africa, of course) certain questions come to mind. In Nigeria, for instance, would not the discussion of its response to a South Atlantic pact impel that country to ask again, as Brigadier Garba first asked of his Brazilian hosts in 1977, "Against whom is the South Atlantic being defended?"[56] And should Nigeria assume the role of defender of the black world—exemplifying, as President Shehu Shagari indicated in a recent statement, the muscle of the black world—would we then find Nigeria advocating and implementing intensification of the armed struggle against the apartheid regime *and* its collaborators?[57] Answers to these questions at this point would naturally be conjectural and so must await the emergence of a clear statement of Nigeria's geopolitical position and theorizing from its military establishment that parallels that of a General Golbery do Couto e Silva.

Nigeria is an important reference point because it is that country—given its growing influence as a regional power, its growing volume of trade with Brazil, and its acknowledgment of kith-and-kin ties with Brazil—that we shall look to for some definition of an African policy toward Brazil that casts Africa in a role other than its present reactive one, in which Brazil alone acts as initiator. Nowhere in Africa do we hear about Brazil the kind of observation that the head of Itamaraty's Africa, Asia, and Oceania division, Marcos Castrioto de Azambuja, recently made. In an address before the Foreign Affairs Committee of the Brazilian Chamber of Deputies in 1979, he discussed the imperative of understanding the aspirations and problems of Africa, with specific reference to liberation movements. Observers, too, he noted, must refrain from imposing inapplicable foreign models on Africa.[58]

Africa, of course, has a role in all this—one that to date it has shown no overwhelming desire to assume. It might begin by working to establish more direct lines of communication with Brazil and to encourage the serious study of Brazil in African academic and journalistic circles. Language studies would of necessity support instruction in the history, politics, economics, and sociology of Brazil. It might reasonably be expected that diplomatic representatives in Brazil would communicate to interested parties at home news of significant developments, but they are severely hampered by their relatively small numbers, the immense size of Brazil, the distance of its capital city from the major centers of Afro-Brazilian life and sociopolitical activities (São Paulo, Rio de Janeiro, Salvador, and Rio Grande do Sul) and, a concomitant problem, rudimentary knowledge about Afro-Brazilians. What is needed is an awareness of the history of Afro-Brazilian struggles for equality that is at least comparable to that of the North American counterpart.

In Brazil itself, Africa might seek to establish joint cultural centers, perhaps under the aegis of the Organization of African Unity, which would unquestionably go some way toward filling the present gap between historical Africa and present-day Africa in the minds of Brazilians. Bahia, we would suggest, is the ideal site for such a center.[59] An inevitable outcome of this initiative would be a better-informed group of Brazilians who are interested in a dynamic relationship between Brazil and Africa, one that would equally inevitably question, and perhaps even lobby to alter, existing trends in their country's conduct of relations with Africa. Brazil's response would certainly be of interest. And should Africa itself decide to emphasize kith-and-kin ties with Afro-Brazilians as articulated policy and to stand on its head this oft-repeated ingredient of Brazil's own policy, how, one wonders, would Brazil respond to this new twist in the business of manipulating historico-cultural and racial dimensions in the furtherance of foreign policy? The fluidity of political incumbency in postcolonial Africa means changes of regime are far more likely to occur there than in Brazil, a prospect that must be taken into account when projecting the future directions of African-Brazilian relations. The potential for confusion and excitement is assuredly great.

In June 1980 Foreign Minister Saraiva Guerreiro made a seminal visit to five countries in East and Southern Africa. His aim was to solidify the political dimensions of Brazil's gains in Africa, thereby demonstrating that his country's interest in Africa went well beyond mere commerce.[60] This journey of "conquest," in the not atypical hyperbole of Brazil's press coverage of African affairs, highlighted for some writers certain basic inconsistencies in Brazil's relations with Africa, particularly in the matter of South Africa. That the South African ambassador to Brazil resides in social "isolation" in Brazil can be of little concern to him as he reviews the figures totting up the dramatically increased trade between Brazil and South Africa. Also in June 1980, the president of Guinea-Bissau, Luis Cabral, went to Brazil.[61] And President Figueiredo himself will go to Africa in 1981, the first Brazilian president to do so.

What happens in the interim warrants careful and critical attention on the part of Africans. For it is only when such reasoned assessments begin to be made that a genuine African-Brazilian relationship, characterized by relative equality in conceptualizing and executing policy designed to be beneficial to both sides, can develop.

Notes

1. See Philip T. Curtin, *The Transatlantic Slave Trade: A Census* (Madison: University of Wisconsin Press, 1969). See also J. Michael Turner, "Les Brésiliens: The Impact of Former Brazilian Slaves upon Dahomey" (Ph.D. diss., Boston University, 1975), and idem., "Brazilian and African Sources for the Study of Cultural Transferences from Brazil to Africa during the Nineteenth and Twentieth Centuries," in *The African Slave Trade from the Fifteenth to the Nineteenth Century*, General History of Africa: Studies and Documents, Vol. 2 (Paris: UNESCO, 1979), pp. 311–330.

2. See José Honório Rodrigues, *Brazil and Africa* (Berkeley and Los Angeles: University of California Press, 1964); Adolfo Justo Bezerra de Menezes, *O Brasil e o mundo asio-africano* (Rio de Janeiro: Edições GRD, 1960); Jânio Quadros, "Brazil's Foreign Policy," *Foreign Affairs* 40, no. 1 (October 1961):19–27; Keith Larry Storrs, "Brazil's Independent Foreign Policy 1961–1964: Background, Trends, Linkage to Domestic Policies and Aftermath" (Ph.D. diss., Cornell University, 1972); and Wayne Selcher, *The Afro-Asian Dimension of Brazilian Foreign Policy* (Gainesville: University of Florida Press, 1974).

3. See Anani Dzidzienyo, "The World of the Afro-Brazilians," *West Africa*, 5 March 1973, p. 301.

4. See Selcher, *The Afro-Asian Dimension*; also John A. Marcum, *The Angolan Revolution: Volume II: Exile, Politics and Guerrilla Warfare 1962–1976* (Cambridge, Mass., and London: M.I.T. Press, 1978).

5. See Anani Dzidzienyo, "A África, vista do Brasil," in *Afro-Ásia*, no. 10–11 (1970), pp. 79–97.

6. See Anani Dzidzienyo, "Brazil's View of Africa, I," *West Africa*, 13 November 1972, pp. 1532–1533; "Brazil's View of Africa, II," *West Africa*, 20 November 1972, pp. 1556–1557; "Barbosa's West African Tour,"*West Africa*, 4 December 1972, p. 1626.

7. See "Operação Tama conquista novos mercados," in *Nações amigas* 1, no. 1 (August 1978): 5–8.

8. See Dzidzienyo, "Barbosa's West African Tour."

9. See "Brazil Goes Africa," *West Africa*, 20 January 1978, p. 175; Marx Gruberg, "Subsaharan Africa: Potential Market, Vexing Political Challenge," *Brazil Herald*, 7 September 1977, p. B12; "Descoberta da África," *Veja*, 27 July 1977, pp. 28–29; "Recognition of the People's Republic of Angola (MPLA Government)," *Africa Currents*, no. 4 (1975-1976), p. 18; "Brazil: Africa Adventure," *Latin American Political Review*, 9 August 1974, p. 246.

10. The classic postulation of Brazil's geopolitical ideas has been propounded by General Golbery do Couto e Silva, who has served as the most influential political adviser to President Figueiredo and his predecessor, President Geisel. See his *Aspectos geopolíticos do Brasil* (Rio de Janeiro: Biblioteca do Exército, 1957); and *Geopolítica do Brasil* (Rio de Janeiro: Editora José Olympio, 1967). See also Ronald Schneider, *Brazil: Foreign Policy of a Future World Power* (Boulder, Colo.: Westview Press, 1976), especially p. 196; "Latin Letter," *Latin America Political Report*, 30 September 1977, p. 299; "South Atlantic: Defending the Sea Lanes of the West," *Latin America Political Report*, 30 April 1976, p. 130. The latter article pointed out that the proposed pact should not be confused with the Pacto Atlántico Sur, signed in 1956 by the governments of Argentina, Brazil, Paraguay, and Uruguay, which was concerned solely with training exercises. See also Daniel Waksman Schnica, "Pretoria y sus aliados: el idilio de los conos sur," *Cuadernos del Tercer Mundo* 2, no. 12 (May 1977):52–55; David Fig, "Apartheid's Hands Across the Atlantic," *Guardian* (Manchester), 18 June 1979, p. 14; and finally, three articles by Clovis Brigagão: "Brazil's Foreign Policy: The Military Command, Itamaraty Embellishes, Multinationals Gain," *International Peace Research Institute* (Oslo), no. 18, 1978; *Brazil's Foreign Policy: The Last Fifteen Years* (Stockholm: Institute of Latin American Studies, 1978); and "Objetivos y contenidos de las relaciones entre el sur de África y Latinoamérica," *Estudios de Asia y África* 14, no. 1 (January–March 1979):158–171.

11. In an interview Fonseca dismissed the necessity of a South Atlantic pact to secure Brazil's coastal defenses; see "Não é preciso um pacto no Atlântico sul," *Veja*, 25 April 1979, pp. 28–29. See also Carlos Conde, "Brasil iniciava ofensiva contra apartheid," *O Estado de São Paulo*, 10 June 1977.

12. See Schneider, *Brazil*, pp. 3–25; Norman Bailey and R. Schneider, "Brazil's Foreign Policy: A Case Study in Upward Mobility," *Inter American Economic Affairs* 27 (1974):3–26; William Perry, *Contemporary Brazilian Foreign Policy: The International Strategy of an Emerging Power* (Beverly Hills, Calif., and London: Sage Publications, 1976); Jacques d'Adesky, *Analyse des échanges commerciaux Brésil-Afrique 1958–1977: problèmes et perspectives* (Rio de Janeiro: Conjunto Universitário Cândido Mendes, Centro de Estudos Afro-Asiáticos, 1979). [The latter has also been published in Portuguese: "Intercâmbio comercial Brasil-África (1958–1977): problemas e perspectivas," *Cadernos Cândido Mendes: Estudos Afro-Asiáticos* 1, no. 3 (1980): 5–34. All citations are to the French edition.]

13. See "Brazil—Just Plant and Anything Grows," in *Africa Guide* (Saffron Walden, Essex: World of Information, 1979), pp. 30–33; Vladimir Reisky de Dubnic, *Political Trends in Brazil* (Washington, D.C.: Public Affairs Press, 1968), especially p. 136.

14. See Wayne Selcher, *Brazil's Multilateral Relations: Between First and Third Worlds* (Boulder, Colo.: Westview Press, 1978), p. 219.

15. See "Brazil—Just Plant"; "Brazil Goes Africa"; d'Adesky, *Analyse des échanges*; Peter Eisner, "Brazil and Africa Seek Closer Ties," *Los Angeles Times*, 2 March 1980, p. 21; "Brazil: Wooing Africa," *Africa Confidential*, 23 April 1980, p. 8; "Brazil in Africa: Radical Politics Boost Business," *Latin America Economic Report*, 22 June 1979, p. 186; "Land Reform in Africa, If Not at Home," *Latin*

America Weekly Report, 5 June 1980, p. 8; Jorge Pontual, "Brasil e África, do comércio à política," *Jornal do Brasil*, 8 May 1980. Although the journey of Dom Eugênio Salles was not, strictly speaking, part of the official "offensive," the timing is nonetheless interesting in the light of our theme. See "Cardeal vai à África para comprender o sincretismo religioso dos brasileiros," *Jornal do Brasil*, 3 July 1980; and "Cardeal volta da África e diz que viagem teve objetivos missionarios," *Jornal do Brasil*, 14 July 1980.

16. See Gabriel Manzano Filho, "Final de festa," *Veja*, 18 June 1980, p. 46; and "Land Reform in Africa."

17. For an account of the visit of General Abisoye in 1978, see "Nigéria envia militar para negociar compra de armas," *O Estado de São Paulo*, 9 November 1978; for that of General Shehu Yar'adua, see "Figueiredo garante que não muda relações com a África," *Jornal do Brasil*, 11 January 1979, p. 16.

18. See "Land Reform in Africa."

19. See Mirna Grzich, "Nigeria, é bom bocado do empresário brasileiro," *Isto é*, 14 December 1977, p. 37; d'Adesky, *Analyse des échanges*; "Brazil Goes Africa"; "Operação Tama," and in the same issue of *Nações amigas*, "Tama and Pelé: The Best from Brazil," p. 9; "Land Reform in Africa"; and finally, "Nigerian Connection Pays Dividends," *To the Point International*, 9 March 1979, p. 42.

20. See *O Estado de São Paulo*, 7 July 1979, p. 1; and Eisner, "Brazil and Africa."

21. See d'Adesky, *Analyse des échanges*, p. 58.

22. In an interview published in *Nações amigas* 1, no. 1 (August 1978):8–9.

23. See *O Estado de São Paulo*, 7 July 1979, p. 1.

24. See "Brazil—Just Plant"; "Brazil in Africa"; and *To the Point International*, 9 March 1979, p. 42.

25. See d'Adesky, *Analyse des échanges*, p. 58; "Brazil in Africa"; "Land Reform in Africa"; and "Brazil—Just Plant."

26. See "Brazil: Wooing Africa"; and Pontual, "Brasil e África."

27. Ibid. See also "Final de festa."

28. See Eisner, "Brazil and Africa"; and Pontual, "Brasil e África."

29. For a discussion of trade with South Africa, see Fig, "Apartheid's Hands Across the Atlantic"; "Fincando a bandeira," *Veja*, 11 June 1980, pp. 34–38; and "Brazil Goes Africa."

30. See "No fortim negro," *Veja*, 23 April 1980, pp. 32–35; and "O Brasil vai em busca da África," *Isto é*, 4 June 1980, p. 28.

31. See interview with Ambassador Sérgio Corrêa da Costa, head of Brazil's mission to the United Nations, in *African Mirror*, 1 December 1977, pp. 31–32.

32. Statement made in welcoming President Kaunda of Zambia. For report, see "Brasil quer fim dos govêrnos de minoria racial," *Jornal do Brasil*, 30 August 1978, p. 8.

33. See George Sheppard, ed., *Racial Influences on American Foreign Policy* (New York: Basic Books, 1971); Basil Ince, "The Racial Factor in International Relations of Trinidad and Tobago," *Caribbean Studies* 16, no. 3-4 (October 1976–January 1977):5–28; and Thomas Skidmore, *Black Into White: Race and Nationality in Brazilian Thought* (New York: Oxford University Press, 1974).

34. Among the notable exceptions are Wande Abimbola, "The Yoruba Traditional Religion in Brazil: Problems and Prospects" (Department of African Languages and Literature, University of Ife, 1976), cited in Abdias do Nascimento, *"Racial Democracy" in Brazil: Myth or Reality* (Ibadan: Sketch Publishing, 1977), p. 143; Olabiyi Babalola Yai, "Alguns aspectos da influência das culturas nigerianos no Brasil em literatura, folclore e linguagem," *Cultura* 6, no. 23 (1976); and Samuel Yaw Boadi-Siaw, "Development of Relations Between Brazil and African States 1950–1975" (Ph.D. diss., University of California, Los Angeles, 1975).

35. See "Sekou Touré in Brazil," *West Africa*, 3 March 1980, p. 420; and "Senghor in South America," *West Africa*, 14 November 1977, p. 2333. The latter is a report of an Itamaraty communiqué; the former appeared a month after Touré's visit.

36. See "Professor Explodes," *Daily Times* (Lagos), 23 January 1977; "The Black Man's Burden in Brazil," *Daily Sketch* (Ibadan), 28 January 1977; "The Plight of Blacks in Brazil," *Nigerian Observer*, 28 January 1977.

37. Dzidzienyo, "World of the Afro-Brazilians," "Brazil's View of Africa, I," "Brazil's View of Africa, II," and "Barbosa's West African Tour."

38. "Brazil Goes Africa."

39. "Brazil: The Beginning of Black Power," *Africa*, January 1980, pp. 70–71.

40. "Dans la patrie du roi Pelé les descendants des esclaves restent des citoyens de seconde zone." Siradiou Diallo, "Brésil: un racisme sournois," *Jeune Afrique*, 26 December 1979–2 January 1980, pp. 56–59.

41. See Gerald Bender, *Angola under the Portuguese: The Myth and the Reality* (Berkeley and Los Angeles: University of California Press, 1978), pp. xxii–xxiii, 199–214; John Stockwell, *In Search of Enemies* (New York: W.W. Norton, 1978), pp. 49, 184; and Marcum, *Angolan Revolution*.

42. Marcum, *Angolan Revolution*, pp. 314–315.

43. See "Land Reform in Africa."

44. In a speech at an MPLA congress in Luanda, Prestes recalled the "historic links between the Angolan people and the most exploited stratum of the Brazilian workers, those of African origin, the descendants of slaves." *West Africa*, 14 November 1977, p. 2333.

45. See interview with Aquino de Bragança, "Relação com Africa é criticada," *Jornal do Brasil*, 17 September 1979, p. 8.

46. See "Estudantes negros fazem protesto pelo tratamento que receberam da policia," *Jornal do Brasil*, 13 September 1979.

47. Personal communication with the ambassador. See "O embaixador africano," *Sinba* 2, no. 3 (1979):6.

48. See especially "Nós e África," *Jornegro* 1, no. 4 (September 1978):1; "África e armas," *Tição* 2, no. 2 (August 1978):7; "Quem deveria ter representada o Brasil no festival de arte na Nigéria?" *Sinba* 1, no. 1 (July 1977):1. In a different category is *Afro-Chamber*, published by Câmara de Comércio África-Brasil; this magazine focuses primarily on business and trade. Its founder, Adalberto Camargo, is a businessman and (unusual for an Afro-Brazilian) a member of the Federal Chamber of Deputies. He has visited Africa on several occasions and ac-

companied Foreign Minister Guerreiro on his tour of Africa in the spring of 1980. He has hosted many dignitaries from the continent. For accounts of those occasions, see *Afro-Chamber* 2, no. 3 (1979):6, 31–32.

49. See "Pelé continúa o mesmo quem mudou?" *Jornegro* 1, no. 1 (March 1978):6. The issue has been commented on even in the alternative press; see, for example, Rubem Confete, "Olga de Alaketo: objeto de consumo do poder," *Lampião da esquina* 2, no. 18 (November 1979):11. For a general discussion of official manipulation of Afro-Brazilians, see the chapter entitled "Etnia afrobrasileira e política internacional" in Abdias do Nascimento, *O Quilombismo* (Petrópolis: Editora Vozes, 1980), pp. 155–208. See also Nascimento's "*Racial Democracy.*" José Maria Nunes Pereira cautions against the merchandising of Afro-Brazilian culture in Brazil's relations with Africa in "Cultura negra semanas afrobrasileiras," *Revista de cultura vozes* 71, no. 9 (November 1977): 45–53.

50. See Manuel Diégues Júnior, *A África no vida e na cultura do Brasil* (Brasília: Brazilian Ministry of External Affairs, 1977).

51. "O sítio racista," *Jornegro* 2, no. 6 (1979):15.

52. See "Pelé continúa"; and Confete, "Olga de Alaketo."

53. In *O Quilombismo* and personal communication with authors.

54. James Rosenau, "Muddling, Meddling, and Modelling: Alternative Approaches to the Study of World Politics in an Era of Change," *Millennium* 8, no. 2 (1979):130–143.

55. See Ronaldo Munck, "State, Capital and Crisis in Brazil: 1929–1972," *Insurgent Sociologist* 9, no. 4 (1980):39–58. The recent visit of Pope John Paul II occasioned intensive press coverage and discussion of Brazil's developmental problems. See, for example, "A face cruel do Brasil," *Veja*, 16 July 1980, pp. 84–92; "John Paul Is Our Voice," *New York Times*, 13 July 1980, p. 20E; Jonathan Power, "A Working-Class Hero and . . . an Archbishop Who Gave His Palace Away," *Manchester Guardian Weekly*, 6 July 1980, pp. 8–9; and Warren Hoge, "Pontiff in Brazil Urges Fair Division of Region's Wealth," *New York Times*, 7 July 1980, p. A1.

56. "Palavras duras," *Veja*, 1 May 1977, p. 20.

57. President Shehu Shagari, quoted in *West Africa*, 7 July 1980.

58. *Jornal de Brasília*, 8 June 1979, p. 14.

59. See Dzidzienyo, "A África vista do Brasil."

60. See "Sucesso no Kilmanjaro," *Isto é*, 11 June 1980, pp. 29–31; "No fortim negro"; "Fincando a bandeira"; and "Final de festa."

61. For an account of President Cabral's visit, see "Mão dupla: Brasil e Guiné," *Veja*, 25 June 1980, pp. 48–49.

9
Brazil and India as Third World Middle Powers

Michael A. Morris

Brazil and India occupy distinctive positions as Third World middle powers because they possess greater breadth and diversity of power and influence, domestically and internationally, than any other developing states. Although they occupy similar positions in the international system, their histories, societies, and political and economic systems all differ sharply. The United States and the Soviet Union differ as well in all these areas, yet their similarity in position in the international system as superpowers is widely recognized.

The theme of Brazil and India as Third World middle powers will be developed by moving from the general to the specific. The general position of Third World states in the international system will be examined first, from which a more specific threefold categorization of Third World states will be made in a subsequent section. This will allow the distinctive positions of Brazil and India in the Third World to be specified further in the rest of the chapter through three kinds of comparisons between these two and other Third World states. The first comparison involves domestic affairs; the second, foreign affairs; and the last, ocean affairs.[1] On the basis of these comparisons, a final section will formulate some conclusions about Third World middle powers.

Third World States in the International System

Power has properly been a major concern of students and practitioners

An earlier version of this paper was delivered at the Eighth National Meeting of the Latin American Studies Association, Pittsburgh, Pennsylvania, April 5-7, 1979. Basic research for the paper benefited from field investigation in both Brazil (1974–1975) and India (summer 1977), with assistance from the Organization of American States and the Conjunto Universitário Cândido Mendes and the Faculty Research Committee of Clemson University.

of international relations. Powerful states have been central actors on the international scene, while weak states, until quite recently, were generally either in the spheres of influence of great powers or were dependent on or colonized by them. The extensive literature on Third World dependency, much of which finds its roots in Latin American conditions and thinking, illustrates this rather rigid international hierarchy of power. The Third World, particularly the smaller or less powerful developing states, still remains subordinate in many ways to the industrialized, developed center. Some important changes in great power–lesser power relationships have nevertheless been occurring. As the international system evolves from a bipolar order toward a multipolar one, great powers find it more difficult to influence lesser powers' policies directly and decisively. At the same time, some Third World states have been developing more independent or assertive foreign policies than previously.

Latin America illustrates this larger Third World trend toward a more flexible international power hierarchy. Relations among Latin American states and between these states and various other regions and powers have been growing as traditional dependency on the United States loosens. Growing intra–Latin American relations and expanding, more diversified external ties have produced greater regional foreign policy autonomy and a relative decline in U.S. influence. Yet another new element in the regional power hierarchy is the emergence of Brazil as the premier power in South America.

India, like Brazil, has emerged as a significant power in recent years and has had serious diplomatic problems with great powers in pursuing a relatively autonomous foreign policy course. In recent years, the sphere of autonomy of both these rising Third World powers has increased and superpower ability to pressure them has declined. Both Brazil and India have accordingly been able to alter their international status from "objects" to "subjects," capable of advancing their own interests both within their own regions and beyond.[2]

Three Categories of Third World States

Changes lessening the traditional dependency of Third World states are, of course, relative. Within the Third World, some states have been emerging as powers in their own right, like Brazil and India, while many others remain very weak and vulnerable. Accordingly, three categories of Third World states may be distinguished in terms of the quantity and quality of their power.

Small Third World States

Small Third World states cannot realistically aspire to status comparable to that of big powers and will remain highly vulnerable in a harsh international environment for the foreseeable future. A recent essay concluded that India's large size and complex elites, despite the country's widespread poverty, support much more significant productive forces, hence, influence, than small Third World States.

> The basic differences [among Third World] states hinge on the level of development of productive forces, not on the extent of poverty. India is no doubt more poverty-stricken than Tanzania, but there is no comparison between them in the level of productive forces; countries like India, with a long-standing and powerful bourgeoisie and fairly significant, concentrated proletariat, are infinitely more complex societies than those of West Africa, for example.[3]

Third World Oil Exporters

Third World oil-exporting states frequently mentioned as emerging powers include Iran (at least until the recent deposition of the Shah), Nigeria, Saudi Arabia, and Venezuela. But their influence and power are derived predominantly from oil revenues, rather than from a diversified agro-industrial base, as in the cases of Brazil and India. None of these states is consequently likely to be able to exert as much international influence across as many issues as Brazil and India. Venezuela and Iran, oil-exporting neighbors of Brazil and India respectively, can illustrate further the extent and limits of the international influence of Third World oil exporters.

Venezuela played a leading role in the formation of the Organization of Petroleum Exporting Countries (OPEC) and has continued to be active in international petroleum matters. It has begun to play a more active role in the Caribbean basin as well in recent years through petrodollar diplomacy. But Venezuela has not been able to make a significant impact on other international issues or in other regions; indeed it is somewhat uneasy about the broader-based emergence of its southern neighbor, Brazil.[4]

Until the deposition of the Shah, Iran was the leading Third World arms importer and was widely touted as a regional challenger to India in the Indian Ocean. Sizable oil revenues did permit Iran to build up a significant military establishment, but the national power base was still narrow and precarious. For example, with the purchase of sophisticated foreign weaponry came thousands of foreign military technicians for training personnel and servicing and maintaining the equipment. Because of the departure of most of these technicians after the revolution, Iran's ability to utilize the most sophisticated weaponry was impaired.[5]

The situations of Brazil and India compare more than favorably with that of Iran, as fairly broad-based national development has permitted much less reliance on foreign military technicians and much greater progress toward weaponry self-sufficiency through domestic arms production. More broadly, because Brazil and India are both less dependent and more involved in many areas than are the Third World oil exporters, they are able to exert greater international influence on many more issues even though both are heavily dependent on oil imports.

Mexico's overall candidacy for middle power status would appear more viable than any of the other Third World oil-exporting states because its recent emergence as a major oil producer is complemented by more broadly-based development. But Mexico's power base and international influence still compare unfavorably with those of Brazil and India, as subsequent sections of this chapter document. Its proximity to a superpower compounds other problems in forging an influential, relatively autonomous international role.

Third World Middle Powers

Brazil and India constitute a final group of Third World states because they, and they alone, have a broad, diversified power base and concomitant international influence. Domestically, both states enjoy broad-based development, although they depend heavily on oil imports. Internationally, both have emerged as the premier powers in their respective subregions (South America and South Asia), and both have been quite successful in projecting influence beyond their regions on more issues than any other Third World states. These domestic and international dimensions of Brazilian and Indian power and influence will each be examined in some detail, but first a few special cases need to be contrasted with these two Third World middle powers.

Third World oil-exporting states, as noted, constitute a special case. Another special case involves Third World states that possess some other significant attribute or set of attributes of national power. For example, some states have experienced remarkable economic development, such as Hong Kong, Singapore, South Korea, and Taiwan, and still others have made some important strides in social development as well. Yet, all these states rank lower in the international power hierarchy than either Brazil or India. Just as high concentration of a single resource, such as oil, does not suffice for Third World middle power status, neither does a relatively high level of social or economic development alone qualify a Third World state for such status. The aggregate size of their economies and of most key sectors within their economies is relatively small in comparison to that of India and Brazil.

Argentina is a case in point—a sizable, fairly advanced Third World state, yet without sufficient means for middle power status. Brazil has clearly displaced Argentina as the dominant power on the South American continent and aspires realistically to a significant extraregional role as well, which appears beyond the reach of Argentina. Widespread poverty in India and great pockets of poverty in Brazil do contrast unfavorably with the higher per capita income and less widespread poverty in Argentina. Yet, aggregate Brazilian and Indian power is still much greater than that of even relatively advantaged Third World states like Argentina. Brazil's so-called economic miracle and increasingly diversified international outreach have been widely appreciated. Less widely recognized has been the growth of Indian power, domestic and international, in spite of widespread poverty.

> In economic power India is at least the equivalent of a middle-sized European country, despite the gross problems of the development which is needed to provide appropriate support to the 80 percent of the population who are poor. . . . Poverty, as a statistical fact, based on the mean, need not obviate great power status. India is a classic example of this phenomenon.[6]

Three categories of Third World states have been distinguished and ranked with respect to each other; these rankings may now briefly be related to other states in the international power hierarchy. A careful study by Steven Spiegel of all states in the international power hierarchy, as of 1970, will be relied on for this purpose.[7] Spiegel ranked the two superpowers at the pinnacle of the international power hierarchy and listed in descending order five secondary or major powers (China, France, Japan, West Germany, and Great Britain), seventeen middle powers (including Brazil and India), and many minor powers, regional states, microstates, and dependent states. For our purposes, this global ranking of states is acceptable, save a few caveats about middle powers.

Designation of seventeen developed and developing states as middle powers at the same rung of the international hierarchy may be appropriate in terms of approximate aggregate power equivalency, but Third World and industrialized middle powers generally need to be more sharply differentiated because of their different levels of development and geopolitical situations. Spiegel does seem to lean in this direction in distinguishing between thirteen developed middle powers and four Third World middle powers (Argentina, Brazil, India, and Mexico). Reasons were presented earlier for ranking Brazil and India higher at present than Argentina and Mexico. Although Spiegel does not concur with this particular classification of current relationships, he does explicitly recognize that of the seventeen middle powers, only Brazil and India have the potential to cross the threshold from middle power status to secondary or major power status.[8] Because Brazil and India stand out as Third World middle powers, they do appear to be the most viable candidates for moving yet a step higher on the international hierarchy to become major powers. But this possible transition is not our concern, which is instead more factual and present-oriented, focusing on their current middle power status.

International System Comparisons: Domestic Power Base

Neither Brazil nor India ranks well in most indicators of social development, such as per capita income, but both stand very high in terms of aggregate and diversified economic power and on this basis warrant middle power status. Their strong positions in terms of diversified gross economic strength provide a firm domestic power base for projecting international influence. In the longer run, the uneven social-development characteristic of both countries, if not alleviated, might threaten political stability and compromise efforts to accelerate economic progress. The very real problems of both countries should nevertheless not obscure the progress they have made in terms of economic development and international influence and recognition, particularly when it is recalled that many have predicted the fragmentation of India ever since independence and ever-increasing contradictions for the Brazilian development model since 1964. Moreover, some Third World aspirant powers, such as Argentina, Iran, and Pakistan, have been less successful than Brazil and India in dealing with intractable internal problems and sustaining international influence over time. While being cognizant of the multiple domestic problems faced by Brazil and India, I shall focus on two aspects of their domestic power base, the domestic economy and domestic arms production, whose international implications distinguish them from other Third World states as middle powers.

The Domestic Economy

Table 9.1 summarizes some key economic indicators for Brazil and India that illustrate the aggregate, diversified strength of both states. Both

TABLE 9.1

Domestic Power Base: Brazil and India (some selected
aggregate indicators ranking top Third World states)

Gross National Product (in US$ millions for 1978, preliminary)[a]

1. Brazil $187,190
2. India   112,660
3. Mexico   84,150

Crude Steel Production (thousand metric tons)[b]

1. Brazil   11,165 (1977, preliminary)
   Projection for 1980: 15,000+ Projection for 1985: 24,000+
2. India   9,836
   Projection for 1980: 14,000+ Projection for 1985: 19,000+
3. Mexico   5,529
   Projection for 1980: 10,000   Projection for 1985: 13,000+

Land Area (in thousand square kilometers)[c]

1. Brazil   8,512
2. India   3,288

Population (in millions of persons in mid-1977)[c]

1. India   631.7
2. Indonesia   133.5
3. Brazil   116.1

Sources:

[a] 1979 World Bank Atlas (Washington, D.C.: World Bank, 1979).

[b] Statistical Yearbook: 1978 (New York: United Nations, 1979), p. 335.

The projections for crude steel production are based on Central
Intelligence Agency estimates, as reported in "Steel: A Third World
Surge", Newsweek, October 29, 1979, p. 45.

[c] World Development Report, 1979 (Washington, D.C.: World Bank, 1979).

Brazil and India have gross national products considerably larger than those of any other Third World states, and their economies are also quite diversified, particularly in contrast with the major Third World oil-exporting states. Although Brazil and India are heavily dependent on foreign oil, both states are quite well endowed with a variety of other resources. Brazil is generally recognized as the most industrialized developing country, with increasingly diversified agricultural production and exports. India's economy is also very large and diversified in Third World terms. A relatively sophisticated industrial base has been developed and agricultural production has been increasing, so that by the mid-1970s India "was ready for a new period of sustained accelerated growth."[9] Both states have been hit hard by rising oil prices in recent years, but the diversity of their economies will probably be able to sustain further growth. Both are also subcontinents with large populations and their sizable areas dominate their respective sub-regions.

Domestic Arms Production

The relatively well-developed industrial and technological infrastructures of Brazil and India have supported a domestic arms-production effort whose breadth and depth stand out in the Third World. The extent of domestic arms production will be sketched here, and the international implications of the resulting strong military postures of Brazil and India will be explored later. (See also Chapter 3.) Brazilian and Indian domestic arms production and research range from small conventional weapons production up to space and nuclear energy programs with possible military applications. For example, India's armaments industry has been regarded as "the largest in the Third World, after China's, in value, volume, diversity of production, and R and D effort," and "Indian space activities are, next to China's, certainly the most ambitious in the Third World."[10] Several studies have also compared the broad spread of Brazilian and Indian arms production favorably with a narrower range of conventional weapons produced by other Third World states.[11] Brazilian and Indian indigenous weaponry production and research capabilities contrast even more favorably when their ambitious space and nuclear energy programs are included in the balance.

Both Brazil and India are aiming toward substantial self-sufficiency by the late 1980s for their relatively large armed forces, with imports of some sophisticated weapons continuing thereafter. Brazilian arms and military supplies exports in 1979 were valued at $300 million, with plans to export over $1 billion yearly by the 1980s. Although Brazil's entry into the arms trade as supplier dates only to the late 1970s, it ranked second (after Israel) among Third World states in total value of weapons exports in the 1970–1979 period, with 21 percent of the Third World export total during those years. India's arms exports during the same period represented only 1 percent of Third World sales,[12] but the potential for expansion is good.[13]

International System Comparisons: International Influence

Brazil's emergence as a middle power, with rapid growth of national power and international interests, has been described in exuberant terms.[14] The Brazilian economic boom from the late 1960s through the early 1970s dramatized this emergence. The ability to sustain growth in the late 1970s in spite of more adverse economic circumstances confirmed earlier impressions of Brazilian staying power, although projections about Brazil's growing international importance are now less ambitious.

Confidence in India's emergence as a middle power was stimulated by the favorable outcome of the 1971 war with Pakistan and the 1974 peaceful nuclear explosion. The bifurcation of Pakistan, India's traditional regional rival, projected India into a position of dominance on the subcontinent and infused the country, including national analysts of foreign affairs, with a confidence previously lacking about the emergence of the country as a significant power.[15]

Books and articles dealing separately with Brazil and India as emerging Third World powers began as a somewhat experimental, speculative exercise out of the mainstream of writing on each of the two states' foreign affairs. As these writings made their case in increasingly cogent terms, and as each state continued to expand domestic power and international influence as well, the concept and implications of middle power status have tended to become incorporated into mainstream foreign policy thinking.[16] This chapter relies on these separate literatures while also extending them, as their focus on national foreign policy is narrower than my comparative focus. I shall now compare the international emergence of both Third World middle powers from several perspectives.

Multilateral Relations

Brazilian and Indian multilateral relations provide a good overview of their international behavior and position, as all kinds of international issues, whether economic, political, or military, come to the attention of multilateral forums. Brazil and India have been particularly prominent Third World states in numerous international forums. India has played a leading role in the nonaligned movement since the 1950s, while Brazil has been prominent in a variety of international organizations. Brazil and India, along with Algeria and Peru, were accordingly singled out for comparison in a recent study as particularly influential Third World states at the United Nations.[17] Their 1965–1975 voting records at the United Nations General Assembly Plenary were compared, with particular attention to 1975, and some broader conclusions were derived from the comparison. Both Brazil and India tended to lean toward Third World positions, although India followed a Third World line much more on colonial and trusteeship issues than did Brazil. On some issues, India tended to lean toward its preferred superpower, the USSR, while Brazil leaned toward the United States. But on economic issues, Brazil, India, and the USSR (as well as Algeria and Peru) all voted similarly against the United States, and on political and security issues, Brazil, India, and the United States voted consistently against the USSR. On the basis of these recent UN voting patterns, neither Third World middle power could be called servile to either superpower. India and Brazil, in voting very similarly on economic issues, generally endorsed Third World positions, yet with qualifications.

Brazil did lean more toward Third World positions at the United Nations after 1970, but continued to discriminate among issues and to disassociate itself from radical Third World views. Brazil has been more inclined toward those developing states holding moderate to conservative views, and Brazilian participation in all major international organizations has reflected an uneasy balance between First and Third World positions in flexibly pursuing complex national interests.[18]

India has supported Third World positions much longer and more solidly than has Brazil. But India no longer seeks leadership of the nonaligned movement with the moral fervor of the Nehru era. A prominent Indian diplomat candidly expressed current Indian views toward nonalignment and multilateral relations: The original emphasis of the nonaligned movement on emotional issues such as colonialism and racism, as expressed by Nehru and others, did not suffice to maintain Third World unity, although eventually concrete economic demands came to offer an effective rallying point through more pragmatic groups, such as the Group of 77. India, like most Third World states, prefers gradual improvement of its position in such ways through orderly change rather than radical transformation. But India also stands out in the Third World as a middle power with distinctive interests, as in the case of Indian opposition to the Nonproliferation Treaty.[19]

India's past influence in multilateral Third World bodies may appear more prominent than her current role. Because India had considerable success, particularly during the 1950s, in leading the nonaligned at conferences, Leo Rose has posed the following question: "Is India thus less of a world power than it was two decades ago?"[20] Rose responds in the negative, that Indian influence in the Third World during the 1950s through international bodies tended to be transitory in nature. Subsequent Indian international influence, if less dramatic, has rested on a dominant subregional position from the 1970s and gradual, pragmatic extension of economic ties.

Foreign Policy Trends

Some of the shared Brazilian and Indian behavior patterns identified in the survey of multilateral relations can be related to a larger evolution of foreign policy. Three periods in the emergence of Brazil and India as Third World middle powers may be discerned.

In the first period, which extended well into the 1950s, both Brazil and India were heavily dependent on external powers. Brazil was historically dependent on Great Britain and later on the United States, although some important qualifications should be made. Close relations with the United States and considerable subordination to its policies were facilitated by the common perspectives of Brazilian and U.S. elites. Brazil was willing to subordinate its policies to those of the United States in return for U.S. support for Brazilian regional primacy.

Dependency on Great Britain was particularly marked for India, which did not have responsibility for foreign policy until independence in 1947. Even as a colony, however, dependency was somewhat reciprocal because of the central role India played in the British Empire. After independence, Indian weaknesses and strengths again produced an ambiguous status. Independence did remove formal obstacles to the development of a national foreign policy, which indeed was active on many fronts in the early years, but Indian freedom of maneuver was still constrained for years afterwards because of pressing regional problems related to the colonial legacy of partition and other difficulties. Thus, from an early date prominent Brazilian and Indian assets tended to lead all concerned to think of both states as potential regional leaders and to lessen their dependency, although truly independent status, much less regional primacy, was never consolidated in the first period.

In the second period, Brazil and India, though they still had not attained regional primacy, attempted to play broader, extraregional international roles. Initial attempts to project Brazilian and Indian influence beyond their respective subregions (South America and South Asia) date from the 1950s. President Kubitschek first began to dream of a wider international role for Brazil in the late 1950s, and during the 1961–1964 "independent foreign policy" phase under Presidents Quadros and Goulart, numerous initiatives were made to project Brazil as a leader of a Third World bloc that could negotiate with the established powers on terms of equality. Paralleling these developments, from the 1950s Prime Minister Nehru relied largely on his personal influence and moralistic positions to gain a preeminent position for India in the nonaligned movement.

Both Brazil and India were still relatively weak, so that these initial attempts to project Brazilian and Indian influence beyond their respective subregions rested on a rather precarious base. On the regional level, both Argentina and Pakistan could still realistically aspire toward parity with their larger neighbors, and on the international system level, the bipolar order did not favor upwardly mobile Third World powers. Cold War politics tended to subordinate interests of lesser powers to the alliance leader, so that the room for maneuver of economically weak powers still heavily dependent on foreign aid, such as Brazil and India, was all the more constrained. Such Third World states, drawn toward ideologically oriented alliances against their will and lacking the power but not necessarily the ideological conviction of the superpowers, responded in kind with the rhetoric of nonalignment or foreign policy independence. Insofar as Brazil and India were able to project influence extraregionally, this accordingly tended to result from personal influence or ideological leadership rather than from intrinsic strength. In the rough-and-tumble world of international politics, personal dynamism and ideological fervor were inadequate substitutes for power. National capabilities to support a rise in status were insufficiently developed, and regional rivalries constrained any significant extraregional roles, as did a rigid international system. Each of these conditions for the projection of power internationally changed significantly in the third period.

In that period, both Brazil and India emerged as Third World middle powers. Brazil's economic boom during the late 1960s and early 1970s helped mobilize latent national potential and achieve subregional primacy in South America. India's economic development has not been as dramatic as that of Brazil, but it has been fairly steady, and the 1971 war resulting in the bifurcation of Pakistan did consolidate its subregional primacy in South Asia. The 1974 peaceful nuclear explosion further symbolized India's emergence as a middle power. By the early 1970s, both Brazil and India had emerged as Third World middle powers enjoying regional primacy, including recognition from other regional states and from the major external powers. The international system, now increasingly multipolar in character, had also evolved in ways favorable to upwardly mobile Third World powers. Looser bloc alignments tended to deemphasize ideology and permit a more complex, flexible international hierarchy. With solid national bases generating greater resources than previously, firm positions of regional primacy for the first time, and a more open international system, Brazil and India were able to transcend traditional regional rivalries and turn more to larger, extraregional concerns. Projection of influence into the larger international arena is now regarded by both Brazil and India as resulting gradually from a substantial, growing national power base and from a regionally secure position.

While Brazil's extraregional activities have tended to be more pronounced than those of India, both states have been careful and pragmatic in developing extraregional relations. Neither power has tried to take advantage of its new-found status by engaging in international adventurism, although both have been drawing small neighboring states into particularly close relationships that tend to set limits on these states' behavior. Depending on the point of view, this might be described either as an emerging sphere of influence or as the natural concomitant of an emerging power in proximity to small states.

Table 9.2 expresses systematically some of the regional relationships shaping the international projection of both Third World middle powers. Regional marine relationships as well as regional landmass relationships are expressed in this table, because of important similarities of structure; these will be discussed later in the context of the international system comparison on ocean affairs.

Economic Affairs

Brazilian and Indian involvement in the international economy is considerable. Both Brazil and India have considerably diversified the content and geographical destination of their exports, both have been burdened with a heavy oil import bill, and both have used their influence, if moderately and pragmatically, in support of demands for reform of the international economic order. They have accordingly been the two most active developing states in the Multilateral Trade Negotiations, and "Brazilian diplomats count their country's participation, with India, as one of the chief proponents in the creation of UNCTAD to be among its most important contributions to the UN system."[21]

At the same time, the economic structure and policies of the two countries are quite different, and the nature of their relationships with the international economy differs accordingly. Brazil's essentially market, export-oriented economy has led it to take opposite stands in international financial institutions from those of countries with statist or regulatory economies, such as India. Similarly, the proposal for an iron ore cartel made by India and several other developing states contrasted with Brazil's recommendation for voluntary producer-consumer cooperation.[22]

Differences in Brazilian and Indian policy preferences have affected the

TABLE 9.2

Regional Dominance of the Third World Middle Powers

Continental Land Masses		
(1) Regional systems	Latin America	Asia
(2) Regional sub-system	South America	South Asia
(3) Regional hegemon	Brazil	India
(4) Regional power rival	Argentina	Pakistan
(5) Potential buffer states or incipient spheres of influence (of the regional hegemon)	Bolivia, Paraguay, and Uruguay	Bhutan, Nepal, and Sikkim (absorbed by India in 1974)
(6) Other regional states	Chile, Colombia, Ecuador, Guyana, Peru, Surinam and Venezuela	Bangladesh and Sri Lanka
(7) Intrusive external powers	United States; Soviet Union much less	Soviet Union and the United States; to a lesser degree, China
(8) Great power colonies or client states	French Guiana (colony of France)	Afghanistan (1979-1980 invasion and occupation by the Soviet Union)
Ocean Space		
(1) Marine Regions	South Atlantic	Indian Ocean
(2) Leading littoral state naval power	Brazil	India
(3) Aspirant regional naval powers	Argentina, Nigeria, and South Africa	Australia, Indonesia, Iran, and South Africa
(4) Other littoral and island-states	About two dozen	About two dozen
(5) Land-locked states dependent for access to contiguous ocean basin	About ten	About ten
(6) Intrusive external powers	US and USSR	US and USSR; to a lesser degree, France
(7) Great power colonies or client states	Great Britain: various island dependencies; USSR: several client states on the West African littoral	US: Diego Garcia; USSR: several client states; France: several island dependencies

extent of participation by each in international economic affairs as well. Foreign trade is a case in point. While the Indian economy has been inward-oriented until quite recently, Brazilian policymakers have regarded expansion of exports as a crucial stimulus for economic growth. Consequently, Brazilian exports ranked third among all developing states in 1977, with oil exports boosting Saudi Arabia and Iran into first and second places, while Indian exports occupy only fourteenth place.[23] Similarly, in the same year Brazilian imports again ranked in third place among all developing states, close behind Saudi Arabia and Iran, while those of India rank only in tenth place.[24] By the late 1970s, with the mounting pressure of costly oil imports, India's development strategy did place greater emphasis on exports, which began to grow rapidly. Continuing rapid growth of Indian exports, with a concomitant rise in imports, has been predicted.[25] Relations with foreign investors also exhibit dissimilarities. Brazil ranks first among all developing states as a recipient of foreign investment, while India has not encouraged multinational corporations to play a major role in the economy.[26]

Because of these and other complexities, the participation of Brazil and India in international economic relations tends to relate to their emergence as middle powers in distinctive ways. Brazil's heavy involvement in the international economy has been an integral part of its emergence as a middle power, both stimulating domestic growth and promoting external relations, yet at the same time creating some new vulnerabilities and dependencies. India's involvement in international economic affairs has been more limited than that of Brazil, but India has been cautiously moving toward more active participation in order to reap benefits, while hoping to limit new dependencies.

Military Affairs

Military affairs constitute yet another facet of the Brazilian and Indian emergence as middle powers. In each case, an impressive military establishment has been developed without undue burden on the economy or heavy demands on the available labor pool.[27]

Conventional arms. Brazilian and Indian conventional military capabilities compare favorably with those of other states, both in their respective subregions and in the Third World at large. (See Chapters 2 and 3 for relevant comparisons.) The effects of significant Brazilian and Indian conventional military strength within and beyond their respective regions have nevertheless tended to differ. Brazil's strategic environment has been much less hostile than that of India, so that the conventional military balance in South America has not had such an immediate, decisive effect on national security as in South Asia, where the two leading powers have fought successive wars. Moreover, formidable geographical obstacles tend to insulate other South American states from any threat posed by the growth of Brazilian conventional military capabilities. The great powers have accordingly not been drawn into regional wars in recent times in South America to the extent that they have in South Asia. It is in the hostile strategic environment of South Asia that India's growing conventional military capabilities have had a direct, immediate impact, on the great powers as well as on neighboring lesser powers.

India's emergence in the 1970s as the predominant regional power in South Asia has affected the access of all the great powers previously active in the area—China, the United States, and the Soviet Union. India had previously had problems in developing satisfactory relations with both superpowers and even had a border war with its major power neighbor, China, in 1962. Some problems have continued, but India's regional power did help it shape the great power presence in South Asia more nearly in accord with its own interests.

The Soviet invasion and occupation of Afghanistan in late 1979 and 1980 in itself does not appear to have altered basic great power patterns of behavior in South Asia. While the Soviet invasion dismayed China and the United States, Indian influence in this state on the periphery of South Asia had not been dominant and close Indo-Soviet relations continued despite mildly phrased official Indian concern about the occupation and resultant conflict. However much one may condemn the Soviet invasion, it still appears true that the period since 1971 "has been a period of very limited involvement by the major external powers" in South Asia, and that "India has been successful in gradually curtailing outside efforts to influence Indo-Pakistani relations or the regional balance of power."[28]

Nuclear weaponry. A single facet of national power is not decisive in determining international status, whether it be oil or nuclear weaponry. It is the strong national bases and diversified interests of both Brazil and India that sustain their regional primacy and extraregional influence, not actual or potential nuclear capabilities. Strictly speaking, there are still no Third World nuclear powers, as India's 1974 peaceful nuclear explosion has intentionally not been followed up with the development of a nuclear strike force. (China is not considered here as a Third World state.) Explosion of the so-called peaceful nuclear device nevertheless did enhance Indian prestige, particularly among developing states, with only Pakistan among Third World states condemning India's explosion. Brazil shares a common aspiration with India for world power status, so that such prestige considerations constitute a strong motivation for Brazil to follow in India's footsteps and employ a peaceful nuclear explosive (PNE) as well. Both states have also argued that PNEs would keep them abreast of the modern technology required for their economic development.[29]

Brazil and India share motivations for going nuclear, but security reasons have been more prominent in the case of India. India's strategic environment has included recurring Indo-Pakistani armed conflicts and frequently hostile relationships with the great powers. In contrast, Brazil has been faced with a simpler, less violence-prone challenge of readjusting relations with the United States and managing relatively low-key disputes with its neighbors.

A review of Sino-Indian relations indicates that India's 1974 nuclear explosion was directed more toward Beijing (Peiping) than toward Islamabad, which ceased to pose an immediate threat after the 1971 war. After the Sino-Indian border clashes of 1962, India signed the test ban treaty in August 1963 with the hope that its nuclear abstinence would be an example for China. Instead, in October 1964, China detonated an atomic device, which India regarded as a threat, and then "China's first hydrogen bomb explosion on July 1, 1967, deepened India's distrust of China and strengthened pressure in parliament for building an Indian bomb."[30] This background of hostile Sino-Indian relations reinforced Indian determination not to sign the 1968 Nonproliferation Treaty and eventually to explode a nuclear device.

Although Pakistan was not a major consideration in India's 1974 peaceful nuclear explosion, the Indian initiative still affected this regional power rival directly. Pakistan has since apparently come to regard the acquisition of nuclear weapons as imperative, both to counter the alleged threat of its larger nuclear neighbor and to boost its own international status, seriously deflated after its dramatic defeat by India in 1971. In view of the overall disparity between Indian and Pakistani resources, both nuclear and nonnuclear, acquisition of nuclear weapons by Pakistan would not be likely to alter the regional balance in its favor. Only an Indian invasion of Pakistan might be deterred, were this unlikely option ever contemplated, while all the other power ratios favoring India would remain unaltered. Even a nuclear arms race on the subcontinent would certainly favor India, just as the conventional arms race has. A Pakistani bomb would trigger further development of an Indian nuclear capability, which is much more advanced in research, development, and delivery capabilities.[31]

India's nuclear example also appears to have made a considerable impression on Argentina, the regional power rival of Brazil. It has been argued that India's nuclear explosion constitutes a shortcut to enhanced international status, so that Argentina could benefit from nuclear weaponry in similar fashion.[32] Enhancement of international status is regarded as particularly pressing in Argentina because of the current overall power imbalance with Brazil. Just as the Indian nuclear explosion was apparently made to help redress the regional balance with China, the argument runs, so might an Argentine nuclear weaponry capability have a similar regional effect in redressing the balance with Brazil in South America.[33]

Speculation that Argentina could tip the regional balance of power in its favor by gaining a nuclear capability before Brazil does seems erroneous for reasons similar to those in the Indo-Pakistani case. It is true that Argentina's nuclear program is generally regarded as somewhat more advanced than that of Brazil, although important Brazilian progress toward an independent nuclear capability, including the 1975 agreement for nuclear cooperation with West Germany, has been rapidly narrowing the gap over the past several years. An Argentine decision to go nuclear would trigger these Brazilian weaponry capabilities, just as the Indian nuclear explosion has impelled Pakistan toward a bomb.[34]

In such a situation, any advantage the regional power rival (Argentina or Pakistan) would gain over the regional hegemon (Brazil or India) by exploding a bomb would be fleeting. Nuclear weapons would not cancel out other factors of national strength generally favoring the regional hegemons, and a regional nuclear arms race would also certainly favor the regional hegemons as well, due to their long-term preponderance of national resources and strength.[35]

Nuclear weaponry capability is consequently not a key ingredient in determining the positions of Brazil and India as Third World middle powers. Both are middle powers without nuclear strike forces and both would retain this status even if their regional power rivals were to go nuclear. Their middle power status is nevertheless closely associated with the nuclear issue. The positions of both states as middle powers have influenced their policies toward nuclear questions, just as the responses of the great powers and the regional power rivals have been influenced by their distinctive middle power positions.

International System Comparisons: Ocean Affairs

Several important parallel developments in the emergence of Brazil and India as leading Third World sea powers may be discerned. Both states had traditionally neglected the sea, whether as a source of wealth and influence or as a theater of competition and external pressure. But as they began to grow and emerge as middle powers and experience an expansion of interests on all fronts, the importance of the sea and of developing sea power more fully became evident. In the case of Brazil, this occurred from about the late 1960s.[36] At about the same time, India's long-standing security concern with its northern frontiers began to be somewhat more balanced by greater recognition of the importance of extensive national maritime frontiers. For example, a former Indian chief of naval staff recently documented Indian progress in building up all facets of national sea power and called for yet additional efforts.[37]

The very breadth and diversity of elements required for national sea power imply that only large, relatively well-endowed states can realistically aspire to establish such a firm base for exercising influence in ocean affairs. Indeed, only a few Third World states have aspired to become sea powers and Brazil and India stand out in their efforts to achieve this goal, as Tables 9.2 and 9.3 show. Table 9.2 on page 232 compared the regional dominance of Third World middle powers on their respective continental land masses with similar positions in their respective contiguous ocean basins. Of particular interest is the relatively large number of littoral states involved in the ocean basins (the South Atlantic and the Indian Ocean), well over twice the number involved in the continental regional subsystems (South America and South Asia). Table 9.3 focuses on one key aspect of sea power, naval strength, to document Brazilian and Indian naval prominence in their respective contiguous ocean basins. Other refinements should be made, such as age of warships and degree of national naval construction capability, but because of space limitations I shall merely note that naval analysts have generally recognized the leading position of the Brazilian navy in the South Atlantic vis-à-vis other littoral states and that of India in the Indian Ocean, particularly after the fall of the Shah of Iran.[38]

To flesh out this brief case study, I shall conclude with a note about two directions in which this fruitful area of inquiry could be developed further. First, I am developing the above naval comparisons and analysis much further in a book-length study on Third World navies.[39] Second, relationships between naval power and sea power should be analyzed systematically, particularly in the case of rising powers such as Brazil and India, whose naval, maritime, and general foreign policy interests are all tending to expand. Naval power, summarized in Table 9.3, is part of the larger growth of Brazilian and Indian sea power, which is sketched in Table 9.4. A whole series of indicators of sea power shows that the two middle powers stand out in the Third World in most maritime areas. Both middle powers have been Third World leaders in promoting a 40:40:20 formula for liner shipping (a cargo apportionment that encourages LDC shipping), both have built up bulk carrier fleets to carry a

TABLE 9.3   COMPARATIVE NAVAL STRENGTH (1978) - Naval Hardware Comparisons

	(1) Major surface ships (air,car.,cr.,des.,frig.)	(2) Light forces (cor., FPBs, patrol craft)	(3) Submarines	(4) Amphibious forces	(5) Mine warfare forces	(6) Supply ships	(7) Surveying vessels	(8) Other vessels (not fighting ships)
Brazil (leading South Atlantic littoral state naval power)	17	22 (10 additional, small)	10	41	6	5	8	16
Aspirant South Atlantic Naval Powers:								
(1) Argentina	12	17(2 additional,small)	4	33	6	3	3	15
(2) Nigeria	1	14	0	1	0	0	1	1
(3) South Africa	4	7	3	0	10	1	1	5
India (leading Indian Ocean littoral state naval power)	18	40(2 additional,small)	8	7	8	7	3	2
Aspirant Indian Ocean Naval Powers:								
(1) South Africa	SEE ABOVE							
(2) Australia (not a developing state nor much Indian Ocean deployment)	12	12	6	23	3	2	4	7
(3) Indonesia	11	38(8 additional,small)	3	60	7	16	4	8
(4) Iran	7	23	3	5 (also 14 hovercraft)	5	8	1	5

Source: Moore, John, Jane's Fighting Ships (London: Jane's Yearbooks). Successive years of Jane's Fighting Ships were consulted to compare the states listed over time and to develop representative weapons categories. Figures for 1978 are presented here for convenience, although the growth of the Brazilian and Indian Navies is even more evident when their evolution is observed over the last 10 or 15 years.

TABLE 9.4   BRAZILIAN AND INDIAN SEA POWER

Comparative Naval Strength (see Tables 9.2 and 9.3)

Merchant Shipping Tonnage[1] (thousand gross registered tons)

Leading Third World States	Developing State Flags of Convenience (with most national tonnage as flags of convenience)
1. India 5,759	
2. Brazil 3,702	1. Liberia 80,191
	2. Panama 20,749
	3. Singapore 7,489

Length of Coastline of Third World States by Rank (in nautical miles)[2]

Coastal States		Island/Archipelago States	
1. Mexico	4,848	1. Indonesia	19,889
2. Brazil	3,692	2. The Philippines	6,997
3. Chile	2,882		
4. India	2,759		

Economic Zone Size of Third World States by Rank (in square nautical miles)[3]

--Exclusive Economic Zone (corresponds to area between baseline and 200 nautical miles)

Coastal States		Island/Archipelago States	
1. Brazil	924,000	1. Indonesia	1,577,300
2. Mexico	831,500		
3. Chile	667,300		
4. India	587,600		

Fish Catches of Third World States by Rank (thousands of metric tons, 1977, preliminary)[4]

1. India	2,540.0 (2nd in value among developing countries)
....	
11. Brazil	790.1 (8th in value among developing countries)

Sources

1. Statistical Yearbook: 1978 (New York: United Nations, 1979), pp. 552-555.

2. Office of the Geographer, U.S. Department of State, Sovereignty of the Sea, Bulletin No. 3, April 1965.

3. Office of the Geographer, Bureau of Intelligence and Research, U.S. Department of State, Theoretical Areal Allocations of Seabed to Coastal States (Washington, D.C.: U.S. Government Printing Office, 1972).

4. Food and Agriculture Organization, Yearbook of Fishery Statistics (Rome: Food and Agriculture Organization, 1978). Statistical Yearbook: 1978, pp. 155-157.

large share of their growing international commerce, and both have supported these shipping interests with considerable national merchant marine and naval construction capabilities. Both have become more involved as well in the sea as a source of protein, offshore oil, and even deep seabed minerals. These extensive ocean interests have also helped project Brazil and India into influential positions at the Third United Nations Conference on the Law of the Sea.[40]

Third World Middle Powers in the International System

The similar positions of India and Brazil as middle powers in the international system have elicited some similar behavior patterns. A related theme in the international relations literature is that similar positions of states, whether superpowers, great powers, middle powers, small states, or micro-states, tend to promote common behavior patterns.[41] Size is undeniably a key factor affecting foreign policy behavior, either when small size cannot be converted into much effective power, or when power advantages are realized from larger size, as in the cases of Brazil and India, but large size alone does not suffice for middle power status. Brazil and India are particularly large Third World states, but they did not measure up to middle power status until the late 1960s to early 1970s, when the latent power potential of each finally was sufficiently mobilized to produce a rise in status. The evolution of the international system from a bipolar order to a multipolar one also favored the upward mobility of both states. A common international context and a common position within that context were fundamental forces affecting the behavior of both states similarly.

Generalizations about behavioral similarities of both Third World middle powers in the international system can be derived from such evidence. In particular, three common periods in the evolution of Brazilian and Indian foreign policy toward middle power status were identified, with both states clearly gaining middle power status for the first time in the third period. A steady buildup of national power, together with opportunities presented by a more open international system, permitted low-key consolidation of regional primacy by both middle powers in this third period. With regional primacy consolidated generally without aggressive tactics, both middle powers were able to transcend traditional regional rivalries and turn to larger, extraregional concerns, again without engaging in international adventurism. Both middle powers have been careful and pragmatic in developing extraregional relations, because projection of international influence into the larger international arena has been regarded by both Brazil and India as resulting gradually from a substantial, growing national power base and from a regionally secure position. Domestic, regional, and global trends therefore all reinforce the conclusion of Brazilian and Indian policymakers that pragmatic, gradual consolidation of middle power status, regionally and extraregionally, is the most appropriate foreign policy strategy.

The similar positions of the two Third World middle powers have tended to produce similar behavior patterns, but basic differences between the two states exert a countervailing influence. The obvious fundamental differences between Brazil and India in practically all facets of civilization and political economy[42] are bound to shape foreign policy in each state differently. In such different national settings, key foreign policy similarities are all the more significant.

Foreign policy similarities between the two Third World middle powers may also be distinguished from foreign policy traits shared respectively by smaller states and by the great powers. Unlike the mirror relationship between the superpowers, burdened by protracted competition and constant parry and riposte, similarities between the two Third World middle powers have resulted from neither interaction nor competition. An action-reaction syndrome has often evoked parallel superpower responses to crises,[43] but Brazil and India, located on opposite sides of the globe, have had very limited interaction. Even the Indian peaceful nuclear explosion appears to have affected Argentina more than Brazil. Given the absence of significant interaction or competition with each other, middle power similarities are particularly striking.

Small states often act the way they do because of impotence, and even unconventional or daring moves they may make are likely to do so insignificant for major actors that no response is probable. In contrast, the Third World middle powers enjoy considerable freedom of movement because of significant resources at their disposal, yet they may also experience greater restraints or negative reactions than small states because of the broader impact of their actions on others. In spite of such constraints, Brazil and India appear justified in their new, confident mood that time will work in their favor. They have accordingly been content to rely on gradual expansion of international influence within the existing order and low-key pressure for reforms favoring their interests. But the rise of Third World middle powers does involve system change. Gradual expansion of influence, while appearing low-key to the middle powers, may be unsettling for smaller neighboring states and may seem too assertive for the great powers.

Both regionally and extraregionally, the distinctiveness and complexity of position of the middle powers have tended to result in ambivalent behavior. Both Brazil and India have been drawn toward the great powers for recognition and support of continuing upward mobility, as the gap separating the middle and the great powers remains large. While regarding the great powers as sources of coveted power and wealth, the middle powers have also been wary of them as inveterate supporters of an inequitable international order and practitioners of intervention in others' affairs. The two middle powers have accordingly felt compelled to reduce their former dependency on great powers by diversifying their foreign relations and pursuing self-sufficiency in crucial areas, while regarding their own rise in status as a harbinger of more peaceful, equitable international relations.

Middle powers' relations with smaller states, particularly those in the Third World with whom they come into contact most frequently, have been ambivalent as well. Both Brazil and India have tended to regard Third World solidarity favorably, although complexity of interests was shown to qualify their Third World support. While generally acting with restraint, the middle powers have not hesitated to forge a buffer zone of client states on their periphery nor to assert Third World leadership, foisting their own interests on the group when particular gains were in the offing. The middle powers have also generally been more willing and able than smaller states to confront the great powers, yet they have valued interests shared with great powers. Middle powers have accordingly been much more discriminating and problem-oriented in picking quarrels with great powers than have the self-styled Third World radicals, who have tended to oppose the United States indiscriminately regardless of the issue.

While such ambivalent middle power behavior has caused exasperation at times among both great and lesser powers, it is generally acknowledged that Brazil and India have on the whole been adept in advancing their own unique set of interests. Their balancing act between small and great powers, among First, Second, and Third Worlds, has been difficult, yet skillful. They have consolidated and maintained regional primacy, recognized by all great powers and acquiesced in by the smaller powers, and have had considerable success in promoting more extensive, diverse extraregional interests. This contrasts with an earlier (second) foreign policy period, when national power was not as great and efforts to raise status were more dramatic, yet less effective. The more recent growth of power and rise in status have been accompanied, for ill or for good, by greater appreciation of the uses and limitations of power. More power used more efficiently does contain greater potential for ill, but on balance, both Third World middle powers have used their newfound power prudently and reasonably. This does not presage an era of more peaceful, equitable international relations, as these middle powers are themselves sometimes wont to believe. But practically all concerned have been able to adapt to a significant system change with much less disruption than could well have been expected in a fluid, violence-prone international system.

Notes

1. A note should be made about sources. A step-by-step logical framework has been set forth in this article to demonstrate that Brazil and India occupy distinctive positions in the international system as Third World powers. Although this involves a series of systematic comparisons about Brazil and India, most citations refer only to India. This is because previous work of the author, on which this article builds, extensively cites the relevant literature on Brazil and because readers of this book on Brazil are also probably much more familiar with Brazilian than Indian sources. Readers interested in background references for this article relating particularly to Brazil may consult Michael A. Morris, *International Politics and the Sea: The Case of Brazil* (Boulder, Colo.: Westview Press, 1979).

2. Baldev Raj Nayar, "Treat India Seriously," *Foreign Policy* 18 (Spring 1975):133–154.

3. Gérard Chaliand, *Revolution in the Third World* (New York: Penguin Books, 1979), p. xvi.

4. Robert D. Bond, ed., *Contemporary Venezuela and Its Role in International Affairs* (New York: New York University Press, 1977).

5. Richard Halloran, "U.S. Report Says Forces No Longer Effective: Disarray Seen in Iran's Military Services," *International Herald Tribune*, November 19, 1979, p. 1.

6. Stephen P. Cohen and Richard L. Park, *India: Emergent Power?* (New York: Crane, Russak & Company, 1978), p. 12.

7. Steven Spiegel, *Dominance and Diversity: The International Hierarchy* (Boston: Little, Brown and Co., 1972).

8. Ibid., pp. 102–103.

9. John W. Mellor, "The Indian Economy: Objectives, Performance and Prospects," in John W. Mellor, ed., *India: A Rising Middle Power* (Boulder, Colo.: Westview Press, 1979), pp. 105, 115–116.

10. Onkar Marwah, "Comment," in Mellor, *India*, pp. 213, 218.

11. *Strategic Survey: 1976* (London: International Institute for Strategic Studies, 1976), p. 22; Peter Lock and Herbert Wulf, *Register of Arms Production in Developing Countries* (Hamburg: Arbeitsgruppe "Rüstung und Unterentwicklung"), p. xii. *The Military Balance, 1979–1980* (London: International Institute for Strategic Studies, 1979), pp. 101–103.

12. *World Armaments and Disarmament—SIPRI Yearbook, 1980* (New York: Crane, Russak & Company, 1980), pp. 86, 88–89.

13. S. Sapru, "Arms Industry Heading for Self-Sufficiency, Eventual Exports,"

International Herald Tribune, December 24, 1979, p. 8S.

14. Ronald Schneider's *Brazil: Foreign Policy of a Future World Power* (Boulder, Colo.: Westview Press, 1976) summarizes the literature on Brazil's emergence as a major power in a bibliographic essay on pages 227–229. Also see the Preface to this book.

15. See notes 2, 6, and 9. Also see an article by Bhabani Sen Gupta, "Waiting for India: India's Role as a Regional Power," *Journal of International Affairs* 39 (Fall 1975):171–184.

16. For example, two of the finest recent general surveys of Brazilian and Indian foreign policy incorporate the middle power theme as an integral part of the analysis: Brady Tyson, "Brazil," in Harold Eugene Davis and Larman Wilson, eds., *Latin American Foreign Policies: An Analysis* (Baltimore, Md.: Johns Hopkins University Press, 1975), pp. 221–258; and Leo E. Rose, "The Foreign Policy of India," in James N. Rosenau, Kenneth W. Thompson, and Gavin Boyd, eds., *World Politics: An Introduction* (New York: Free Press, 1976), pp. 199–221.

17. Wayne Selcher, *Brazil's Multilateral Relations: Between First and Third Worlds* (Boulder, Colo.: Westview Press, 1978), pp. 189–193.

18. Ibid., especially Chapters 6 and 9.

19. Sisir Gupta, "Great Power Relations, World Order, and the Third World," *Foreign Affairs Reports* 27 (July-August 1978):110–154.

20. Rose, "Foreign Policy of India," pp. 218–220.

21. Selcher, *Brazil's Multilateral Relations*, pp. 97, 99.

22. Ibid., pp. 147, 121.

23. *World Development Report, 1979* (Washington, D.C.: World Bank, 1979), pp. 140–141.

24. Ibid.

25. Hannan Ezekiel, "India's Trade Prospects and Potentials," in Mellor, *India*, pp. 265–293.

26. *World Development Report, 1979*, pp. 152–153.

27. *The Military Balance: 1979–1980*, pp. 94–97.

28. William J. Barnds, "South Asia," in Rosenau, Thompson, and Boyd, *World Politics*, pp. 525–526, 520.

29. John R. Redick, "Nuclear Proliferation in Latin America," in Roger Fontaine and James Theberge, eds., *Latin America's New Internationalism: The End of Hemispheric Isolation* (New York: Praeger Publishers, 1976), p. 283.

30. Ernest Lefever, *Nuclear Arms in the Third World: U.S. Policy Dilemma* (Washington, D.C.: Brookings Institution, 1979), pp. 29–31.

31. Onkar Marwah, "Comment," p. 213.

32. A Canadian article to this effect was translated and reprinted approvingly in a leading Argentine military journal. Barrie Morrison and Donald M. Page, "La Opción de la India: El camino nuclear para alcanzar el poderío mundial," *Estrategia* 31-32 (November 1974-February 1975): 74–82. On this same point, see also Paul Buchanan, "Argentina: At the Threshold in the Southern Cone?" *Arms Control Today* 9 (October 1979):5–6.

33. Luis Garasino, "Explosión Atómica de la India. Proyección Eventual en América Latina," *Estrategia* (May-June 1974):91–98. For similar arguments

relating Argentina and India, see C. H. Waisman, "Incentives for Nuclear Proliferation: The Case of Argentina," in Onkar Marwah and Ann Shulz, eds., *Proliferation and the Near-Nuclear Countries* (Cambridge, Mass.: Ballinger Publishing Co., 1976), pp. 284–290.

34. John Redick has made just this comparison between the nuclear proliferation situation in Latin America involving Argentina and Brazil and that in South Asia involving India and Pakistan. Redick, "Nuclear Proliferation," p. 299.

35. Stephen M. Gorman, "Security, Influence, and Nuclear Weapons: The Case of Argentina and Brazil," *Parameters* 9 (March 1979):63, 64. Another recent study concluded as well that a South American nuclear arms race would soon tip in Brazil's favor. Lefever, *Nuclear Arms*, p. 117.

36. See Morris, *International Politics and the Sea: The Case of Brazil.*

37. S. N. Kohli, *Sea Power and the Indian Ocean: With Special Reference to India* (New Delhi: Tata McGraw-Hill Publishing Company, 1978), pp. vii–viii.

38. For Brazil, see note 36. For India, see W. J. Crowe, "The Persian Gulf: Central or Peripheral to United States Strategy?" *United States Naval Institute Proceedings* 104 (May 1978):203. (Vice Admiral Crowe is Deputy Chief of Naval Operations [Plans, Policy and Operations] of the U.S. Navy.) See also John E. Lacouture, "Seapower in the Indian Ocean: A Requirement for Western Security," *United States Naval Institute Proceedings* 105 (August 1979):36.

39. The study is being carried out while the author is on leave from the Department of Political Science of Clemson University at the Stockholm International Peace Research Institute (SIPRI) from 1979 to 1981.

40. Barry Buzan, *Seabed Politics* (New York: Praeger Publishers, 1976), pp. 130 and 147 n. 17; and Edward Miles, "The Structure and Effects of the Decision-Process in the Seabed Committee and the Third United Nations Conference on the Law of the Sea," *International Organization* 31 (Spring 1977):230.

41. For example, this theme is developed in Spiegel, *Dominance and Diversity*, and in Saul B. Cohen, "The Emergence of a New Second Order of Powers in the International System," in Marwah and Shulz, *Nuclear Proliferation*, pp. 19–33.

42. George Rosen examined similarities and differences between the political economy of India and that of Latin America and concluded that differences predominate so that appropriate policies likewise differ in each case. George Rosen, *Latin American and Indian Political Economy Compared: Some Comparisons Derived from K. B. Griffin's "Reflections on Latin American Development"* (Santa Monica, Calif.: Rand Corporation, 1966), Rand paper P-3383.

43. For example, see Spiegel, *Dominance and Diversity*, p. 209, and Mohammed Ayoob, "The Superpowers and Regional 'Stability': Parallel Responses to the Gulf and the Horn," *The World Today* (May 1979):197–205.

Index